Web 2.0 Tools and Strategies for Archives and Local History Collections

Kate Theimer

Neal-Schuman Publishers, Inc.

New York · London

Published by Neal-Schuman Publishers, Inc.
100 William St., Suite 2004
New York, NY 10038

Printed and bound in the United States of America.

The paper used in this publication meets the minimum requirements of American National Standard for Information Sciences—Permanence of Paper for Printed Library Materials, ANSI Z39.48-1992.

Library of Congress Cataloging-in-Publication Data

Theimer, Kate, 1966-
  Web 2.0 tools and strategies for archives and local history collections / Kate Theimer.
      p. cm.
  Includes bibliographical references and index.
  ISBN 978-1-55570-679-1 (alk. paper)
  1. Archives—Information technology. 2. Archival materials—Data processing—Handbooks, manuals, etc. 3. Archives—Automation—Handbooks, manuals, etc. 4. Web 2.0. 5. World Wide Web—Handbooks, manuals, etc. 6. Online social networks—Handbooks, manuals, etc. 7. Libraries—Information technology. 8. Digital libraries—Design—Handbooks, manuals, etc. 9. Blogs—Handbooks, manuals, etc. 10. Web sites—Design—Handbooks, manuals, etc. 11. Wikis (Computer science)—Handbooks, manuals, etc. I. Title.

CD973.D3T54 2010
006.7'54—dc22
                                                              2009045942

Contents

List of Figures

Preface

Many archives and other cultural heritage institutions are stuck in a "Web 1.0" mind-set. This needs to change.

To remain relevant, archives and local history organizations need to shift their thinking about how they make their collections accessible to researchers. In these days of decreasing budgets and increasing competition for resources, archives and local history organizations must take advantage of the range of low-cost Web 2.0 tools to open up (at least virtually) our closed stacks and let users discover and interact with our collections in the ways they want to.

Web 2.0 Tools and Strategies for Archives and Local History Collections focuses directly and exclusively on how organizations with archival and historic manuscript collections can use social media to share their activities and collections on the Web. My goal is to offer practical, commonsense advice in nontechnical language that shows both what Web 2.0 tools can do for your organization and what it takes to use these tools. Archivists from 21 institutions, ranging from the national archives of Australia and the United Kingdom to local historical societies in the United States share their experiences implementing specific Web 2.0 tools in sidebar interviews.

The book provides descriptions of all the major Web 2.0 services—blogs, podcasts, image-sharing sites, video-sharing sites, microblogging, wikis, and social networking. For each tool, there is an overview of its functionalities, analysis of the implementation requirements, and thoughtful discussion of how it's being used by a range of archives, historical societies, and special collections. Recognizing how quickly technical specifics change on the Web, I took the approach of organizing my discussion of the different ways each tool can be used into broad categories, emphasizing the underlying purpose, in addition to specifics. The discussion focuses on what the tools are being used for—the goals that they are achieving—rather than the specifics of how they function, so that the analysis I'm providing will continue to be relevant even as Web 2.0 tools inevitably evolve.

Implementing Web 2.0 doesn't take place in a vacuum. *Web 2.0 Tools and Strategies for Archives and Local History Collections* recognizes that to be successful you need to consider your available resources, management requirements, and policy issues. The need to "set the stage" for using Web 2.0 is discussed, including a walk-through of reviewing your existing Web presence, technical resources, and available hardware and software. Other planning topics addressed are the need to ground any new Web 2.0 efforts in your strategic plan and to consider what audiences you want to attract. Starting something like a Twitter, Flickr, or Facebook account may take only a few minutes, and starting a blog may seem like a fun thing to do one afternoon, but a successful Web 2.0 implementation needs to be part of an organization's workflow. I address important areas such as establishing systems to measure your results, getting institutional buy-in, considering legal issues, defining tasks and assigning workload, creating policies, preserving work products, and publicizing your efforts. An informative essay at the end of the book also provides an overview of recommended resources on Web 2.0 and its implementation in archives and historical organizations.

In assembling the content of this book, I wanted to make it as useful as possible for my friends and colleagues in the field—archivists at institutions of all sizes who want to learn about Web 2.0 tools but don't have a lot of time to spend "playing around." *Web 2.0 Tools and Strategies for Archives and Local History Collections* will be useful to anyone working in archives, special collections departments, historical societies or organizations, local history collections in public libraries, or museums that want to explore new ways to interact with the public. Although it's targeted to people working in smaller or mid-sized organizations, the information and concepts are applicable to larger organizations, too.

You can use this book to learn about Web 2.0 basics and tools and get ideas for how you might implement them in your organization. In addition, I hope the information provided here allows you to see new ways of using Web 2.0 tools beyond what others are already doing. Structuring the discussions around the purpose for which archives are using Web tools should help you assess the potential of new tools as they appear on the market. You can also use this as a guide for working through the steps needed to get ready for an implementation—putting Web 2.0 in the context of the unique world of archival materials and raising important questions about what you need to do to make it work.

Web 2.0 Tools and Strategies for Archives and Local History Collections is organized with framing chapters that provide context, background, and additional information around the central chapters that describe the major Web 2.0 tools and how archives are using them. The Introduction reviews the changes and opportunities the Web (both 1.0 and 2.0) has brought for archives and historical organizations. Chapter 1 introduces "Web 2.0" and the key concepts behind it and reviews some of the common myths and misperceptions about social media. Chapter 2 provides an overview about what makes a good "Web 1.0" site for your organization, to ensure that the new users you attract with Web 2.0 will find a usable and professional Web site representing you. This chapter also reviews other issues you should take into account in your planning: both technical—like building on your existing digital assets and inventorying your hardware, software, and IT support—and administrative—such as working with your strategic goals and identifying your intended audiences.

Chapters 3 through 9 each focus on one Web 2.0 tool or service: blogs (Chapter 3), podcasts (Chapter 4), Flickr (Chapter 5), YouTube (Chapter 6), Twitter (Chapter 7), wikis (Chapter 8), and Facebook (Chapter 9). These chapters all follow a common structure—a brief definition of the tool and an overview of its functionalities, followed by a substantial discussion of how archives and historical organizations are using the tool, and then concluding with a review of steps needed for implementation. Each chapter contains interviews with people from archives and related historical organizations who have successfully implemented the Web 2.0 tool in question. These interviews cover topics such as the steps the archivists took to prepare, the major benefits and challenges they have experienced, and the lessons they learned. Chapter 10 contains similar briefer discussions of four Web 2.0 tools that are not being commonly used by archives and historical organizations but that are important to be aware of: mashups, widgets, online chat, and Second Life.

Chapter 11 raises a critical issue, and one that is all too often ignored—how to measure the success of what you've done. It introduces the concepts of measuring outputs and outcomes, places the methods in the context of a Web 2.0 implementation, and provides some suggestions for how to approach the thorny issue of measuring social media success. Chapter 12 reviews the range of management and policy concerns that are necessary to plan for in any successful Web project: getting institutional buy-in, dealing with copyright issues, defining tasks and assigning workloads, creating policies, planning for preservation, learning what your users want, and publicizing your efforts.

The Conclusion returns to the broad issues raised in the Introduction about the impact of the Web, discussing the major challenges it holds for archives. It presents an argument that the key to success—and the greatest challenge—lies in each organization finding the right balance between the archival principles and traditions embedded in the old way of doing things and the opportunities of the new Web. The essay presented in the Appendix provides a critical overview of what I think are some of the most useful resources available on Web 2.0 in general, as well as recommendations on where to look for the best thinking on use of these tools by archives and historical organizations.

Web 2.0 Tools and Strategies for Archives and Local History Collections isn't just *about* Web 2.0—it was written *using* Web 2.0 research. In gathering information for the book, I raised questions and had discussions on my blog, ArchivesNext, and on my Twitter and Facebook accounts. I developed my understanding of how Web 2.0 tools work through my own firsthand experience creating my own blog and wiki and using tools like Facebook and Flickr. When there was a tool I had not used, I asked my blog readers and friends on Twitter and Facebook for help (in addition to using traditional Web tools for research). I also used the feedback I've gotten from the many people I've talked to about Web 2.0 in workshops I've taught and from conversations with my colleagues. These archivists shared their own success stories, as well as their concerns, questions, and fears. I've incorporated the stories I heard from people about the planning they wished they had done to suggest topics to be included in the chapters on planning and management.

One of the aspects of *Web 2.0 Tools and Strategies for Archives and Local History Collections* that I'm most pleased to share are the many examples of organizations using Web 2.0 tools right now to reach new audiences and advance their missions. They provide real-world demonstrations that Web 2.0 tools can have real results. For example, the National Archives of the United Kingdom is located in London, but through its podcasts and wiki, as well as the images it shares on Flickr and the videos it shares on YouTube, it provides information to people around the world. And using Web 2.0 tools doesn't just get your message out; it also gives your audience a vehicle for giving information back to you. Using Twitter, the Nova Scotia Archives not only shares news about what they are doing but they also participate in conversations with others about Nova Scotia and its history. The experiences of the many archives using Flickr show that people want to engage with historical content, whether by sharing their opinions or providing new identifying information.

I hope my efforts to share these examples and my own practical experience provide you with the background you need to feel confident approaching Web 2.0 and its many tools and services. You should have a clear understanding of why these tools are useful for archives, be able to knowledgeably decide which ones would work best for your organization, and have a basic understanding of what it will take to implement them. If you are skeptical about the hype surrounding Web 2.0, this book should demonstrate through examples of real-world implementations why Web 2.0 is worth exploring. If you're nervous that Web 2.0 will require more technical skills or resources than they have, I think you'll see how simple most tools are to use. But I also want to caution and inform people who want to rush into Web 2.0 implementation to ground your efforts in your strategic goals and do the preparation and planning necessary to ensure your project succeeds. Ultimately, I hope *Web 2.0 Tools and Strategies for Archives and Local History Collections* can demystify Web 2.0, supply a framework for how to evaluate the usefulness of both existing and new Web tools, and spark new ideas about how to be part of the new interactive Web.

Acknowledgments

This book would not have been possible without my own social network of friends and colleagues on Facebook and Twitter and the wonderful community of people who have engaged in discussion of these issues with me on my blog, ArchivesNext. A friend joked that this would be a crowd-sourced book, and in some ways, it is. The world of Web 2.0 is too large for anyone to keep up to date on everything that's happening, and so I am happy to be part of a community of archivists working toward integrating Web 2.0 technology and thinking into our archival institutions.

In particular I would like thank Howard Batchelor, Alan Bell, Linda Clark Benedict, Rebecca Goldman, Beth Harris, Steve Heaps, Paul Lasewicz, Euan Semple, Rob Sieczkiewicz, Jerry Simmons, Jennie Thomas, Ann Thomason, and Eddie Woodward, who all supplied inspiration, assistance, or information. David Dexter, Robin Riat, Richard Urban, and Christian van der Ven were all generous in their responses to my queries about Second Life.

All the people who responded to my request for interviews about their use of Web 2.0 tools, sharing their experience and advice, made a substantial contribution to the value of the book. They are:

Sara Piasecki, Oregon Health & Science University
Stephen Fletcher, University of North Carolina at Chapel Hill
Gavin Freeguard, The Orwell Prize
Emma Allen and Joshua Shindler, The National Archives (UK)
Heather McClenahan, Los Alamos County Historical Society
Lin Fredericksen, Kansas State Historical Society
Julie Kerssen, Seattle Municipal Archives
Amy Schindler, The College of William and Mary

Katrina Harkness and Joshua Youngblood, State Library & Archives
    of Florida
Mark E. Harvey, Archives of Michigan
Ann Cameron, Gill Hamilton, and James Toon, National Library
    of Scotland
David Hovde, Purdue University
Matt Raymond, The Library of Congress
Lauren Oostveen, Nova Scotia Archives
Molly Kruckenberg, Montana Historical Society
David Smith, Archives New Zealand
Tracey Baker, Minnesota Historical Society
Michele Christian, Iowa State University
Colleen McFarland, University of Wisconsin–Eau Claire
Tim Sherratt, National Archives of Australia
Matthew Davies, National Film & Sound Archive (Australia)

I'm grateful for the time and thoughtfulness of those who reviewed and commented on drafts of individual chapters: Rob Jenson, Jeanne Kramer-Smyth, Andrea Medina-Smith, Nancy Melley, Aimee Morgan, Lauren Oostveen, Sara Piasecki, Arian Ravanbakhsh, Amy Schindler, Pam Whitenack, and Tanya Zanish-Belcher.

I also want to give special thanks to the indefatigable and encouraging Alison Stankrauff, who read and commented on most of the chapters in the book.

The contributions of Jim Gerencser are too numerous to describe; without his support and assistance, I would never have been able to complete this work and would never have struck out on the unusual path that led to it. This book is dedicated to Jim, and to all the archivists like him, who are not afraid to try something new.

Archives and the Web: Changes and Opportunities

The latest glossary published by the Society of American Archivists (SAA) provides many definitions for the word "archives." The SAA glossary allows for the use of the term to describe records ("materials created or received by a person, family, or organization, public or private, in the conduct of their affairs and preserved because of the enduring value . . ."), organizations ("the division within an organization responsible for maintaining the organization's records of enduring value" and "an organization that collects the records of individuals, families, or other organizations"), a profession ("the professional discipline of administering such collections and organizations"), and even buildings ("the building [or portion thereof] housing archival collections") (Pearce-Moses, 2005: 30). Interestingly, all of these definitions focus primarily on the need to preserve, maintain, administer, and house archival materials, but none makes explicit that archives are preserved, maintained, administered, and housed so that they may be *used*.

The professional discipline of archives has both an inward and an outward focus. Archivists are responsible for acquiring, processing, and preserving their collections, but they are also responsible for ensuring that those collections are used by as many people as possible. Archives are defined as being materials that are preserved because of the "enduring value contained in the information they contain or as evidence of the functions and responsibilities of their creator" (Pearce-Moses, 2005: 30). Archival materials are not usually preserved because of their intrinsic value (their value as objects); they are preserved because of the use to which they can be put. Archives are *for* use.

Because archives and historical collections exist to be found and used, for most archivists, the rise of the Internet and the World Wide Web has been a welcome means of expanding the audience for their collections. The Web is a powerful platform for promoting repositories, sharing information about collections, and reaching out to potential new users. It did not change the archival principles that underlie the traditional tasks archivists perform. What the Web has changed, for almost every archives, special collection, local history collection, or historical society, is the way it interacts with the public.

How has the Web changed how we interact with our users? I think we have seen the greatest changes in terms of:

- how users locate material that interests them,
- volume and type of reference requests,
- user expectations about how they want to conduct their research,
- user expectations about the speed of the reference process,
- shift in workload from researchers to archivists, and
- increase in workload on archivists.

For most people who work in archives and historical organizations today, these changes are taken for granted as an accepted part of how we do business. However, before considering the range of possibilities Web 2.0 brings to archives, it's worth going back and reviewing how broadly Web 1.0 affected our jobs and institutions—in some cases in ways we have yet to fully adjust to.

Before the Web, almost all researchers who wanted access to material in an archives would have to begin by corresponding with the archivist to identify how much material was of potential interest. Then the researcher would either have to travel to the archives to review the materials (or pay a local researcher to do so) or else pay for photocopies to be made of all possibly relevant materials (and pay for their postage). The Web has transformed several aspects of this process. First, the Web made it easy for archives to share information about collections—like finding aids and collection catalogs—online. This allowed users to discover for themselves with relative ease what information an archives might have. Then, with the digitization of holdings, users could get direct access not only to information about the records but also to some of the actual records themselves. For many users, interaction with the archivist and travel were no longer necessary.

Thanks to Google, if you put information on the Web today, people who are interested in it will find it, and you. For most archives, sharing descriptions of collections on the Web has brought an overall increase in the number of reference requests. In addition to finding they have more users, most repositories also find they are attracting a new kind of user, one who often has no previous experience working with special materials. Their requests often begin, "I found you by doing a Google search for . . ." Responding to requests from these kinds of users often requires the archivist to explain some basic facts about archives, such as the level of intellectual control of the materials and the fact that not everything is digitized and searchable. Working with these inexperienced users is generally a different kind of reference interaction than working with professional researchers.

Increasingly, users of all types expect the Web sites for archives, special collections, and historical organizations to function like the other Web sites they use. They want everything to be easy to discover, access, and share. Many first-time users expect an archives to function like a library, with item-level control of all its holdings. When they ask an archives if it has something, they expect the archivist to be able to give them an answer, not a lengthy explanation about how they will have to come and look for it themselves. Users also expect materials to be digitized and online. In the twenty-first century, telling a user he or she will have to travel to you to get an answer to questions is becoming less and less acceptable.

Furthermore, as e-mail replaces "snail mail" as the preferred method of communication for most researchers, it means that users are placing their requests with greater ease and speed, and they are placing them 24 hours a day. The Web brought archives not only more users, but users who are communicating more quickly, and often expecting responses just as quickly.

Identifying what information an archival collection holds on a specific subject requires research. In the past, it was the archivist's job to describe the content of collections in general terms; it was the researcher's job to locate the particular material desired. Serving new, inexperienced users and attempting to meet the increased expectations of today's audience has meant that the burden of doing the work of locating relevant materials often shifts from user to archivist. While most archivists may not be doing actual research for users (although that does happen), archives are targeting their resources to providing more and better online description and more digitization of collections. The traditional model, in which the archivist processed collections, produced hard-copy finding aids, and then waited for users to come to them has transformed into archivists proactively producing and pushing out information and digitized content, trying to pull people in rather than waiting for them to show up. Finding and telling the stories contained in collections used to be the province of researchers; now, to make the archives a compelling and relevant online destination, archivists are finding it's also part of their job to promote the value of their holdings.

These changing conditions have meant new kinds of work for archivists, in addition to what was traditionally required. Today's archives must produce content for the Web—online exhibits, digitized collections, EAD (Encoded Archival Description)–encoded finding aids, and possibly also the blogs, Flickr photostreams, and YouTube videos inspired by Web 2.0. Archivists must respond not only to letters and phone calls but also to reference requests received via e-mail and online chat. The products of the Web and the other virtual mountains of electronic records being created must also be managed, appraised, acquired, processed, preserved, and made accessible—no small task for any archives. The need to share data among archives led to increased standardization in how collections are described—leading to the need for training in the standards and increased scrutiny of descriptive products to ensure they meet the standards. Archivists have had to learn how to use new software to create Web sites and to format finding aids in EAD. Meanwhile, the wonders of technology have done little to change the fundamental responsibilities that have always faced archivists—to acquire, process, preserve, and make available the materials they are charged to collect.

All of these changes may make it seem like the Web has brought nothing but trouble for archives and historical organizations, but this is hardly the case. What it has done is put them on the same playing field with other information providers such as libraries and museums—as well as sites like Wikipedia. In the past, archives and special collections generally appeared hard to access, with limited hours and restrictive policies. All too often they had a reputation for being places that were not very welcoming to people who were not serious scholars. They were "special" places, and those coming to visit were expected to abide by special rules that didn't apply in other places. On the Internet, a Web site for an archives, special collections department, or historical organization can be found and accessed just like any other site. This accessibility brings opportunities. Although most archivists and history professionals are familiar with the possibilities inherent in the Web, it's worth reviewing them before embarking on a discussion of the new tools that Web 2.0 gives us, which build on and expand these opportunities.

The Web allows archives to be discovered by more people—and by more diverse people—than would ever have been possible in the past. If you agree that archives exist so that their collections can be used, then the Web is the best thing that ever happened to them. Digitization of collections and online exhibitions mean that people around the world can see and learn from archival materials. Partnerships with companies like Ancestry and Footnote, who digitize and provide access to millions of archival records, mean greater visibility for our holdings and greater use by an interested public. Web 2.0 tools provide a wealth of further options for connecting people with our documents, photos, sound, and moving image collections.

The Web has brought about a sea change in how people find out about what's in our holdings. Before the Web, many archivists created descriptions of collections targeted to meet the needs of historians—our primary users. Those descriptions, or summaries of those descriptions, were shared primarily through published scholarly channels. If you were interested in something outside the mainstream of scholarship or if you were not familiar with how to do scholarly research, you had little chance of locating relevant archival material. Today, millions of people can discover what collections you have by simply typing search terms into their favorite search engine. The channel for discovering collections is open to everyone, and if an archives describes its collections well, people will find them.

The Web has also transformed what is required to "publish" information—creating new opportunities for other people to publicize your collections. In the past, sharing information about archival materials took place largely through formal publication, which was primarily done by professional scholars and dedicated hobbyists. With the Web, anyone with an interest in a topic, however narrow or specialized, can publish a blog, contribute to Wikipedia, or start their own Web page, and if the topic is right, share information about relevant material in your collections. The support the Web provides for people to network means that those with common interests can easily share knowledge about where to find good resources.

There is a user out there for everything in an archives' collections; it's just a question of connecting the right user with that material. In 2004, Chris Anderson introduced the concept of applying the "long tail" to online commerce. In short, he argued that although the largest volume of consumers will be interested in only a relatively small number of products, and for each of the less popular products there will be a much smaller number of interested consumers, if you add up the total number of consumers for all of the "less popular products" the potential revenue for all the products along this "long tail" of demand will be significant. A requirement for the "long tail" to work is that you need to make sure the people looking for the less popular items can find them—a requirement more easily met with the advent of the Web (Anderson, 2004).

The concept of the "long tail" can also be applied to archives (Lasewicz, 2007). In most archival repositories, the bulk of the reference requests will probably be for a relatively small percentage of the collections, usually those that have material on popular topics or that are the best publicized; the rest of the holdings receive little use. This is not because those collections have material that is of no interest. It is because the people who might be interested in using them don't know about them. One potential the Web has for archives is the capability to match the most users with the most materials.

Archivists frequently complain that when their profession appears in the popular media—movies, television, or books—the archivist is all too often a stereotype: old and pale, living in the past, obsessed with his documents, unable to deal with technology, catering only to researchers he finds worthy. Archives are invariably referred to as "dusty" or "musty" (or both). They are hidden-away places, seldom visited, quiet and dark. By embracing technology and the opportunities that the Web provides, archivists can begin to break down these stereotypes, showing that we are not, in fact, out-of-touch guardians of crumbling paper, but rather open, engaged, and tech savvy. Unlike the hard to find and restrictive places in the real world, on the Web archives are always open, and people can browse through the collections as much as they want. While campaigning against a stereotype may seem like a minor concern, the public perception of archives has serious implications for funding and public support. In these times of shrinking financial resources, an archives cannot afford to have the public and its funders think that archives are for only a few scholars and that archivists are out of step with the times.

Breaking down stereotypes and connecting more people with more materials are just some of the opportunities that resulted from "Web 1.0." As you will read about in the upcoming chapters of this book, Web 2.0 has only enhanced these possibilities for greater visibility, providing increased opportunities for the discovery of materials and for promoting the archivist and the archives as valuable and relevant contributors to the culture of the Web.

The Web, in both its 1.0 and 2.0 incarnations, has brought many challenges along with these opportunities. Archives and historical organizations face issues such as increased user expectations, maintaining archival principles in the digital world, copyright concerns, bridging the digital divide, and finding a balance between serving the needs of the physical and digital worlds. These complex challenges will be discussed in the conclusion.

It is worth remembering, as you think about the challenges presented by the Web, that we have no choice but to address them. The Web becomes more closely integrated with our lives every day, and those who seek to turn back the clock to a time when archives were places that were governed by different rules are fighting a losing battle. The question for archives and other historical organizations is how they can best adapt and take advantage of the Web as it continues to evolve, through Web 1.0, Web 2.0, Web 3.0, and beyond.

REFERENCES

Anderson, Chris. 2004. "The Long Tail." *Wired* 12, no. 10 (October). Available: www.wired.com/wired/archive/12.10/tail.html (accessed May 27, 2009).

Lasewicz, Paul. 2007. "Even Worst Sellers Have Value: What Amazon Means for Archival Reference Processes." Paper presented at the annual meeting of the Society of American Archivists, Chicago.

Pearce-Moses, Richard. 2005. *A Glossary of Archival & Records Terminology.* Chicago: Society of American Archivists.

CHAPTER 1

Web 2.0 Basics

"Web 2.0" is a buzzword. Like all buzzwords, it gained popularity because it's useful for capturing the meaning of something. But it also has been overused and become something of a cliché. The technology cognoscenti have now moved on and are talking about Web 3.0 (the semantic Web) and even Web 4.0. But for most of us, "Web 2.0" accurately describes the Web we know and use.

The origins of the term are a bit disputed, but its most prominent early use was by O'Reilly Media, which sponsored the "Web 2.0" conference in 2004 (Wikipedia, "Web 2.0," accessed 2009). The term "2.0" refers to the system used by software developers to signify new versions of software—that is, by assigning a new number (rather than using, say, 1.8 or 1.9), the developers signal that this software release has significant changes and differences. "Web 2.0," then, was used to signify that the Web had begun a fundamental change in the way people were able to use it.

WHAT IS "WEB 2.0" ALL ABOUT?

There is no agreed-upon definition of "Web 2.0." While O'Reilly Media may have popularized it, the term was not created by one company or type of software. Rather, it describes a confluence of changes in Web design and functionality that resulted in fundamental differences in the ways developers and users approach the Web. The most significant of these changes are the following:

- "Network as platform" or "cloud computing"—applications and data "live" on the Web, not on your local computer. This has two significant results for users: it decreases the need for computers with a lot of memory because less information and software are stored on your local system, and you can access both applications and data from anywhere you have an Internet connection.

- Open standards, open source, openness in general—Web applications using shared standards and releasing their code to developers results in greater interoperability between applications, as well as an explosion of opportunities for developers to create "add on" applications tailored to work on popular Web sites.

- Creation of syndicated content—use of RSS (described in the next section) allows sites to "push" customized content out to users rather than users having to visit individual sites to "pull" content out of them. This allows you to identify what information you want automatically delivered to you rather than having to regularly check for it on different Web sites.

- Customized Web experience for users—Web sites draw on user profile information to create customized Web views. Customization allows sites to present information that will be most relevant or that you have selected (for example, local weather reports or news headlines or recommendations for products or services).

- Broad use of interactivity—Web sites allow (and encourage) users to interact with posted content, using features such as commenting, tagging, ranking, making lists, and allowing many options for redistribution and sharing. The shift from the Web as primarily a vehicle for passively sharing published content to a vehicle for people to interact with and reuse that content is one of the most visible characteristics of Web 2.0.

- Prevalence of user-created content—the rise of sites like Wikipedia, Flickr, and YouTube, and tools like podcasting and blogging, which allow users to publish and share content, made individual people just as much a force in publishing on the Web as traditional information providers.

- Integration of user-to-user connection—broad-based use of the Web as a way to connect people to each other, not just to information sources. Sites like MySpace, Facebook, Twitter, and Second Life exist purely as a forum for users to connect with other users. In addition to the popularity of social networking sites, users have also come to expect social networking and sharing functions to be available on any site providing other Web 2.0 services (like Flickr and YouTube) and any major media or corporate site (like *The New York Times* or *The Washington Post*).

A good example of how these different elements come together is the hugely popular online retail site amazon.com. Once you create an account, it remembers you and presents you with a customized homepage when you enter the site. Based on the products you look at and buy on the site, amazon.com makes recommendations for other products it thinks you may also enjoy. You can customize your own experience by creating shopping or wish lists. You can sign up to have amazon.com contact you when products you are interested in become available. You can also interact with the information Amazon provides by rating products or writing a review. In addition to contributing reviews, you can also publish your own lists and recommendations to share with other users. If you have your own blog or Web site, you can even choose to add a widget to your site that promotes amazon.com products (and generates revenue for you).

In 2006, *Time* magazine selected "You" as its "Person of the Year," recognizing the enormous changes Web 2.0 technologies and practices had made in the Web. In his cover story article, Lev Grossman summed up the changes:

> It's a story about community and collaboration on a scale never seen before. It's about the cosmic compendium of knowledge Wikipedia and the million-channel people's network YouTube and the online metropolis MySpace. It's about the many wresting power from the few and helping one another for nothing and how that will not only change the world, but also change the way the world changes. (Grossman, 2006)

WEB 2.0 BUILDING BLOCKS

A technical discussion of the underpinnings of Web 2.0 would include references to protocols, software, APIs (application programming interfaces), and programming languages. This section will not delve into these technical matters but rather describe some common Web 2.0 tools that are user-facing.

RSS (or "Really Simple Syndication")

RSS enables people who create Web content to establish a "feed" for it, to which interested users can subscribe, meaning that they are automatically notified when new content is available. In more technical terms, RSS is:

> a family of web feed formats used to publish frequently updated works—such as blog entries, news headlines, audio, and video—in a standardized format. An RSS document (which is called a "feed", "web feed", or

"channel") includes full or summarized text, plus metadata such as publishing dates and authorship. (Wikipedia, "RSS," accessed 2009)

You can create an RSS feed for Web 2.0 products you create, like blogs and podcasts. When you visit sites like blogs, popular news sites, or virtually any kind of Web site that updates its content, you will probably see options for subscribing.

To conveniently manage and read the content you subscribe to, you will want to set up an account with a "feed reader" (also known as an "RSS reader" or "aggregator") such as Google Reader (www.google.com/reader) or Bloglines (www.bloglines.com). (Increasingly, desktop e-mail systems are also offering support for subscribing to RSS feeds.) These readers collect the latest information from the feeds you subscribe to and then provide the updates to you in an easy-to-use interface.

Tagging

A "tag" is a descriptive word or phrase applied to a piece of digital information, such as a Web page, blog post, or digital image, video, audio, or other electronic file. Tags are applied by creators and users of digital content and are used to help people find materials they are interested in. There are no formal standards for creating tags, so they are essentially user-applied keywords (as opposed to formal subject headings or hierarchical classifications). When a creator applies tags, the tags will probably describe the general content or special qualities of the digital object. User-supplied tags may operate in this way too, but they may also reflect the user's own personal way of finding materials (such as their own abbreviations or categorization schemes, or just "good site" or "to do"). The ways in which tags are applied and used vary for different Web 2.0 tools, but they are a common feature of many of the tools you will read about in this book.

One of the more interesting ways to reuse tags is to create "tag clouds," which are graphic representations of the tags used to describe something, with more frequently used tags appearing larger and in brighter colors. Figure 1-1 shows a tag cloud of words commonly used to describe Web 2.0.

Social Bookmarking

Bookmarking has long been a feature of many Web browsers. Creating a bookmark for a Web page gives you a way to make a note of material that interests

Figure 1-1. Tag Cloud of Terms Used to Describe Web 2.0

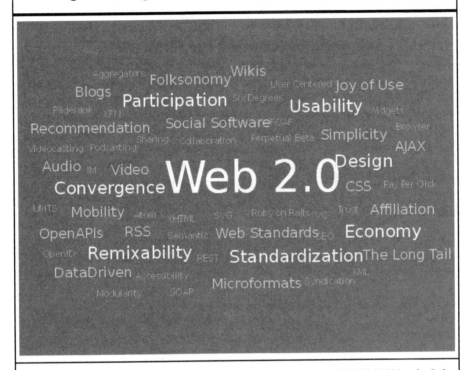

Source: Author: Luca Cremonini; www.railsonwave.it/2007/1/2/web-2-0-map/; www.railsonwave.com/assets/2006/12/25/Web_2.0_Map.svg.

Note: This cloud-map picture (constructed by Luca Cremonini on December 25, 2006, for railsonwave.com) has been recreated in SVG format from the image of Markus Angermeier (http://kosmar.de/archives/2005/11/11/the-huge-cloud-lens-bubble-map-web20/; http://kosmar.de/wp-content/web20map.png).

you. Prior to Web 2.0, Web browsers provided users with tools for keeping and organizing bookmarks, but not for sharing them. The innovation of social bookmarking is that when you apply tags to sites using these tools, your bookmarks are stored on the Web rather than your browser. This means that your bookmarks can be shared with or discovered by other users of the social bookmarking service and that you can access them from any computer with Internet access.

One of the earliest and most prominent of these bookmarking sites is Delicious (or del.icio.us; http://delicious.com), which is credited with coining the term "social bookmarking." Another site is StumbleUpon (www.stumbleupon.com), which works in a similar way but allows users to share reviews and recommendations of Web content. Digg (www.digg.com) and Reddit (www.reddit.com) are "social news sites"; that is, they allow users to submit and vote on items like news stories or other links to Web resources. The service "AddThis" (www.addthis.com; Figure 1-2) has created a widget (see Chapter 10) that provides you with a choice of using virtually any of the current social bookmarking tools to tag a Web page.

An interesting use of social bookmarking in an archival setting is the Delicious account established by the U.S. National Archives' education staff

Figure 1-2. Display of Social Networking Services Available on "AddThis"

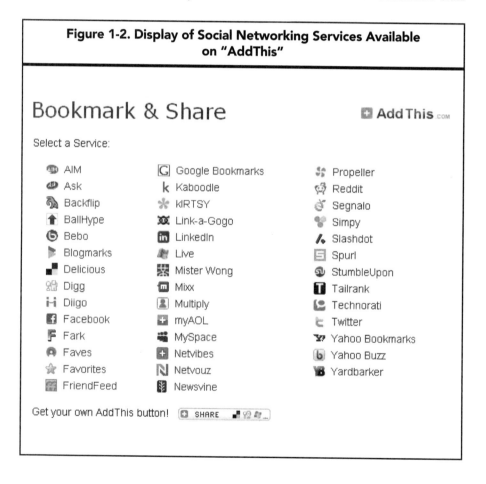

(http://delicious.com/NationalArchivesEducation) to share resources with the teachers who attend their workshops and other programs. Archives' staff use tags like "NHD08" to flag resources that relate to the theme of National History Day in conjunction with topical tags like "dictatorsvillains." Most of the resources tagged are digitized images or documents from the National Archives' own holdings, so the education staff are promoting the use of the archives' collections while providing a valuable service to teachers and students.

MYTHS AND MISCONCEPTIONS ABOUT WEB 2.0

Today, most people who use the Web regularly are accustomed to the term "Web 2.0" and the concepts it describes. Even people who don't use services like Twitter or Facebook have probably heard or read stories about them in the media. While one would think that by this time most people had overcome their suspicions about using these kinds of Web tools, you may still encounter people who have reservations. Some of the most common myths and misconceptions about Web 2.0 are discussed to help you address these issues.

"Those Sites Are Scary and Dangerous"

People may have formed this opinion based on stories in the media about bad things happening to someone who shared too much personal information on social networking sites. Everyone should exercise the same kind of discretion on these new kinds of Web sites as they would in any other public forum, but for some people (particularly young people) the ease with which you can share information leads to lapses in judgment. Information you post in any Web forum can be shared, even if the forum itself is private. Be discrete about the information you share (including pictures and video). From an institutional perspective, there is little chance that a well-monitored presence in a Web 2.0 forum would lead to anything scary or dangerous. It's true that on many sites other people can post pictures or messages that your institution might not approve of (for example, comments on videos posted on YouTube or images on Flickr). If you are monitoring your presence, you will probably see them quickly and remove or modify them. Even if people see them before you have a chance to take them down, most users of Web 2.0 sites understand that an institution cannot be held responsible for the actions of private individuals. In addition, organizations like archives and historical organizations are not the most popular of Web 2.0 participants and so are unlikely targets for spam or vandalism.

"Only Kids Use That Stuff"

While it's true that many Web 2.0 tools originated as sites that were most commonly used by high school and college students, they have long since matured out of that stage of development. Recent studies by the Pew Internet & American Life Project show that:

- Forty-eight percent of Internet users have been to video-sharing sites such as YouTube and the daily traffic to such sites on a typical day has doubled in the past year (Rainie, 2008).
- The share of adult Internet users who have a profile on an online social network site has more than quadrupled in the past four years—from 8 percent in 2005 to 35 percent now (Lenhart, 2009).
- Twitter and similar services have been most avidly embraced by young adults. Nearly one in five (19 percent) online adults ages 18 to 24 have used Twitter and its ilk, as have 20 percent of online adults 25 to 34 (Lenhart and Fox, 2009).
- Currently, 19 percent of all Internet users say they have downloaded a podcast so that they could listen to it or view it later (Madden and Jones, 2008).

These and similar studies show that Web 2.0 tools are, indeed, more popular among younger people than among those over 35; however, their use is steadily increasing among older Web users. It's also important to remember that, as time passes, the people who were "the kids" yesterday are today's young professionals. In addition, anything that "kids" use, such as Twitter or Facebook, is also likely to be something that their parents and other family members start using to keep in touch with them. Web 2.0 tools certainly were used first and are used most heavily by the young, but it isn't true by any means that they are the only people using them.

"It's Just a Fad"

Some people think that because the media hype about Web 2.0 and some of its sites was so prominent, the "buzz" can't possibly be justified. They may also think that the huge numbers of users attracted by sites like YouTube, Twitter, and Facebook are too big to last and that when the novelty wears off the sites will wither and die. Although the media may have exaggerated the importance of Web 2.0 and overhyped some of its more popular sites, this has no bearing on the fact that the way users interact with the Web has fundamentally changed. No individual Web site is guaranteed to last, and there is a good chance that many of the specific Web sites or tools discussed in this book will not exist five years from now. However, given their broad popularity (and the amount of money being invested in them), there is a good chance many of them will continue to exist and evolve for years to come. All of the Web 2.0 tools discussed in this book have been in existence and stable for several years. Although it's difficult to predict the longevity of any individual site or tool, the services being offered and the overall impact of Web 2.0 are here to stay.

"If I Give My Content Away, People Will Misuse It"

This is a concern voiced more often by cultural institutions than by individuals, and it really centers on the issue of control over how their materials are used. Some institutions have been afraid to share digital content over the Web because they are concerned people will infringe on their copyright by redistributing it without proper credit or that people will deface or modify the content in an offensive or irresponsible way. It is certainly possible that either of these things can happen if you share your digital content. Some institutions, particularly in the early days of the Web, put watermarks on their digital images to address some of these kinds of concerns. There are no studies or assessments that identify the percentage of digital content cultural institutions have shared that has been misused. However, it is worth noting that the largest and most prominent cultural institutions in the world share images of their content online. They seem to think, as most organizations with an educational or outreach mandate do, that the opportunities presented by sharing their collections outweigh the potential risk.

"If I Give My Content Away, I'll Lose Money"

This is another concern raised by organizations like archives and historical societies that include as part of their revenue stream profits made by charging for copies of items in their collections. Some organizations provide copies on a cost-recovery basis and so are not dependent on reproduction fees as a source of revenue. For other institutions, the loss of this revenue is a significant concern. Again, no surveys or studies have yet been done that show how sharing digital surrogates of collections affects income. For most archives, the quality of the images shared on the Web is not high enough to meet the standards needed for high-quality publication, so most people or organizations wanting to publish an image will still need to purchase a high-resolution digital version. It's true that people who want to have a digital image of a picture or document for their own reference purposes would not need to purchase one if a copy were available online. If revenue from people purchasing reference copies constitutes a significant source of income for your institution, you may want to take that into account in deciding what images to include in your Web 2.0 projects. However, the majority of organizations who have shared their materials would probably say that the benefits they've gained from the exposure and the value the public has gained from having access to their collections far outweigh any revenue they may have lost.

These myths and misconceptions about Web 2.0 are rapidly fading away, and many people are already turning their attention to Web 3.0. Over time the term Web 2.0 will fall out of fashion, and tools like RSS, tags, and social networking may be replaced by things that are even more powerful or simple to use. But the concepts of openness and sharing on the Web that that term embodies are here to stay, and for the foreseeable future Web 2.0 is the Web we will be using. All archives and historical organizations need to become accustomed to operating in this new environment and begin to explore its diverse opportunities for interacting with their users.

REFERENCES

Grossman, Lev. 2006. "Time's Person of the Year: You." *Time* (December 13). Available: www.time.com/time/magazine/article/0,9171,1569514,00.html (accessed May 25, 2009).

Lenhart, Amanda. 2009. "Adults and Social Network Websites." Washington, DC: Pew Internet & American Life Project (January 14). Available: www.pewinternet.org/Reports/2009/Adults-and-Social-Network-Websites.aspx (accessed May 30, 2009).

Lenhart, Amanda, and Susannah Fox. 2009. "Twitter and Status Updating." Washington, DC: Pew Internet & American Life Project (February 12). Available: www.pewinternet.org/Reports/2009/Twitter-and-status-updating.aspx (accessed May 30, 2009).

Madden, Mary, and Sydney Jones. 2008. "Podcast Downloading 2008." Washington, DC: Pew Internet & American Life Project (August 28). Available: www.pewinternet.org/Reports/2008/Podcast-Downloading-2008.aspx (accessed May 30, 2009).

Rainie, Lee. 2008. "Increased Use of Video-Sharing Sites." Washington, DC: Pew Internet & American Life Project (January 9). Available: www.pewinternet.org/Reports/2008/Increased-Use-of-Videosharing-Sites.aspx (accessed May 30, 2009).

Wikipedia. "RSS." Available: http://en.wikipedia.org/wiki/RSS (accessed May 25, 2009).

Wikipedia. "Web 2.0." Available: http://en.wikipedia.org/wiki/Web_2.0 (accessed May 25, 2009).

CHAPTER 2

Evaluating Your Current Web Presence and Setting Goals for Web 2.0

Before thinking about how Web 2.0 tools can help your institution, it is necessary to ask some basic questions about what you want to achieve and what resources you have available. This chapter asks questions about five areas of your institution's current infrastructure and plans. Being able to answer questions about your current Web site, existing Web resources, technical resources, strategic plan, and intended audiences will give you a firm foundation for planning your new ventures with 2.0 tools.

ASSESSING YOUR CURRENT WEB SITE

Before embarking on any new Web 2.0 projects, you should assess your existing Web presence. The point of many of your new outreach efforts will be to bring new visitors to your Web site to learn more about your organization. If your Web site is hard to navigate, lacks important information, or looks dated, you will lose the interest of many of these potential new users. Your Web site is your only public face for many of your potential patrons. You should make sure it portrays your organization as welcoming, capable, and informative.

Some archives and historical organizations implemented a Web site design and structure many years ago, with no subsequent updates, leaving them with a site that looks out of date and unprofessional. Other organizations have not kept up with the expectations of users, who turn to the Web as a source of complete and timely information. While it's true that few organizations can put all their collections online, most organizations can put all of the available information about *themselves* online.

It's also important to acknowledge that many archives and historical organizations are part of a larger institution—such as a college, university, or local or state government—and so must work with a mandated design or template. If you fall into this category, you may not be able to address some of the concerns discussed in this chapter. However, you should still be able to ensure that you are providing users with complete information. (And you can also provide specific feedback to your organization about how the mandated template does not meet your needs.) Almost every organization has some kind of constraint on how much it can modify its Web site—because of organizational requirements, lack of resources, or lack of expertise. The information provided in this chapter will help you address some of the areas that you can improve.

Does Your Web Site Answer the Key Questions—Who, What, When, Where, and How?

While you may think that anyone who visits your Web site is there because they already know who you are and want to learn more, it's important to remember that many users will not enter your Web site through your "front door," but will land on one of your pages as the result of a Google search. These kinds of new visitors, as well as those who come to your site with more background, should be able to easily locate essential information about your organization, either on the homepage or within one click. Users should easily be able to find the following information:

Who your organization is:
- Your organization's name and mission statement
- Organizational structure and governance—Is it a membership organization? Is it part of a larger organization?
- Names of the leadership, board, and staff
- Multiple forms of contact information—e-mail addresses, phone numbers, and fax numbers for departments or key staff

What your organization has:
- Information about your collections—broad statements about the general collecting areas, short descriptions of major collections, online finding aids, an online catalog, and digitized content
- Information about size of the collection and the media and records types represented

- Information about what your collections *do not* include (if there are gaps in your collections, or if users frequently expect something to be there that is not)

Where you are located:
- Mailing address and street address
- Maps, driving directions, information about parking and available public transportation
- Links to information about your community—to other archives, libraries, and historical sites, for example

When people can access materials:
- Hours of operation, including any seasonal variations and special closings
- Information or recommendations about accessing materials, such as pull times or the need to check to see if materials are stored off site
- If an appointment is required to access the materials, information about how to make an appointment, including how much advance notice is required

How people can get access to what they want:
- Policies and procedures
- Recommendations on how to plan a visit
- User or reference guides, if available
- Explanations about how things are organized—for example, how do archives work? What is a record group? Why don't you describe every item?
- Information about how people can gain access to materials if they can't visit in person
- Information about accommodations available for people with disabilities

Some of these points may be more relevant to larger organizations and some to smaller, but while you may not want to include all this information, this is a good checklist for you to review in assessing your current Web site. The goal is for someone with no knowledge of your institution (and possibly no understanding of what an archives is) to be able to understand who you are, what you have, and how to gain access to materials.

Does Your Site Look Professional and Current?

In the early days of the Web, many nonprofit organizations had Web sites designed for them by volunteers or staff with little or no professional training. At that time, having a presence on the Web was the most important thing; how it looked was secondary. Today's audiences are more sophisticated, and Web sites with poor design, outdated design features, or just a "dated" look reflect poorly on their institutions. Your Web site needs to reflect that it is an essential part of your operations. Check to make sure that your site:

- has a clear graphic identity and appealing color scheme that is continued on all pages;
- does not use outdated design features, such as frames, scrolling marquee, flashing or colored text, and animated GIFs;
- uses only one or two different fonts that are professional and contemporary in style;
- has current information about upcoming programs, exhibits, and events (and does not list events from the past as "current");
- has your latest newsletters, annual reports, or other publications;
- does not have links that don't work; and
- shows a "last updated" date.

For many people, your Web site will be the first (and perhaps only) impression they get of your institution. You should make sure it reflects an organized, efficient, modern institution that is a credible source of information.

Is Your Web Site Usable?

Perhaps the most important aspect of your institution's Web site is that visitors can use it. While this may seem obvious, there are many basic aspects of usability that some archives have not taken into account in their Web site design. Here are some questions you should ask about your site:

- Does it have a complete site map?
- Is there a search box for the site available on every page?
- Does it have a toolbar to provide consistent, easy access to other parts of the site?
- Is contact information available on every page?
- Is the font easy to read?
- Does the site maintain the same look and functionality in different Web browsers?

- Do all the pages load reasonably quickly, even with a slow Internet connection?
- Do all the pages print appropriately? (With different Web browsers?)
- If it is part of a larger organizational site, how easy was it to find the site for your archives?
- Does it avoid the use professional jargon? (Remember, not everyone knows what finding aids or record groups are.)

Anyone who is active on the Web knows the frustration of encountering a site that is difficult to use. For many people, especially casual visitors, the aggravation caused by some of these issues may mean they just turn to another site for the information they need. Although you may not be able to fix all these problems on your site right away, these are issues to be aware of that you should try to improve as you update your Web site.

ASSESSING YOUR EXISTING DIGITAL RESOURCES

In addition to assessing how well your current Web site represents your organization, you should also consider your other digital assets. Today, most institutions have created descriptions or finding aids in electronic form and digital versions of some of their holdings—which may or may not already be online. When you are considering implementing Web 2.0 tools, you should consider how these tools can best take advantage of your existing digital presence and assets. You may also be able to leverage your existing digital resources to "jump start" your new Web 2.0 efforts.

Online Catalogs and Finding Aids

If you have described your collections in an online catalog that is available on the Web or posted finding aids for your collections on your site, you should make sure your Web 2.0 implementations contain links back to these descriptions. If you write about items in your collections on your blog posts, you should ensure that people who are interested in these collections are easily able to locate the relevant information. Although many of the people who will enjoy your Web 2.0 implementation may never have the time or energy to explore further, you should always bear in mind that your Web 2.0 presence can be a way to draw new users to your catalog or finding aids. For these people, your use of Web 2.0 will encourage them to dig deeper, and your Web site should make it as easy as possible for them to learn more. If attracting new users for your collections is one of your motivations for implementing a Web 2.0 tool, then you should make sure your catalog and finding aids are easy for new users to find and navigate. Wherever possible, you should also try to create linkages back from your collection descriptions to your 2.0 tools, for example, linking to a relevant blog post or Flickr image from the catalog description or finding aid.

If your collections are described in a catalog or in finding aids that are not posted on the Web, you will still want to create connections between the materials you incorporate in your Web 2.0 implementations and these resources. If your local catalog has unique identifier numbers, you should include them in your descriptions of materials in your Web 2.0 tools. When referring to hardcopy or electronic finding aids, you should explain that these are available for consultation in the archives and provide the citation information. Although moving a catalog online is a major undertaking, you might consider using your Web 2.0 implementation as a spur to post all or some of your finding aids on the Web. Being able to link your new Web 2.0 audience directly to an online finding aid would be a valuable way of promoting the use of your collections and is something you might want to consider in your planning.

If your collections are not yet described well in a catalog or finding aids, it may be a difficult choice whether to devote resources to Web 2.0 outreach efforts when the essential task of establishing intellectual control of your collections is not yet completed. However, you will find some models in this book of how you can also use tools such as blogs and wikis as a way of sharing information about the collections you are processing. Opening up your process of arranging and describing materials by writing about them in a blog is a way to engage users and share information before you are able to make a complete description available. Tools such as wikis can also be used to support processing by providing a means of sharing information about procedures and making descriptions available to everyone on a team. While not a substitute for a properly constructed finding aid, information shared through blogs and wikis gives users a different perspective on the collection and on the ways archivists work to make them accessible.

Digitized Collections and Online Exhibitions

Today, most archives and historical organizations have digitized some part of their collections, if only a small number of popular images. However, many institutions have digitized large collections of documents and images, both to provide easier access to the content of the materials and to preserve the original from overuse. Having digital images of items in your collections provides you with an obvious resource for participating in image-sharing sites such as Flickr. However, you can also tap into this resource to support a blog that regularly features images or create a video from stills to post on YouTube. Digitized archival film or video content is, of course, also a natural choice for sharing on sites like YouTube. Digitized audio files are great source materials for podcasting and can also be used in the soundtrack if you create your own videos.

In online exhibitions, digitized holdings are combined with descriptive text that usually offers more information than a basic catalog record would provide. The opportunities presented by the digital content are the same as previously described, but the contextual information from an exhibit can be reused, for example, in a "mashup" (see Chapter 10) that allows users to browse information about holdings by seeing it tied to locations on a map.

ASSESSING YOUR TECHNICAL RESOURCES

Although many Web 2.0 tools require little technical expertise and don't require you to use any software on your local system, it is a good idea to consider what technical resources you have access to as you consider what tools you might want to implement in your own organization. One of the hallmarks of most Web 2.0 resources, like Flickr, Facebook, and many blogs, is that they are very easy to use, and most people don't need any support or training to be successful with them. However, it's always useful to revisit what your resources are, especially when considering new projects.

Professional Technical Support

Unless you are working in a very small archives, you probably have access to some form of professional technical support—whether in-house or outsourced. However, in many organizations having access to technical support does not always translate into having a cooperative and supportive technical environment; archives are sometimes not very high on the list of an organization's information technology (IT) priorities. Your own experience may give you an indication of how much support you can expect from your IT department, but you should not assume that when you approach it about Web 2.0 projects you will get the same kind of response that you've had before. You may very well find that your technical support staff already have experience (perhaps from their own personal projects) implementing Web 2.0 tools, and you may find them more interested in helping you than they have been in the past. You may learn that they have already implemented similar tools in other parts of your organization, and so your request may not be as complicated as you think. You may also be asking different kinds of questions than you have previously; in many cases, you may not be asking for help but only for permission or guidance. In any case, when you are ready to consider the specifics of a Web 2.0 implementation or want to discuss the pros and cons of different tools, set up a meeting with your technical support staff and see what they can do to help. It may be more than you expect.

Staff and Volunteers with Skills

Just as your technical support staff may have experience implementing Web 2.0 tools on their own time, so might members of your own staff and volunteers. Tools like blogs, Flickr, Facebook, and wikis are no longer new and exotic for many Web users. If you ask your staff and volunteers, you will probably find that many of them have some experience working with the Web 2.0 tools you are considering. If you expand your network to the friends and family of your staff and volunteers, you are almost certain to find someone who can help advise you or share their own experience. While you may not be able to rely on people like these to help you actually implement the tool you choose, they can help answer questions, show you around a site, and give you some feedback on your first efforts. Or, depending on the circumstances, you may be able to call upon them to help you set up your implementation. It's important to remember that, unlike the applications needed in the "Web 1.0" days, most Web 2.0 tools are being commonly used by a great many ordinary people on the Web. If you don't have access to professional technical support, you may have other options all around you.

Hardware and Software

For most of the Web 2.0 tools described in this book, you should not need any unusual hardware or expensive software. However, as you begin to think seriously about what you want to do, it is a good idea to know what you have to work with. Do you have access to computers with processing power sufficient for your needs? If you want to edit digital files or be active in Second Life, you will want to make sure you have a computer with a reasonably fast processor and enough memory. If you plan on uploading large image, audio, or video files to the Web on a regular basis or participating in Second Life, you will probably want to have a fast Internet connection. You will also want to make sure you have adequate storage space for any digital files you are creating, as well as media, such as external hard drives or CDs, to use for creating backup files.

Many Web 2.0 resources don't require you to use any special software at all—they operate completely on the Web. Each tool is different and has its own requirements, but in general you should explore what kinds of software you already have available for editing digital images, audio, and video. Some basic software is often already available, bundled on computers you may already have, and other software may be downloaded for free (or at a minimal charge) from the Web. Before you purchase any specialized software for a Web 2.0 project, you should always check to see if there is a comparable freeware product available.

UNDERSTANDING YOUR STRATEGIC PRIORITIES

In considering an implementation of a Web 2.0 tool, just as with any new program or outreach effort, you should ask how it serves your institution's strategic priorities. Some institutions have undertaken strategic or long-range planning that has resulted in formal planning documents, whereas others have a less formal planning process. In any case, every archives or historical organization should have some kind of documentation of its most important goals for the future—or at least a shared understanding of what those goals are. Your goals may include things such as:

- increasing use of materials in your collections;
- increasing the number of visitors to your physical location;
- building public recognition for your institution (or "building your brand");
- promoting the history of your locality or of a collecting area;
- supporting new scholarship on the subject areas of your collections;
- building a broader advocacy base for your institution; and
- increasing financial donations or donations of materials.

Almost any kind of Web 2.0 implementation could help achieve many of these goals. For example, a popular podcast about the materials in your collection could build public recognition for your institution, promote the history of your area or collecting area, and probably also support new scholarship and build a broader advocacy base, at a minimum. A Flickr account with many interesting images from your collection could increase the use of materials from your collection and build public recognition, and it might also result in new scholarship about those images and possibly even new donations of similar materials.

Most use of Web 2.0 tools contributes primarily to achieving goals that are more outwardly focused, such as the ones listed earlier. In addition to these kinds of goals, most archives also have goals related to their own internal processes, such as accessioning and processing collections and responding to reference requests (these are very likely goals related to "outputs," as will be discussed in Chapter 11). While the connection may be less obvious, some Web 2.0 tools have the potential, when used creatively, to make contributions to these kinds of goals as well. One of the hallmarks of most Web 2.0 tools is their flexibility. Blogging software, for example (as described in Chapter 3), can be used to create a blog that also serves as a tool to easily create and update catalog descriptions or to create a system for logging and tracking reference requests and making reference responses easily available for reuse. Posting images on Flickr and creating descriptive tags can make it easier for archivists, as well as the public, to locate and share relevant images. Creating a subject area wiki or a wiki for commonly used resources (such as the DuBoisopedia or the Montana History Wiki, respectively; see Chapter 8) can save time for reference archivists in answering common reference questions on popular topics. As you read the following chapters describing specific Web 2.0 tools and how they have been used by other institutions, you should be thinking of which ones could best be used to help you meet your own strategic goals.

IDENTIFYING YOUR AUDIENCES

As you consider how Web 2.0 tools can help you meet your organization's strategic goals, you should also be thinking about how they can help you serve your target audiences. There are many ways of describing your potential audiences, but two broad groupings that can help you frame your analysis are:

- traditional audiences versus new audiences, and
- local audiences versus distant audiences.

Neither of these juxtapositions (traditional versus new or local versus distant) represents needs that are totally separate; you can meet the needs of both kinds of audiences at the same time. However, different tools and different uses of the tools do sometimes have more advantages for one type of audience rather than another. If serving or attracting one type of audience should take precedence, then it is important for you to factor that into your thinking about implementing Web 2.0 tools.

Existing Audiences versus New Audiences

If your institution wants to focus on maintaining and serving the audience who already knows about you, you might want to create Web 2.0 products that emphasize areas you know your audience is interested in. For example, if you create a blog you might choose to write posts that delve deeper into topics that appeal to your existing audience (but which might not appeal to casual readers) rather than writing on topics that introduce your collection or have broader popular appeal. In contrast, to attract new audiences you might want to create a blog that features a "document of the day" and set up an associated Twitter account. A collaborative wiki (such as "Chinese-Canadians: Profiles from a Community"; see Chapter 8) can also be used to attract interest and participation from a new audience of potential users of your resources.

Local Audiences versus Distant Audiences

If you have decided that you are most interested in serving your local audience, you may select images and video to post on sites like Flickr and YouTube that have a strictly local focus rather than seeking out material to post that has a broader appeal. Images of your town's main street through the decades, for example, would appeal primarily to a local audience, whereas images taken from a tourist scrapbook documenting a trip to Egypt in the 1870s would be of potential interest to a wide variety of distant users who may never have heard of your archives. Framing your decision making in this way, you might decide that the potential local audience doesn't justify the resources needed to create and broadcast a podcast, or you might decide that the opportunities presented by a podcast to reach people all over the world does justify the investment.

As was discussed in Chapter 1, it is not wise to assume that your existing or local audiences won't be interested in or able to use Web 2.0 tools and sites. The demographic reach of popular sites such as Flickr, Facebook, and Twitter, and the easy availability of tools such as blogging software, means that more and more people from every age group and socioeconomic status are familiar with and are using Web 2.0 products. As previously noted, studies such as the Pew Internet & American Life Project (www.pewinternet.org) consistently document how much the Web dominates the way people seek information and the prevalence of Web 2.0 tools. If you want to be a Web destination for today's users, you need to make sure your site speaks to their needs and gives them the kinds of information they want in the forms they want it.

CHAPTER 3

Using Blogs

WHAT IS A BLOG?

The term "blog" originated as an abbreviation of "Web log." Blogs are Web documents (usually a unique Web site) created by software that allows material to be published on a Web site in the same manner as log—or diary—entries are written in a journal. When a new entry is published, it appears at the top of the Web page, moving older entries down, and eventually off, the site's first page.

Blogging software was first introduced in the late 1990s, and in their earliest days blogs were primarily used by technology writers and other "early adopters." At that time, "blogger" was sometimes used as a derogatory term, and the information conveyed by blogs, particularly news information or political commentary, was often perceived to be unreliable. Today, blogs have gained widespread acceptance as a mainstream vehicle for Web communication and are used by major corporations, publications, and writers.

There are two options available for creating a blog. You can use a service that provides both online software and hosting, or you can install software on your own server (or server space you rent) and host the blog yourself. The most commonly used services that combine blogging software and hosting are the following:

- Blogger (owned by Google)
- LiveJournal
- TypePad.com
- WordPress (through WordPress.com)

Of these, Blogger and WordPress are the most popular. The most common software programs used by bloggers on their own servers are the following:

- Moveable Type
- Textpattern
- WordPress (through WordPress.org)

All of these services are available at no charge. The ease with which people can use free services such as Blogger has led to the creation of millions of blogs—a very small percentage of which remain active for any substantial amount of time. Blogging is very easy to begin but not so easy to continue. It takes a commitment to writing on a regular basis. While often a challenge to maintain, blogs are powerful tools for Web communication and one of the simplest of Web 2.0 tools.

Parts of a Blog

The term "blog" refers to a whole Web site. A blog is composed of a series of "entries" or "posts." Posts are identified by a title and by the date on which they were published. Posts can contain any mixture of text, embedded images, audio, or video content. Most blog posts—particularly those created by archives—contain primarily text or a mixture of text with images. Each blog usually creates its own conventions about the length of its posts. Most bloggers keep their posts relatively short, in the range of three to five paragraphs, and some blogs routinely feature one-paragraph posts. Bloggers can also employ a "jump" feature—often used for longer posts. Inserting a "jump" means that the entire post is not displayed in an RSS feed or on the blog's Web page; the jump appears as a "read more" link that, when clicked, takes the reader to the rest of the entry.

In addition to the title (which serves as a permanent link back to that specific post), each post will have an author identified. A blog may have multiple authors or contributors who write posts. Most bloggers assign categories in the form of tags to each of their entries to allow them to be accessed by subject. Categories should be consistently applied and easy to understand.

The way a blog is laid out and its visual elements are usually governed by a "template." These templates enable the creator of the blog to select the layout and visual style that best suits their needs. Content can be switched from one template to another very easily. Almost all blogs have a header section at the top that contains the blog's name, sometimes an image, and usually some basic administrative information. Blogs generally have either a two- or three-column layout—because one of the "columns" contains the blog entries, this means that the blog either has one or two additional columns (or sidebars) for other kinds of information. For example, the "Historical Notes from OHSU" blog shown in Figure 3-1 (shown later in the chapter) is a two-column layout, while "A View to Hugh" in Figure 3-2 (shown later in the chapter) uses a three-column layout.

Sidebar Content

Sidebars can contain a variety of additional features. The most common are the following:

- A search tool for the blog
- A "blogroll"—links to other blogs
- A link to an "about" page, which provides a short description of the purpose of the blog and who sponsors it
- A list of the tags or categories used to classify blog posts that also allows users to click on a tag to pull up all relevant posts
- Links to the blog "archives"—usually in the form of a list of past months and the number of posts in each month
- A calendar for the current month, with days on which there were posts to the blog highlighted in some way
- An indication of the copyright or use restrictions placed on the information in the blog, often in the form of a Creative Commons license (see Chapter 12)
- Links that allow people to subscribe to the blog or the blog's comments or to tag posts with social bookmarking services (as discussed in Chapter 2)
- A "tip jar"—a link to a way people can make donations (This is not very common among archives blogs.)
- Advertisements, including ads for pertinent books available on amazon.com
- One or more "widgets" (see Chapter 10)

Blog Comments

When a blog is established, the administrator can choose whether to allow readers to comment on the blog posts. Blogs that allow comments usually require the person leaving a comment to provide some kind of name or identifier and an e-mail address. The e-mail address is not publicly displayed but is provided to the blog creator. Most blogs also allow people leaving comments to provide a link to their Web site in addition to an e-mail address. If a Web site is provided, the commentor's name will appear as a hyperlink leading to the commentor's Web site. A "trackback" is a type of comment that links back to another blog post that references the original post.

Most blogging software allows the administrator to determine whether comments will be moderated or unmoderated. If comments are moderated, they must be approved by the administrator before they appear on the site. If comments are unmoderated, they appear on the site immediately. Once posted, any comment can be removed by the blog administrator at any time.

It is highly recommended that blogs that allow comments employ a spam filter. Blogs are frequent targets for spam comments. Spammers sometimes make an effort to compose comments that appear to be real, but usually they are just long strings of words that they think people will be searching for—often words associated with pornography or gambling. Employing a spam filter and moderating comments should ensure that no spam comments appear on a blog.

HOW CAN YOUR INSTITUTION USE A BLOG?

The functionalities provided by blogging software are very simple—publishing information on the Web that appears in sequential order, with the newest material appearing first. This simple structure makes blogs very easy for most people to understand, and it also lends itself to many different uses. Archives and historical organizations are using blogs to share information about their collections and activities, highlight processing projects, publish date-based archival content, and provide innovative ways to support archival processes like description and reference while including a public-facing component. These are certainly not the only ways blogs can be employed, but they are the most common.

Institutional Blogs

Institutional blogs are sponsored by organizations like archives, historical societies, and special collections as a general outreach tool. They can range in tone and content from impersonal blogs that are reminiscent of a newsletter to blogs that reflect the personalities of the individual staff who contribute and the variety of events and collections at the institution.

The most basic form of institutional blog is strictly a forum for posting official communications, such as press releases and other general information. These blogs are used for sharing information about hours, exhibits, events, and collections and usually do not stimulate (nor are intended to stimulate) comments or discussion. This type of blogging is the least labor intensive for staff but also will be of limited interest to anyone outside the archives' existing user community. It is primarily a way to share information with people who already know about your organization, not a means of attracting new audiences. These types of blogs are, however, an effective way to communicate information to your user community without having to maintain an e-mail distribution list.

Other organizations invest their institutional blogs with more personality—for example, having staff write under their own names and in the first person. Blogs like these can have posts that discuss new acquisitions or collections that have recently been made available. These kinds of blogs also sometimes feature digital images of the objects or locations related to the blog posts. A "document of the day" (or week) can be a feature of blogs like these.

This type of institutional blog takes time and commitment from staff, but the return on the investment can be quite rewarding. Staff have an opportunity to share their own knowledge of the collections more broadly and informally with a wide audience. Among the oldest and most successful institutional blogs is "Historical Notes from OHSU" (Figure 3-1), produced by Sara Piasecki at the Oregon Health & Science University (http://ohsu-hca.blogspot.com). Active since 2006, "Historical Notes" has promoted knowledge of the collections and mission of its institution far beyond its traditional audience.

Another model is "Coca-Cola Conversations" (www.cocacolaconversations .com), the blog written by Phil Mooney, the archivist of the Coca-Cola Company. This blog provides its organization—in this case, a for-profit business with a long history—a chance to build on its own corporate image by drawing on its history and the expertise of its archivist. In his opening post, Mooney (2008) wrote:

> We'll talk about people who collect Coke memorabilia, the items they collect and the stories they tell. We'll talk about recipes made using Coca-Cola and our other drinks. We'll talk about what's happening today with Coke—and how it relates to things from our past. And we'll talk about the new World of Coca-Cola in Atlanta, which just opened last summer.
>
> We hope to give you a look into the Secret Formula of Coca-Cola—but not literally! While we can't show you the actual formula famously in an Atlanta vault, we can give you an insider's look into the world of Coca-Cola.

Figure 3-1. "Historical Notes from OHSU" Blog

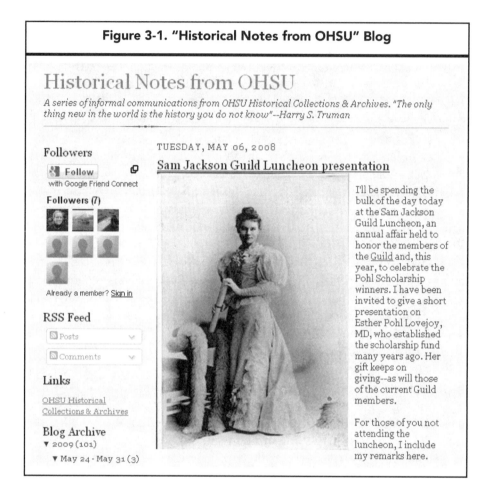

Historical Notes from OHSU

A series of informal communications from OHSU Historical Collections & Archives. "The only thing new in the world is the history you do not know"--Harry S. Truman

Followers

[Follow]   with Google Friend Connect

Followers (7)

Already a member? Sign in

RSS Feed

Posts
Comments

Links

OHSU Historical
Collections & Archives

Blog Archive

▼ 2009 (101)

▼ May 24 - May 31 (3)

TUESDAY, MAY 06, 2008

Sam Jackson Guild Luncheon presentation

I'll be spending the bulk of the day today at the Sam Jackson Guild Luncheon, an annual affair held to honor the members of the Guild and, this year, to celebrate the Pohl Scholarship winners. I have been invited to give a short presentation on Esther Pohl Lovejoy, MD, who established the scholarship fund many years ago. Her gift keeps on giving--as will those of the current Guild members.

For those of you not attending the luncheon, I include my remarks here.

You can comment on what I say and send me questions—and I hope you do! You can even email a photo of a Coke piece you have and wonder about. We'll do an appraisal on this site and I'll tell you what I know.

People read these blogs because they have an association with the organization or the subject matter of the collection. For many readers, interacting with the blog authors and other readers via the comments, or simply following the news and progress that's being reported, means that these blogs strengthen their connection to the sponsoring organization. Blogs can also provide a venue for reaching out to the organization's community by presenting questions to the readers—such as a photo that needs identification. Take, for example

Interview with Sara Piasecki
Historical Collections & Archives
Oregon Health & Science University

What made your organization decide to start a blog?

I decided to start the blog when, after a few years of working in HC&A at OHSU, I realized that library staff from other units didn't really know what we did—and that they would never know what we do or what collections we have unless we told them. Mostly, I wanted to share the fun and excitement that we were having on a daily basis. Only secondarily did it occur to me that folks outside of OHSU would be interested as well.

What information, tools, and processes did you need?

I had already set up an account for Google Docs, so it seemed natural to use the Blogger platform to start our blog. It's free and it's easy, so I was able to go in, pick a template, and start posting in a very short amount of time.

How did you determine what content to include?

When I started, I thought that I would share one cool thing I encountered on any given day, with emphasis on collections and processes (for my "intended audience" of library staff). As my readership grew and I got more feedback, I started to think more about what might be of interest generally. Now, the posts are all over the map, from collection gems to screeds on archival issues of the day to conference reports to new donations to obituaries. I occasionally try to tie posts in with larger issues or events at OHSU, in Portland, or in the profession.

What challenges did you face?

One of the challenges is, of course, time. Another is balancing access to information with the privacy of donors and the wishes of a (justifiably) image-conscious university.

What kinds of positive results have you had? (And, any negative ones?)

The results have been far more positive than I could ever have imagined when I conceived the blog. Patrons we never would have reached before now stumble across us in Web searches. Readers from all sorts of communities (historians, librarians, archivists, healthcare workers, genealogists) have contacted us because of something they saw in some post or other of mine. We've received donations of materials from as far away as New York and Arizona. Awareness of our collections and services among the OHSU community has risen exponentially, and though that has come

(cont'd.)

Interview with Sara Piasecki (continued)
about in combination with other outreach efforts, the blog is definitely a part of it. Another wonderful aspect of blogging is the ability to tap into extramural expertise: when we posted about some mysterious Russian LPs we had received, two readers quickly responded with translations of the jacket text. Negative results? Not yet.
About how much time does it take?
It really depends on the topic and can take anywhere from five minutes (look at this cool picture!) to two hours (annotated bibliographies of a donation).
What advice would you give an organization wanting to use something similar?
Organizations are like people: each one is very different, so your mileage may vary. If you're in the sort of organization where everything needs to be discussed before it gets implemented, make sure you talk to stakeholders first. Think about how often you plan to update it: daily, weekly, monthly? Volume for volume's sake is unappealing, but people will lose interest if you only post a couple of times a year. The best advice I can give you is: Don't stress about posting! It's ok to have typos, it's ok to have short posts some days, it's ok to go out on a limb and say you don't know much about some item in your collections. Most of all, it's ok to show a little personality!

Rensselaer Polytechnic Institute's "RPI History Revealed" (http://rpiarchives .wordpress.com), which regularly publishes "Mystery Images" and had readers successfully identify seven out of ten of the first mystery images. The "Sandusky History Blog," sponsored by the Sandusky Public Library, also is very successful with its "Mystery Photo" posts (http://sanduskyhistory.blogspot .com).

Processing Blogs

Processing blogs are sponsored by an archives or special collection as a more specialized form of outreach tool. They may be written by one or more contributors, and their tone is usually a more personal one. They are used for sharing information about what archivists find as they are processing a collection (usually one specific collection), and they often stimulate comments and discussion.

One of the most successful of the processing blogs is "A View to Hugh" (Figure 3-2), a blog related to the Hugh Morton Photographs and Films Collec-

Figure 3-2. "A View to Hugh" Blog

A VIEW TO HUGH
Processing the Hugh Morton Photographs and Films

HOME   ABOUT   CONTACT

Recently Written

Remembering WW2, part 2
"For A Few Glorious Moments..."
Mother's Day Montage
World's Largest . . .
Camp Yonahnoka, part II
The Wilds of Alaska
Series 1: North Carolina Places
UNC vs. Villanova: 1982 and 1985
Azalea Festival memories
Hugh Morton's Short Run For Governor

Recent Comments

Childrens Beds: I dont know if you knew this but Graham graduated from Nort...
Elizabeth Hull: Charlie Yogenfloster? That is priceless! I wonder if that wa...
Julia Morton: Hugh would rise up and smite me for telling you this in irre...
Jack Hilliard: I'm really glad to learn that so many of Hugh Morton's warti...
Jack Hilliard: Two of Hugh Morton's classic photos of UNC All America Charl...
Jack Hilliard: Beautifully written, Amber. I like the way you matched Hugh...
: Bodie Island Lighthouse has been approved for restoration. ...

Categories

Animals (11)
Azalea Festival (2)
Behind the Scenes (36)
Biography (17)
Camp Yonahnoka (3)
Celebrities (13)
Events (32)
Filmmaking (1)
Grandfather Mountain (20)
  Highland Games (3)
  Singing on the Mountain (3)
Jazz (3)
Landmarks & Attractions (22)
Music (4)
Nature (15)
Photojournalism (15)
Politics (6)
Sports (14)
  Basketball (7)
  Football (5)
  Golf (1)
  Hang Gliding (1)
Tourism & Development (8)
UNC (17)
Who Am I? (10)
WWII (5)

Archives

May 2009
April 2009
March 2009
February 2009
January 2009
December 2008
November 2008
October 2008
September 2008

From Grandfather Mountain to Chapel Hill

November 1, 2007 | Subscribe to this post
Posted by Stephen Fletcher in Behind the Scenes, Biography

The life's work of photographer Hugh Morton has a new home: the North Carolina Collection Photographic Archives in Wilson Library at the University of North Carolina at Chapel Hill. It took two trips in four vans filled to the gills to bring it all from the Morton residence near Grandfather Mountain to the university where Morton spent his freshman through junior years as a student. His enlistment in the United States Army in September 1942, at the outset of his senior year, pulled him away to the Pacific and on to what became a celebrated life, but he returned to the campus he loved time and time and time again—and likely always with his camera.

It's also likely that Morton had his camera with him everywhere else he went. We all look for something to "click" in our lives; for Hugh Morton it was his cameras' shutters. We think he clicked them about half a million times. It takes a lot of shutter clicks to fill four vans. Morton made many photographs and shot a lot of motion picture film, too. It will take a good deal of time—measured in years—to organize and make available for use the results of so much clicking. Sometimes *I* "shutter" just thinking about it.

There is so much interest in the Morton collection. The first inquiries started before we opened more than a handful of boxes. The time needed to make such a voluminous collection available compared to the demand for its use beckoned for a non-traditional approach to collection processing. The way it's "supposed" to be done is to open the collection only once it is completed. To make material accessible as soon as possible, we are planning to make parts of the collection available incrementally as we complete them.

We also needed a way to keep people informed about our progress and offer glimpses into the collection's wealth. We are enthused by the public interest and want to transform it into community involvement. So we developed this blog to meet those needs and we hope it "clicks" with you!

Links

ArchivesNext - Blog examining archives and technology
Biographical Conversations with . . . Hugh Morton - An episode from the UNC TV program featuring a one-on-one conversation with Hugh Morton
Duke Digital Collections - Updates and discussion from staff of the Duke Libraries' Digital Collections Program
Grandfather Mountain - Scenic attraction and nature preserve in Linville, NC owned by Morton from 1952 until his death in 2006
Morton Biography from Grandfather Mountain website
NC Collection Photographic Archives
NC Digital Collections Collaboratory - For Digital Librarians in North Carolina to share experiences, exchange ideas, and develop collaborations.
NC Miscellany Blog - Blog of the North Carolina Collection, Wilson Library, UNC-CH
Posterity Project - Blog related to archives, history, civic responsibility, and open access to public records in Tennessee
Processing the Chew Family Papers - Reports on an NEH-funded project to process the papers of the Chew Family at the Historical Society of Pennsylvania.
Southern Short Course in News Photography - America's longest running photojournalism seminar, of which Morton was a founder
Southern Sources - Interesting staff finds, curiosities, old favorites, and other cool stuff from Wilson Library's Southern Historical Collection
UNC Libraries

Feeds

Subscribe to new posts
Subscribe to comments on posts
What is this?

Source: Photograph by Hugh Morton, Copyright University of North Carolina at Chapel Hill Library.

Interview with Stephen Fletcher
North Carolina Collection
University of North Carolina at Chapel Hill

What made your organization decide to start this blog?

The primary reason we created "A View to Hugh" was to inform the general public on our progress with processing the Hugh Morton photographic collection that contains an estimated 500,000 items. We knew the collection would be in high demand but that it would likely take two to three years to make available for use. By creating a "processing blog," we wanted to highlight interesting discoveries we would make along the way and solicit information about unidentified or partially identified photographs, of which there are thousands. We also saw an opportunity to provide glimpses into how photographic archivists work so that the public would understand what is involved in archival processing, especially a collection that large. By writing about the above points, we hoped to foster a discussion with the audience and gain input from our readers, who we hoped would be the public and archivists alike.

What information, tools, and processes did you need?

We needed our IT department's programming knowledge because the blogging software, WordPress, is installed on university servers and must conform to a variety of internal standards and protocols.

How did you determine what content to include?

We made it up as we went along, mostly because we were working with a highly unorganized collection and had no idea what discoveries awaited us. We wanted a friendly, conversational tone (not academic) to the writing that encouraged readership and participation. To that end, we try when possible to make personal connections to the material we discuss, showing by example that photographs are not merely illustrations.

What challenges did you face?

We soon faced an unexpected controversial topic that we had to weather, which we survived by staying focused on the photographs, not the photographer. More broadly, once you go live you need to stay active, so we try to post at least once a week. With a huge, daunting processing job in front of you, it is easy to fall into the trap of thinking that writing for the blog is "just one more chore." You have to remind yourself that, on a higher level, it's building support for the collection and that, in the bigger picture, the blog has aided in the completion of the job.

(cont'd.)

Interview with Stephen Fletcher (*continued*)

What kinds of positive results have you had? (And, any negative ones?)

We have been able to leverage the blog to gain additional media coverage and to build emotional and financial support for the collection.

About how much time does it take?

Three months transpired between our first meetings with IT staff to our first blog post. It took a few weeks to explore the blogosphere and then draw sketches of how the blog might look. Then we surveyed WordPress templates to serve as the base. IT staff then did the necessary coding for design adaptations and worked on behind-the-scenes programming and security matters. Of course we all have other responsibilities, so a dedicated focus on the blog would have resulted in a quicker pace, but we were satisfied with three months.

The time it takes to write posts really varies greatly. Our most popular post, as measured by user comments, is very short, taking about ten minutes to compose. Others have taken an hour or more to write. Each post is reviewed by a second set of eyes for properly functioning links, typographical errors, and style consistency. We check daily for spam and reader comments, and the attention necessary to address these can range from a few seconds to several minutes depending on the nature of the comments. All in all, it is not burdensome.

What advice would you give an organization wanting to use something similar?

Look at lots and lots of blogs to see what you like and don't like, but more importantly gain a sense of the styles and features that meet your particular needs. Once established, involve other staff to share the limelight, and utilize a variety of voices, but maintain a harmonious style. Your writing should reflect your personality, but more importantly your material. Respond to readers' comments to create a dialog, build readership, and convey genuine interest. Write for both archivists and the public, but do so in a manner that is understandable to the public.

---

tion at the North Carolina Collection Photographic Archives, the University of North Carolina at Chapel Hill (www.lib.unc.edu/blogs/morton). A prolific photographer, Hugh Morton was a figure of enormous significance in North Carolina, and the collection his family donated to UNC after his death contained a huge volume of mounted slides, photographic prints, transparencies, negatives, motion picture film, videotapes, audiotapes, and CDs. Knowing that public interest in the Hugh Morton collection would be high, and also knowing that it would take many years to process the disorganized materials well enough to provide access to them, UNC took what was at the time an innovative approach—they would open up their activities in processing the Morton collection via a blog.

"A View to Hugh" succeeds in part because the materials in the collection date from a time within the memories of many of its readers. "Processing the Chew Family Papers," sponsored by the Historical Society of Pennsylvania, benefits from discussing materials that are far removed from today's world (http://chewpapers.blogspot.com):

> The Chew Family Papers is one of the Historical Society of Pennsylvania's largest collections of family papers, spanning approximately 400 linear feet, and covering a period of nearly 300 years. This collection details the family's activities as lawyers and politicians, as well as the events of their daily lives.
>
> The Chews were one of Philadelphia's wealthiest and most influential families. Benjamin Chew (1722–1810), his siblings, and descendants, played fundamental roles in shaping revolutionary and early federal America. They acted as lawyers for the Penn family, served on the Commission to determine the boundary line between Pennsylvania and Maryland, held high public offices, and purchased large amounts of property in the Delaware River valley. As one of the largest slave-owning families in the mid-Atlantic region, the Chews maintained numerous farms and plantations, and kept careful documentation about their practices. (Miller, 2008)

The Chew Family Papers blog is written by three NEH-funded processing archivists; in their posts they discuss the intellectual content of the materials they are processing as well as the physical challenges they present (see posts such as "Conserving the Chew Family Papers" and "Dealing with the Madness"). Their posts convey the excitement archivists feel as they make discoveries in the records, as well as providing information about the content of the collections and the work involved in processing them.

Both of these blogs have multiple authors, a lively tone, and varied content, which can be keys to a successful processing blog. The audience for this type of blog will probably want a combination of information about the processing itself and what kinds of materials the archivists are discovering. However, interspersing these more causal posts with ones that provide more historical context for the documents is important. If you want to appeal to scholars and nonscholars, a balance of types of posts is essential, as is an engaged first-person tone. Readers should feel that they are getting a view "behind the scenes" and a sense that they are alongside the archivists making discoveries and unraveling mysteries.

Archival Content Blogs

The date-based format on which blogs are built lends itself naturally to conveying date-based information, such as reproductions or transcriptions of diaries or letters. Blog entries are usually synchronized with the date of the material they are sharing (in other words, a diary entry may be posted on the same month and day as the original document was written). Although this might seem like an obvious choice for a blog topic and most archives have many collections of diaries and letters, blogs of this type appear to be somewhat unusual so far. It is worth noting that some of the most prominent were created by private citizens, making available their own family documents.

One of the most celebrated blogs of this kind is almost certainly "WW1: Experiences of an English Soldier" (http://wwar1.blogspot.com), in which a grandson published letters written by Private Harry Lamin, 90 years to the day after Private Lamin wrote them while he served in the British army in World War I. The response to this blog was tremendous, including multiple news stories on television and radio and a nomination for "Best Blog of All Time" in the Blogger's Choice Awards. The comments left by readers demonstrate how much the blog has touched them. On November 11, 2008, the 90th anniversary of the end of World War I, they included comments such as the following two (Anonymous, 2008):

> I've been reading your blog for the past year. A very moving account. I love the combination of personal detail with the official accounts of the same events. I've linked to your blog today as part of my own little act of remembrance. I look forward to seeing the rest of Harry's story.

> What an emotional and fascinating journey you've taken us on, Bill. Thank you so much for your dedication and hard work. I feel like a member of Harry's family—waiting each day for letters and worrying when there's no news. I introduced the blog to my father and work colleagues and now Harry's very much the subject of our daily conversations! Once again, thanks for allowing us to experience history in such a unique and fascinating way.

A somewhat different approach was taken by the archives of Hobart and William Smith Colleges in creating the "Abner Jackson Journal 1858–1867" blog (http://abnerjackson.wordpress.com). In this case, only the entries relating to Jackson's tenure as president of Hobart College were published from the journals, rather than every journal entry. Posts to the blog were also not made to coincide with the dates of the journal entries; the relevant journal entries cover nine years, so it was more practical to post them in chronological order, but not with any tie to the particular date. Each diary entry post was given relevant subject tags, such as "Curriculum," "Civil War," and "The Episcopal Church." While this log probably does not have the broad appeal of the World War I letters blog, it enables researchers easy access to the information in Jackson's journal and enables keyword searching by users as well as discovery via search engines.

A diary blog that has received far more attention and comment is the "Orwell Diaries" blog (Figure 3-3; http://orwelldiaries.wordpress.com). *(continued p. 51)*

Figure 3-3. The "Orwell Diaries" Blog

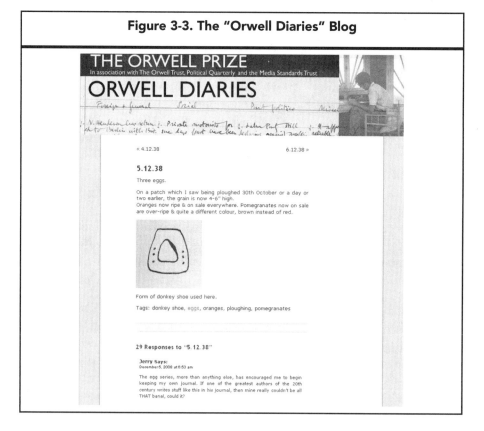

Interview with Gavin Freeguard
The Orwell Prize

What made your organization decide to start this blog?

We felt, with our access to the Orwell Archive (at the University College, London) and having our (then) new Web site, we had an opportunity to give the public access to "Orwelliana" that they wouldn't usually be able to see. We were particularly keen to open up works which many people probably hadn't read, or even heard of, before—his essay on British Cookery proved popular on the main Orwell Prize Web site. Trawling through the archive listings, the domestic and political diaries from 1938–42 jumped out—especially as it was mid-2008, and the diaries started in August 1938, perfect timing! I had a look at them in the archive, a mix of typical Orwell political observation and the more domestic and mundane, and we decided to go ahead with blogging the entries 70 years to the day since they were written.

What information, tools, and processes did you need?

Permission from the literary executor (who we already had a good relationship with via the Orwell Prize) and the cooperation of the Orwell Archive at UCL; a couple of excellent interns who, along with me, typed out the diary entries from the original archival material and Peter Davison's magisterial *Complete Works* and added the links in the posts for further information; photographs (and money to pay for them) from the archive; and some media coverage to ensure that the hard work which had gone into the project wasn't wasted. However good the idea, and however good the blog, it would have been pointless had nobody known about it to enjoy it! The WordPress platform has been excellent, and their team very supportive and helpful. Lately, we've also been tweeting the first few lines of each day's entry at twitter.com/TheOrwellPrize.

How did you determine what content to include?

The content really chose itself—the diary entries written by George Orwell, 1938–42. We have tried to keep it as pure as possible—we could have linked to all the letters, articles, etc., he was writing at the same time, but this would have been too much information, raised rights issues, and, quite simply, have been too much work. We've also included other Orwell archive materials directly relevant to the diary entries (available in the Image Gallery on the site), works by D. J. Taylor, Peter Davison, and Gordon Bowker to provide some context, linked to Web sites with more information on some unfamiliar terms in the entries, and—of course—created the popular Google Map plotting Orwell's location.

(cont'd.)

Interview with Gavin Freeguard (continued)

What challenges did you face?

Given that the idea came relatively late, and quite close to the projected start date, time was an issue! There was no electronic version of the diaries in existence, so everything had to be typed up from scratch. We had originally hoped to provide both text of the diary entries and an image of the entry for that day—but the delicate nature of the archival material and cost made this impossible.

What kinds of positive results have you had? (And, any negative ones?)

I think we've achieved our original aim to open up parts of Orwell's canon that people hadn't previously been aware of—and in so doing, opened up a side of Orwell they may not have been aware of. Running the diaries as a blog has advantages over printing them as a book (although there will soon be an edition published following the success of the blog)—people are much more likely to dip into, or follow from start to finish, these bite-sized chunks rather than a huge, daunting book. As well as giving the diaries a real sense of immediacy, especially as World War Two approaches, they give a real insight into Orwell's life. Orwell once wrote (in his 1939 essay about Charles Dickens, written as the diaries unfold) that "When one reads any strongly individual piece of writing, one has the impression of seeing a face somewhere behind the page." The diaries allow you to gather your own impression of Orwell's face—behind the screen, rather than the page. They show—whether writing about the Spanish Civil War or sloe gin, geraniums or Germany—Orwell's perceptive eye and rebellion against the "gramophone mind" he so despised; a real interest in nature and domestic handiwork, which while surprising to many readers is not a surprise to, for example, his son Richard Blair; and the nature of a writer's life, the kind of compulsion to write, a voracious consumption of everything around him and trying to record everything as it actually is, whatever it may be.

It's also been very positive to see a community build up around the blog—even when the only records of note were about how many eggs Orwell's hens had laid! [See Figure 3-4.] Our "egg-centrics," as one publication lovingly dubbed them, have stuck with us through the lows of one-egg days and the highs of four-egg days (even using that parlance themselves). They're egg-static now the daily egg count sometimes reaches double figures. The community have also asked questions, shared their own experiences, and provided further information around topics mentioned in the posts—one of the best examples is the discussion around "Vasano," a seasick remedy which Orwell took on 4th September 1938. The Orwell scholars who have contributed to the blog have also been very pleased—one of them was even tracked down by an old student as a result!   (cont'd.)

Figure 3-4. Sample Comments from the "Orwell Diaries" Blog

Augustus Carp Says:
December 5, 2008 at 10:44 am

Orwell's problem is that he is trying to run a small sale egg production unit a couple of years before ET Halnan's seminal text on "Feeding Poultry" was published by the War Office in 1940. If he had had the benefit of that valuable pamphlet, I reckon he would be up to about six eggs a day by now. (It later reappeared as Chapter XV of Halnan & Garner's " Principles and Practices of Farm Animals", published by Longman, Green & Co also in 1940.)

dave Says:
December 5, 2008 at 12:02 pm

1000 Pounds for the date he gets 4 eggs.

That egg diagram obviously has some nice freshly ground pepper on it; yummy...

Ed Webb Says:
December 5, 2008 at 1:44 pm

When the breakthrough came,
The three egg day, I complained,
Of pomegranates

art brennan Says:
December 5, 2008 at 1:47 pm

Don't you think the closed shoe would tend to be lost or pulled more often than an open shoe? Also, stones and debris would be trapped more often between the hoof and/or frog and the shoe.

Natalie Says:
December 5, 2008 at 4:48 pm

Overripe pomegranates are really disgusting.

Jonas Söderqvist Says:
December 5, 2008 at 5:14 pm

Ed Webb: Next to the excitment of what Eic is writing next, I'm allways looking forward to read your Haiku poem of the day.

Thank you very much for bringing a smile on my face every evning

Interview with Gavin Freeguard (continued)

We also used the Orwell Diaries blog as an excuse to expand the Orwell Prize, which is Britain's pre-eminent prize for political writing. The Prize has, since 1994, awarded a Book Prize and a Journalism Prize to the entry which comes closest to Orwell's ambition "to make political writing into an art"—so for the 2009 Orwell Prize, we had a Special Prize for Blogs as well. It generated a great deal of interest in the British political blogosphere and 83 entries. The eventual winner, a pseudonymous serving police officer called "Jack Night," received a great deal of praise and positive media coverage.

Indeed, the international media coverage around the launch of the blog (see examples in the side bar links on the blog) and at various stages in the Orwell Prize for blogs (e.g., after the longlisting) has sparked a lot of interesting discussion about whether Orwell would have blogged and, through that, the value of blogging as a medium.

On the negative side, there has been some criticism about the way we've conducted the project (i.e., whether we should be blogging what are "personal" diaries, even though Orwell himself definitely intended that some of them be published) and whether it presents a distorted view of Orwell. On the whole, a lot of the "criticism" has been part of a healthy and interesting debate, which is what the Prize has always existed to promote. A few of the commenters on the blog display what can only be described as a sense of entitlement—that somehow we should run the project exactly as they think it should be done, and they have a right to demand that. We're very willing to listen to suggestions, of course—and some of the comments on the blog have been very helpful.

And being nominated for a Webby was very positive! [The "Orwell Diaries" blog was nominated for a prestigious "Webby" award in 2009 but unfortunately did not win.]

About how much time does it take?

The WordPress platform means that we're able to produce a huge batch of entries in advance, ready to be published when the time comes. It took a few weeks to type up the first batch of entries, and it will take a similar amount of time to take us to the end. In terms of day-to-day maintenance, it's a few minutes to check comments in need of moderation, make sure any images are inserted in the post, and to add a location to the Google Map.

What advice would you give an organization wanting to use something similar?

Keep it simple, give yourself as much time as possible to put it together, listen to constructive criticism, and enjoy the experience!

Unlike the Abner Jackson diary, the blog documenting the life of the writer George Orwell has attracted a loyal following and regular comments. Orwell's diaries begin in 1938 and are being blogged 70 years to the day since each diary entry was written. Created by the Orwell Prize, the preeminent British prize for political writing, the site created for the diaries blog also contains images and documents that supplement the information in the diaries, as well as a Google Map that shows the progress of Orwell's travels. This rich context, the built-in attraction of a famous writer, and the content of the diaries themselves have all no doubt contributed to the success of this blog.

Blogs Supporting Traditional Archival Systems

Several archives are taking advantage of the flexibility of blogging software to create innovative approaches to sharing information about their collections. Among the more unusual uses is Dickinson College's reference blog (http:// itech.dickinson.edu/archives). This blog, although available to the public, is not intended primarily as an outreach tool. The public blog is used to publish summaries of all the reference requests received and their responses. These summaries, along with administrative data about the request, are reused in the administrative "back end" of the blog, which is used for internal tracking purposes. The blog also provides archivists with a tool for searching past answers to help respond to questions on similar subjects. Most importantly, the descriptions of the reference queries supplied on the blog are crawled by search engines and thus are discoverable by users searching for similar information. Thus the reference blog serves internal uses for generating statistics and developing a knowledge base while taking advantage of the "long tail" qualities of the Internet—that while there may be a small number of users for some collections, if you make that information available to them, they will take advantage of it.

Another example of archivists using blogging software as a tool for discovery is UMarmot (see Figure 3-5), an interactive online catalog for the Special Collections and University Archives at the University of Massachusetts Amherst (www.library.umass.edu/spcoll/umarmot). UMarmot takes advantage of blogging software's inherent tools for easily publishing, tagging, and searching data to present short descriptions of the archives' collections. Like all blogs, UMarmot is crawled by search engines like Google, increasing the chances that users will discover its collections. The blog entries can be easily updated as new information is found. Just as with traditional blogs, interested users can comment on blog entries and subscribe to the blog's RSS feed. In ad-

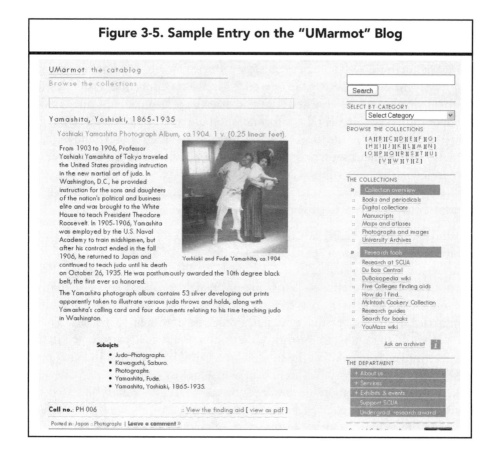

Figure 3-5. Sample Entry on the "UMarmot" Blog

dition, UMarmot contains links to PDF versions of completed finding aids for collections that have been fully processed, but when no finding aid is available the blog entry provides the public with readily accessible information about the archives holdings with a minimal technological investment by the archives.

WHAT DOES IT TAKE TO START A BLOG AND KEEP IT GOING?

The first step you should take as you think about starting a blog is to *identify your goals*. What do you want the blog to achieve for your institution? After looking at the different types of blogs discussed in the previous section, it should be clear that blogs can have different purposes. Do you want to convey simple announcements, or do you want staff writing more detailed posts? Do you want to focus only on your collections, or do you also want to discuss your public programs? Do you want to highlight one collection or many? How do your goals for the blog relate to your institution's strategic plan and goals? Who do you want your audience to be?

Your blog's purpose can evolve over time, but it is essential when you are starting out to have a clear mission statement that you can share with your readers and administration (as Mooney did in "Coca-Cola Conversations"). Your mission statement should include an identification of the blog's target audience. If your blog will have more than one contributor, having a clear definition of your blog's purpose also helps ensure that everyone keeps their posts "in scope."

Next you should *make an inventory of your constraints*. Think about issues such as:

- How much time can staff realistically devote to writing and maintaining the blog?
- How much technical expertise do you have access to (including your own)?
- How supportive is your organization's leadership to the goals you have for the blog?
- How sensitive are you and your administration to risk?

On the issue of risk, publishing a blog is by definition making a public statement about your institution. While it may seem unlikely that any of your blog authors will make a statement that may raise public concerns, this is a possibility you should consider, and you should develop some basic policies for how you would handle such an event. (See Chapter 12 for more discussion about policies.)

Based on the goals and constraints you've identified, you next need to *determine your blogging software and hosting*. You need to decide if you want to host your blog on your own server or through a commercially hosted service. You also need to explore what software is available to you. There are several options for blogging platforms that combine hosting and software, such as Blogger.com and WordPress.com. Here are some factors you need to consider in making these decisions:

- What are your technical capabilities?
- How much do you care about "branding" your blog through its Web address?

- How often do you plan to embed images or video in your posts? (How much server space do you need?)
- Do you have funds available to spend on software or hosting services, or do you need to utilize no-cost options?
- How concerned are you about reliability?

Next, you need to **define the key aspects of your blog**, such as:

- What do you want your blog's full name and Web site address to be?
- Will you accept comments?
- Will people blog under their own names?
- What template do you want to use?
- What do you want to include in your "about" section?
- What e-mail address do you want people to use for feedback or questions?
- How often will you post? (Not less than weekly? More often?)
- What should your policy be about what kinds of comments you will accept and what kinds will be deleted?

In the course of considering these important questions, you may want to revisit and revise your blog's mission statement to make sure your practices are adhering to the goals and audience you've defined for the blog.

While you're considering these key aspects, it is also important to define key roles and responsibilities for the blog, for example:

- Who will write the posts?
- Do you need someone to review or edit the posts?
- Who will respond to comments?
- Who will serve as the blog's administrator?
- Who is responsible for promoting the blog or serving as its "public face"?

For organizations that will have many people contributing to the blog, it may be useful to develop and disseminate "blog guidelines," such as those developed by the University of London Computer Centre's Digital Archives (http://dablog.ulcc.ac.uk/guidelines). Guidelines such as these define appropriate practices for the institution's blog.

In this planning stage you should also begin to determine how you will measure and evaluate the success of your blog. For more information on planning for evaluation, see Chapter 11.

Finally, you need to *plan for your blog rollout*. You may choose to start your blog with very little public fanfare to give yourself an opportunity to establish a blogging rhythm and get some posts under your belt before going public, or you may want to make a media splash with your first post. In either case, you should conduct a series of test posts and comments with your software (to be deleted) to make sure you fully understand it before you "go live."

Think about promoting your blog the same way you would your public programs or publications—such as announcements to your immediate community and local media, articles in appropriate newsletters, etc. However, there are additional ways for you to promote your blog in the online world. For example, have your blog included in the blog aggregator AchivesBlogs (http://archivesblogs.com). Send announcements to archives and history bloggers, such as the American Historical Association's blog (http://blog.historians.org). You can also find out if there are any people blogging about your community or have blogs related to the materials you're discussing; they may also be happy to give your blog some promotion.

Final Tips If You Are Considering Blogging

- Study other blogs to get ideas.
- Have a voice and a point of view.
- Remember to write posts that the public will understand and find appealing. (Avoid archival jargon—or, if you use it, take the time to explain it!)
- Get a spam filter, if necessary.
- Post regularly, and respond to your comments.
- Remember that your blog can evolve.
- Don't be afraid to ask other bloggers for advice.

REFERENCES

Anonymous. 2008. Comments on "At Last the End of Hostilities." WW1: The Experiences of an English Soldier. (November 11). Available: http://wwar1.blogspot.com/2008/11/at-last-end-of-hostilities.html (accessed April 23, 2009).

Miller, Cathleen. 2008. "The Project Unfolds." Processing the Chew Family Papers (February 13). Available: http://chewpapers.blogspot.com/2008/02/project-unfolds .html (accessed May 29, 2009).

Mooney, Phil. 2008. "Welcome to my Blog," Coca-Cola Conversations (January 23). Available: www.coca-colaconversations.com/my_weblog/2008/01/welcome-to-my-b .html (accessed May 29, 2009).

CHAPTER 4

Using Podcasts

WHAT IS A PODCAST?

A podcast is a series of digital audio or video content made available to users on the Web for subscription and/or download. The term "podcast" is commonly used to describe either an individual episode or an instance of a podcast series and the series as a whole. It is also used as a verb to describe the process of creating and distributing podcast series. The term was coined in 2004 by combining "iPod" (the most popular and culturally significant MP3 player) and "broadcast" (Wikipedia, "Podcast," accessed 2009). Although some people object to using the term "podcast" because of the close association the term implies to iTunes products, this has become the most commonly accepted term. You may also hear podcasting described as "audio blogging" or "video blogging" (sometimes shortened to "vlogging").

Key Attributes

The key aspect of podcasts is that they are downloaded by users rather than streamed to users. This means that podcasts can be accessed via computer or portable media devices (such as iPods and other MP3 players) at any time the user chooses. Streaming media must be listened to in one sitting, at a computer; when you hit the "start button," you have to sit and listen to the whole thing in one session or start from the beginning again. With downloaded media, like podcasts, users can "time shift"—choose how and when they access the content. Listening to a podcast is a portable experience, and users control when they listen to the content, for example, while seated at a computer or while commuting, traveling, or exercising. It also enables users to do things like pause, rewind, or skip while listening, which can't be done with streaming media.

Another key aspect of podcasts is that users can subscribe to the content's RSS feed and automatically download new episodes as they become available. Usually a podcast's "archives" (i.e., previous episodes) are also available for download, so new listeners can go back and catch up.

From the perspective of a user, the most essential aspect of a podcast is the digital media file that contains the podcast episode or program—usually an .mp3, .mp4, .m4v, or .mov file. Each media file has descriptive tags containing identifying information, such as the title of the podcast series, episode title, author, and date.

Accessing a Podcast

Individual media files can be accessed in a number of ways. Users can go directly to the homepage for the podcast series, which may take the form of a simple list of available episodes (see Figures 4-2 and 4-3, shown later in this chapter) or a more descriptive blog for the podcast series (Figure 4-4, shown later in this chapter). Users may download and listen to individual episodes, including shows from the "archives," directly from these kinds of sites. However, most users will probably choose to subscribe to their favorite podcasts using podcatching software, such as iTunes or iPodder. Users can also subscribe to a podcast's RSS feed using tools such as Bloglines and Google Reader (as discussed in Chapter 2). When a user is subscribed to a podcast with software such as iTunes, Bloglines, or Google Reader, new episodes of the podcast are automatically downloaded whenever the user accesses the software.

Podcast Structure

Most podcasts are similar in format and style to traditional broadcast series. A podcast series will have a descriptive title, a unifying theme, and a consistent host or hosts. Successful podcasts employ a style and tone that is appropriate for their subject matter and audience. Each episode of a podcast follows a standard format, even if it is as simple as beginning with an announcement of the podcast name and subject, followed by the content, and closing with a reiteration of the podcast name, credits, and contact information. Many podcasts use musical cues to transition between segments, and most use "bumper music" or "bumpers"—that is, music played at the beginning and end of a podcast. Most podcasts are also identified by an image or picture that is associated with the series and appears on the screen of a user running iTunes or using an MP3 player with a screen. All these elements—a podcast's title, format, images, music, and host—combine with the podcast's content to determine how effectively it works for the audience.

Information to Support a Podcast

Many podcasts are supported by a blog that provides a place to put "show notes" and additional information relating to each episode (including corrections and follow-up information). A companion blog for the podcast also provides an easy mechanism for listeners to leave comments and share feedback. As discussed in Chapter 3, allowing blog readers to have discussions in the comments builds a sense of the blog—and by extension your podcast—being part of a community.

Good podcasts usually provide mechanisms for user feedback, including comments, corrections, and suggestions for new topics. These mechanisms can include providing an e-mail address, a telephone number, or relying on the comments feature of the podcast's blog or the comments posted on iTunes (Figure 4-1). Some podcasts include responses to user feedback as part of the content of their podcast programs.

HOW CAN YOUR INSTITUTION USE A PODCAST?

Podcasting allows you to share a wide variety of information about your collections; for example, you can share digitized audio or video archival content and recordings of public programs or tours or create a program specifically to be podcast (or any combination of these). You can also choose to create an ongoing, open-ended podcast series or create a podcast series around a specific topic designed to have only a predetermined number of episodes. The latter format—a podcast that is not ongoing—may be more practical for many archives and historical organizations. You may have a particular event, such as an anniversary or exhibition, or a particular theme or collection that you wish to highlight using a podcast. You could enable users to subscribe to this kind of short podcast series, just as they could to an ongoing series, while new episodes are being added. And, of course, users would still be able to access your series as long as you continue to make it available online.

Podcasting Public Programs

Many organizations offer unique and valuable public programs, such as lectures or tours, that only a limited number of people can attend. Capturing these

---

Figure 4-1. Sample Comments Posted on a Podcast Page in iTunes

CUSTOMER RATINGS

▶ Average rating: ★★★★½ 23 ratings

Rate this podcast: [Select   ‡]

CUSTOMER REVIEWS   16 Reviews ⊕
                                                         Write a Review ⊕

Excellent ★★★★
by Joe Shaw - Jan 21, 2007
I've listened to the first four podcasts and I'm very much enjoying them. As a history fan you can't do much better than the first person recollections and insights of the people who were there. Forget about James Bond, this is the real deal and the... More

Incisive analysis of covert operations ★★★★★
by larkr - Mar 14, 2007
The interviewer, a.k.a. Peter Earnest, does an excellent job of bringing contemporary relevance to past historical operations in the Company (CIA). Each spycast maintains a very objective position on past operations which allows interviewed guests t... More

Early shows somewhat interesting, lately has become very partisan ★★
by IceNorm - Mar 5, 2008
Interesting only in that it shows the depth to which the spy agencys are staffed with people who have their own leftist policy agenda which complely colors their view of world affairs.

---

events and distributing them via podcasting is an excellent way to derive lasting benefits from a one-time event. Distributed on the Web, podcasts such as these can help broaden your local network of members, users, or supporters as well as build a national (or international) reputation for your repository. You can also use this type of podcast as a way to provide an orientation session for your users or offer advice about specific types of research.

An excellent example of this kind of podcasting is the series sponsored by the National Archives of the United Kingdom (Figure 4-2; www .nationalarchives.gov.uk/rss/podcasts.xml). This series captures and publishes talks and events given at the National Archives that are of a broad general interest. They include some talks by historians, who describe the process and results of their research, but the majority of the programs are more directly related to the records housed in the National Archives. These programs focus on specific

Figure 4-2. The National Archives of the United Kingdom Podcast Web Page

Subscribe to this podcast using [Live Bookmarks ▾]

☐ Always use Live Bookmarks to subscribe to podcasts.

[Subscribe Now]

The National Archives Podcast Series

Listen to talks, lectures and other events presented by The National Archives of the United Kingdom.

The National Archives

Catching Victorian and Edwardian criminals on paper

The problem of serious habitual criminals and how to keep track of them greatly exercised the minds of our Victorian and Edwardian forebears. This lecture focuses on the methods utilised by police and government to record and monitor such offenders, and how the surviving records can be used by present-day historians to investigate both historical and contemporary questions concerning serious and persistent crime.

Media files
♪ catching-victorian-edwardian-criminals.mp3 (MP3 Format Sound, 20.3 MB)

Every journey has two ends: using passenger lists

The National Archives' Chris Watts reveals the benefits of using both arrival and departure records when searching for details of our migrant ancestors, as well as demonstrating how the shortcomings of content, indexing and accessibility can be minimised.

Media files
♪ every-journey-has-two-ends-edit.mp3 (MP3 Format Sound, 20.3 MB)

From Mountbatten to Patten: the last proconsuls and the ending of the British Empire

After the Second World War, the role of governors in Britain's overseas territories changed. This talk examines the colourful personalities and mixed fortunes of these proconsuls, and argues that, in spite of their declining power and authority, they performed a key role in managing imperial retreat.

Media files
♪ from-mountbatten-to-patten.mp3 (MP3 Format Sound, 20.3 MB)

record types or series and allow listeners a chance to learn from experts what these records contain and how they might be used. Programs such as these—captured and made permanently available—can be found and accessed by people from all over the world at any time, turning a one-time investment of resources into a long-term asset.

The National Archives of Australia has developed a similar podcast series (www.naa.gov.au/whats-on/audio/index.aspx), which captures talks and events at their institution. One advantage of this series is that in many cases transcripts of the audio content are provided for download. The Australian site also provides information about the size of the audio file and the length of the program, which are useful features.

The New York Historical Society has adopted a strategy for podcasting that is common in the museum world—creating podcasts that complement current exhibitions. For example, the series "Hidden Sites of Slavery and Freedom: A Walking Talking Tour of New York City," culminates with a series of podcasts

**Interview with Emma Allen and Joshua Shindler
The National Archives of the United Kingdom**

What made your organization decide to start this podcast series?

In the past few years The National Archives has been moving its focus from an offline to an online organisation to meet our users' expectation that there should be more records, services, and expertise available online. This move is backed up by statistics: for every document viewed on site at Kew, 170 are viewed online. Similarly, while 20 to 100 people attend the regular talks and events at The National Archives in Kew, there are over 5,000 downloads of each talk. It seemed a natural extension to open up access to our expert talks by podcasting them for a much wider audience.

What information, tools, and processes did you need?

- One of the most important resources you need is access to good speakers who can present interesting subjects in an engaging way. We're fortunate to have a large number of colleagues who are historians, archivists, or academics and are experts in their field.

- To help keep a regular flow of podcasts, we use a production schedule for our planning. It details the recording date, location, speaker, topic/title, description, and the publishing date.

- It is important to get the basic logistics right. If the room does not have recording equipment built in, we'll need to bring a portable recorder and microphone with us, and it is crucial that we get there early in order to carry out a sound check.

- Meeting the speaker beforehand is also vital. If it is the first time that a speaker is going to be recorded for a podcast, we'll need to brief them. The speaker will need to let the audience know that the talk will be podcast, ask the audience to save questions until the end, not rustle papers while talking, and when referring to slides, read aloud any information on screen.

- Whether recording a live event or recording in a studio, we always need to do a significant amount of editing. This can involve removing pauses, coughs, mouse clicks, and other interruptions from a live recording, adding music and titles to the beginning and end of a podcast, or stitching together pieces of an interview. We use Audacity software to edit the raw audio files and professional audio software to "normalise" and clean the audio.

(cont'd.)

Interview with Emma Allen and Joshua Shindler (continued)

How did you determine what content to include?

Unlike the traditional radio show or magazine style podcast, our podcasts are primarily live recordings of regular talks and events that take place at The National Archives. Talks are given on a whole host of subjects: most appeal to an audience interested in history or genealogy; some might only appeal to a specialist in the field of archiving.

When we started podcasting, almost all the recordings were edited and published as podcasts. Now, although we record as much as possible, not all recordings are turned into podcasts. Some are too specialised, while in others the speaker may focus too heavily on a visual presentation, or the sound quality may just not be good enough.

What challenges did you face?

The biggest challenge was achieving an audio quality that meets the listeners' expectations. Unfortunately, the sound quality of the very early podcasts was not good enough, and we received negative feedback via the "contact us" section on our Web site and the iTunes reviews. Some listeners were willing to ignore the poor quality sound in favour of the content, but most weren't. We resolved this problem by purchasing professional audio recording equipment. In particular, a wireless tie microphone really improved the sound, since many speakers like to move away from a podium when speaking.

Educating a speaker to tailor his or her talk to a future podcast audience, as well as those in front of them on the day, is an ongoing challenge. A talk at The National Archives may be attended by anywhere from 20 to 100 people. In its first month available on the Web a podcast will be downloaded by over 2,000 listeners, increasing to between 5,000 and 10,000 downloads over the course of a year.

What kinds of positive results have you had? (And, any negative ones?)

Our podcast page statistics show that we are constantly growing our audience. We consistently place in the top 20 historical podcasts in the iTunes store, and we've had positive feedback via the iTunes store reviews. In addition, we have received excellent recommendations from listeners on genealogical and historical forums.

As a result of positive external exposure, more colleagues within The National Archives have approached the podcast team to record events and talks as a form of external communication. This has made finding quality content much easier; recent highlights include talks from actor and comedian Terry Jones and historian Peter Hennessey.

(cont'd.)

Interview with Emma Allen and Joshua Shindler *(continued)*
About how much time does it take?
When we first started it took a couple of days to source the content, edit the audio, and update the podcast feed. The time decreased as more content was fed to the team and as we became more efficient with editing. As a general rule, it seems to take four times the length of the podcast to record, edit, and publish. As we add more features (transcripts, notes, links, etc.) the process becomes more time consuming.
What advice would you give an archive wanting to use something similar?
Before you start recording, find out what your users want to listen to. This can be a tricky task, and sometimes it is only once you start publishing that you find out that you are not providing the content that your users want. User testing, reviews, and statistics analysis can really help.
Creating a realistic production schedule is essential, and remember not to sacrifice quality for frequency. Start off by releasing podcasts every month and build up to a weekly show. You can always add but you can't take away.
Invest in some professional audio recording equipment, and find a quiet, if not silent, room to use as a recording studio. You may have the greatest content on the Web, but if no one can hear it then no one will listen.
Finally, if you have spent time recording and editing and the results are still not good enough, then don't be afraid to scrap a podcast. Not all recordings will work as podcasts.

that captures talks given in conjunction with the 2007 exhibition "Legacies: Contemporary Artists Reflect on Slavery" (www.nyhistory.org/web/default .php?section=whats_new&page=tour). Given the long-term value and potential public interest in this information, the NYHS wisely invested in making it available in both audio and video podcasts (with transcripts available), and the series is also available via cell phone so that users can listen to the podcasts while actually following the walking tours being described.

Podcasting Digitized Archival Material

A more common use of podcasting takes advantage of the opportunities it provides to share audio or video holdings from historical collections. For example, the various Presidential Libraries (part of the U.S. National Archives and Records Administration) have joined together to sponsor the series "Presidential Libraries Uncovered" (www.archives.gov/presidential-libraries/research/podcasts.html). This podcast series is updated each month with material from the Libraries' collections, each in the presidents' own voices, including excerpts capturing things like policy discussions and conversations with family members. The Harry S. Truman Library and Museum has also created its own podcast series, featuring excerpts from Truman's public addresses (www.trumanlibrary.org/audio/podcasts.php).

Capitalizing on the roots of iPods and other MP3 players as vehicles for listening to music, several historical organizations are using podcasting to share recordings of musical performances. In their series "The Virtual Gramophone," the Library and Archives Canada brings to public attention "lost" treasures of Canada's musical heritage (www.collectionscanada.gc.ca/gramophone/m2-121-e.html). However, "The Virtual Gramophone" is also an outreach tool for an existing digitized collection of over 4,700 audio files, which are also available via searching and browsing of the collection's database. Each "Virtual Gramophone" episode contains music related to a different theme, such as "Drinking Songs," "Marching Bands," or "Fiddlers." When accessing the podcast via the LAC's Web site, you can see that each episode (or "channel," as the LAC calls them) actually consists of many individual music files that can be accessed separately.

Another type of archival holding that is suitable for digitization and distribution via podcasting is oral histories. One of the most notable examples of this type of podcast is the Los Alamos Historical Society's series (Figure 4-3; www.losalamoshistory.org/pods.htm), which shares excerpts from its oral history collection, focusing on the people and events of the building of the world's first atomic bombs. The Los Alamos series demonstrates the potential of podcasting for combining stories that highlight individual lives with larger historical events. This podcasting model, like the Library and Archives Canada series, draws on the archives' existing collections, bringing attention to materials that the public might not otherwise access or even be aware of.

Similar podcasting examples are available at two state archives. The State Archives of Florida has a series highlighting digitized recordings from their Florida Folklife Collection (www.floridamemory.com/collections/folklife/sound_pod.cfm). This series focuses on Florida's rich musical heritage, combining oral histories with recordings of performances at Florida's Folk Life Festivals. The Wyoming State Archives, in its "Wyoming Stories" and "Voices

Figure 4-3. Los Alamos Historical Society Podcast Web Page

New Podcast: MacAllister Hull was part of the Los Alamos Special Engineer District (SED) during the Manhattan Project. His background in college made him eligible for this technical assignment, where he worked with high explosives, as he explains in this podcast (1.23 MB .mp3 file.)

Ken Ewing, a chemical and nuclear engineer who spent his career in Los Alamos, discusses the possibility of surviving Nuclear War in this podcast (1.07 MB .mp3 file.)

Cold Warrior Ken Ewing talks about his work in the development of nuclear weapons during the in 1960s in this podcast (1.56 MB .mp3 file.)

Pop Chalee, a native of Taos, worked on the Manhattan Project and even rode horses with the Oppenheimers. Hear her stories in this podcast (1.3 MB .mp3 file.)

While Amy Gibson worked as a nurse in Los Alamos during the Manhattan project, she got to know physicist Richard Feynman on a personal level. She talks a little bit about his fun and quirky personality in this podcast (.76 MB .mp3 file.)

As a nurse during the Manhattan Project, Amy Gibson dealt more with industrial accidents and a baby boom than radiation issues. She tells about it in this podcast (1.43 MB .mp3 file.)

Frances Dunne, Los Alamos' own version of Rosie the Riveter, worked on airplanes, so she had no trouble working on the Manhattan Project, where her small hands helped get the job done. And she says that she had no qualms about being the only woman in her group in this podcast. (1.08 MB .mp3 file)

Jack Aeby took the only known color photograph of the world's first atomic bomb blast at Trinity site (all the official laboratory photos were in black and white). In this podcast (1.64 MB .mp3 file.), Aeby tells how it came about.

The housing crunch early during the Manhattan Project wasn't terrible for everyone. Some of the scientists and their families got to stay at really nice guest ranches in the Rio Grande Valley, as we hear about in this podcast. (1 MB .mp3 file)

Even though Kay Manley worked on the Manhattan Project and her husband was considered Oppenheimer's right-hand man, she says she still wasn't sure what the project was all about in this podcast. (1.1 MB .mp3 file)

Even 50 years later, Harlow Russ vividly recalls in his first day on the job, where he went, and the important people he met in this podcast. (1.54 MB .mp3 file)

Beckie Diven tells of her adventures in the dorm -- including cooking on top her her toilet! -- in this podcast. (1.64 MB .mp3 file)

Miriam Campbell explains how secuirty was part of every day life during the Manhattan Project in this podcast. (1.37 MB .mp3 file)

Source: Courtesy of Los Alamos Historical Society.

Interview with Heather McClenahan
Los Alamos Historical Society

What made your organization decide to start a podcast?

It was sort of a whim. We have a wonderful oral history collection, and I was looking for ways to use our Web site to attract new audiences. The podcast seemed like a perfect fit. The annual Museums and the Web conference happened to be in Albuquerque in March 2006, and I was able to attend. One of the workshops was by Ken Dickson from the Ontario Science Center on "How to Build a Podcast." I went to it, and he did a terrific job of showing how easy it was. We started our podcast in June 2006. The board has been very supportive—especially since it has been successful.

What did you need to get started?

We had just been given a CD recorder by Los Alamos National Laboratory, so the first thing we had to do was transfer the oral histories from cassette tapes to CDs (a process that is still ongoing!). All the software we use, Audacity and iTunes, was free, downloaded off the Web.

How do you determine what materials to include in the series?

So far, I pick the stories I find most interesting. Each podcast is about 5–6 minutes long, so I'm only doing snippets, not the complete oral histories. If someone is particularly articulate, I might use them for more than one podcast, talking about different things. Most of the podcasts have focused on the Manhattan Project, partly because that's what most of our oral histories are. But we also have some about the Ranch School, homestead, and Bandelier National Monument. I'm a historian, so my goal is to share history with wide audiences. The podcasts have become a really great venue for that.

What challenges have you faced since you started?

Until last spring, we had a problem with size. I didn't realize with voice-only recordings that .mp3 files could be downsized. So we had 6–7 MB files for each podcast, and they really started to add up. I was afraid we would run out of space on our server. Last spring Heather Marie Wells from the Shiloh Museum of Ozark History and I were on a panel together at an American Association of Museums conference. She told me how to customize the conversion and shrink the files. That's been a big help. The only other problem is the quality of the tapes. Some of these were recorded in the '70s. I had one tape break. Some are fuzzy and hard to hear. Audacity is a great program for what it does, but it can't clean up fuzziness and other sound quality issues as well as I would like.

(cont'd.)

Interview with Heather McClenahan (continued)

What kinds of positive results have you had? (And, any negative ones?)

The podcasts have been far and away the most popular aspect of our Web site. We get hundreds of downloads each month, and about 5,000 people hit our RSS feed. I even had one of the subjects contact us. He didn't remember giving us the oral history and was quite surprised to hear himself on the computer. We refreshed his memory, and he thought it was great. We've also been contacted by relatives of some of the subjects. We've had students use them as primary sources for history projects. For us, it's a great way to share the history of Los Alamos and meet our mission. It's getting this wonderful collection of oral histories "out there" rather than just collecting dust on a shelf.

About how much time does it take?

Including transferring the tape to CD, listening to the CD to find just the right podcast material, cutting, pasting, etc., it takes about two hours per podcast. I usually spend a day every few months "canning" several and getting them ready to go. We put up a new podcast about every two weeks.

What advice would you give an organization wanting to start something similar?

Figure out, first and foremost, what is the purpose of your podcast. The point should be to share what your institution is all about, whether it's history, art, science, etc. Listen to some other similar kinds of podcasts to get ideas. Some focus on exhibits, others on their collections. Figure out what's unique and great about your institution, and allow that to shine in your podcasts.

of the Governors" collections (http://wyospcr.state.wy.us/Stories/index.asp), focuses on digitized historical interviews with prominent Wyoming citizens.

Creating Unique Podcast Programs

Creating an ongoing podcast series that is based on primarily original content requires a commitment of time and resources that not many archives have made. One excellent model is "A Kansas Memory," produced by the Kansas State Historical Society (www.kshs.org/audiotours/kansasmemory/kmpodcast.htm). This podcast is designed to complement the materials from the historical society's library and archives that have been digitized and made available in the

Interview with Lin Fredericksen
Kansas State Historical Society

What made you interested in producing a podcast?

We knew a number of people who listen to recordings while driving or gardening or doing tasks around their homes, who prefer this to reading printed items. Audio books have also become an extremely popular item at the public libraries. We hoped we could tap into that user group.

What information, tools, and processes did you need to begin?

We do this with a very minimal budget. We use the same digital recorder that we use to collect oral histories. The readings are all done by staff members. We use Audacity, which can be downloaded free, to edit the recordings. For period and instrumental music, we mostly have permission from groups in this area to use their recordings, and then we credit them on our Web page. Our main cost is staff time.

How do you determine what to include?

We only use documents or recordings that are available online through our www.kansasmemory.org Web site. Those are selected for scanning from the collections by staff members, and many of the topics are tied to the curriculum standards for teaching Kansas History classes. I follow our Kansas Memory updates and ask the digital coordinator for suggestions. We also look at our download statistics and try to select topics that users have shown the most interest in.

What challenges are there?

Some of the challenges were technical; being a newer office building, very few of our offices have walls or ceilings, so it was surprisingly difficult to find a place quiet enough to make recordings. We have a limited pool of staff to draw on, particularly when it comes to subjects like Black and Hispanic history, and most of the historic readings require male voices, when our staff is predominantly female. We have incorporated some of our original oral interview recordings, but sometimes the quality of the recordings is too poor.

What kinds of positive results have you had? (And, any negative ones?)

The sheer number of people who subscribe to the RSS feed and download the podcasts has been a real revelation. For instance, in FY 2008 we had a total of 34,654 Kansas Memory Podcast downloads compared to 6,300 users who visited our library in person. We haven't had as many people actually give us feedback as we would like, and we'd like to hear from our listeners more.

(cont'd.)

Interview with Lin Fredericksen (continued)
About how much time does it take? We decided to let the documents speak for themselves and keep the secondary narration to a minimum, so writing doesn't usually take long. To save time, we sometimes pull all the excerpts out of one collection or diary. What takes the most time is selecting the passages that illustrate the topic best and will hold people's interest. If I had to estimate the time involved, I'd say: • Selection and cropping the excerpts to a manageable length: 4 hours • Research and writing narration to string the excerpts together: 2 hours • Recording: 2–3 hours • Editing: 2–3 hours • Coding the Web and XML pages: 1 hour
What advice would you give an organization wanting to use something similar? Look at what other institutions have done, and brainstorm about the format and possible topics. Plan on a learning curve of several months to establish the process, learn the software if it's new, and figure out the workflow. We wanted to find ways to make our Web site more interactive, and this really isn't an overly difficult or expensive project the way we do it.

Kansas Memory online repository (www.kansasmemory.org). In this series, after an introduction to provide context, excerpts of documents in the collections that relate to the episode's theme, such as "Grasshoppers! Plague of the Prairie" or "The Buffalo Hunt," are read. On the podcast's Web site are links to the complete digitized documents, and a link is also spoken at the end of each episode. The Kansas Historical Society also produces the "Cool Things Podcast," featuring curators discussing significant objects from the museum's collections (www.kshs.org/audiotours/coolthings/index.htm). Although this series focuses on museum objects, it provides another podcast model for archives and historical organizations.

An interesting example of drawing on a corporate archives to support a podcast is the Wells Fargo History Museum's series "Guided by History" (http://blog.wellsfargo.com/guidedbyhistory/Podcasts). This series was developed to publicize and expand on the museum's exhibition "San Francisco Is in

Ashes." Both the exhibition and the podcast draw upon the resources of the Wells Fargo corporate archives. Although the exhibition has closed, the podcast and additional Web resources continue to provide historical information about the San Francisco earthquake of 1906 and its aftermath. However, this site expands its educational mission beyond the historical, providing links to information about how people can prepare for future earthquakes and volunteer to help. The podcast, in this case, is part of a Web package that combines community service with promotion of the Wells Fargo corporate brand and an exhibit at the Wells Fargo History Museum.

In contrast to the resources of Wells Fargo, the Maynard Historical Society in eastern Massachusetts has no paid staff, and its collections are housed in storage, inaccessible to researchers. To promote awareness of the organization, its mission, and the collections, one volunteer, David Griffin, started the Maynard Historical Society podcast (Figure 4-4; http://web.maynard.ma.us/historyblog/archives/category/podcast). The content of the podcast varies from news about the society's activities, to interviews, to discussions of interesting material in the collection. Each episode is accompanied by a post on the Society's blog, usually with many images of the materials being discussed. The Maynard podcast is an excellent example of a podcast, supported by a blog, serving as a low-cost outreach tool for an organization with limited resources.

WHAT DOES IT TAKE TO START A PODCAST AND KEEP IT GOING?

If you are considering podcasting, your first step should be to *listen to a lot of podcasts* to identify what you want to emulate and what you don't. You should listen to podcasts produced by similar organizations, but don't limit yourself too much. A search on iTunes, Juice (http://juicereceiver.sourceforge.net), or Podcast Alley (http://www.podcastalley.com) will help you find podcasts by archives, museums, and libraries, as well as podcasts on virtually any topic of interest to you (cooking, knitting, movies, etc.). Study what you think "works" in these podcasts, for example—how do they use music? How long are they? What kinds of personalities do the hosts have?

In addition to thinking about what kind of "feel" you want for your podcast, you need to *determine what kind of content you want to share*. For example, do you have audio materials or video materials that can be digitized and shared? At the same time you consider your possible content, you need to *con-*

Figure 4-4. Maynard Historical Society Podcast Blog

« Maynard Historical Society Podcast #5   Maynard Historical Society Podcast #7 »

Maynard Historical Society Podcast #6

Written by Dave Griffin on January 2nd, 2009

"Priorities" – Dave Griffin discusses how we will be prioritizing the cataloging and digitization efforts. We are faced with processing thousands of items in the existing collection and they represent a wide variety of conditions and importance to the Society's collection.

To show some of the challenges of prioritization, two boxes recently found in the Collection are used as examples.

These are some photographs of items mentioned in the podcast:

The "Doll's Suitcase" (from the estate of Eva Edwards):

Source: Courtesy of the Maynard Historical Society.

sider what format and duration you want. Do you want to commit to an ongoing podcast series, or would a short series of programs suit your needs (and resources) better? Do you want your podcasts to all be the same format—sharing oral histories or public programs, for example—or do you want to mix up the content of your program?

You also need to *decide whether you want to produce an audio or video podcast*. While video podcasts allow you to integrate visual materials directly into the podcast, they are a bit more complicated to produce and create larger files for users to download. They also do not provide your users with quite the same level of freedom in how they access the podcast. Video podcasts can, of course, be accessed only by computer or by MP3 players with video capability. They also cannot be accessed by users while they are doing other activities, such as driving. However, video podcasts do allow you to *show* as well as tell your story, and they can be redistributed via YouTube and other video-sharing sites in addition to being distributed as podcasts (see Chapter 6.).

Once you have determined whether you want to produce an audio or video podcast, what type of content you want to include, and how often you feel you can publish new programs, you need to *consider the physical requirements*. In general, to produce an audio podcast you will need a computer with a high-quality sound card, a microphone (if you are recording new material), and sufficient file storage space. For software, you will need recording and editing software, FTP software, and podcasting software.

Many podcasters use freely available software for all their podcasting needs. For example, the audio recording and editing software Audacity (www.audacity.com) is very popular with podcasters. Liberated Syndication (www.libysn.com) is another popular provider that offers one-stop shopping for many podcasting services at no charge (or for a small fee, depending on your usage). The technical aspects of podcasting require too much detail to be covered in a book like this one, and the tools and requirements are changing at a rapid rate. If you are interested in learning more, check for resources on the Web or at your library.

In addition to setting up your technical infrastructure you will need to *make some key decisions*, such as:

- What will the title of your podcast be? How will you describe it?
- What kind of tone do you want? Formal or informal? Scripted or nonscripted?
- Will your podcast have a regular host? Do you want one host or two?

- Do you have a target length you would like for a typical program?
- Do you want to have theme music or "bumpers"? (Note that all music must be "podsafe"—as defined later.)
- Do you want to set up a blog specifically for the podcast or use an existing blog?
- Have you chosen a picture or logo to be displayed on your podcast's page for services like iTunes?

You should also *decide how listeners will be able to send you feedback*. User feedback is an important aspect of any podcast, allowing people to ask specific questions, provide corrections or follow-up information, submit suggestions for future programs, and offer general comments. You will probably want to identify an e-mail address to be used for this purpose. If your podcast will be supported by a blog, you may just want to direct listeners to the feedback mechanisms on the blog. Some podcasts also provide a telephone number where listeners can leave feedback via voicemail. This kind of audio feedback is sometimes included in a future podcast. As with any public outreach effort, offering multiple ways for users to provide feedback is a good idea, and, ideally, you should respond to all the feedback you receive, especially as you are building up your audience.

As you might imagine, issues of copyright and licensing come into play when you are broadcasting music—even a small selection of a recording. The podcasting community has come to grips with this problem by creating networks for finding "podsafe" music. Wikipedia defines "podsafe" as:

> a term created in the podcasting community to refer to any work which, through its licensing, specifically allows the use of the work in podcasting, regardless of restrictions the same work might have in other realms. For example, a song may be legal to use in podcasts, but may need to be purchased or have royalties paid for over-the-air radio use, television use, and possibly even personal use. (Wikipedia, "Podsafe," accessed 2009)

To *learn more about your options for finding podsafe music* to use in your podcast, you may want to browse the options at the Podsafe Music Network (http://music.podshow.com).

Depending on the kind of material you want to include in your podcast, you may need to *consider other kinds of rights and permissions issues*. If you are recording a public program for use in a podcast, you will need to have your speakers sign a permissions form that grants appropriate rights for rebroadcast. If you are using an oral history or other form of archival content, your ability to repurpose it may be less clear. The approach that many archives and historical organizations seem to be taking in these cases is to publish the content and be ready to remove it if the subject of the podcast expresses concerns. For more discussion of copyright, consult the "Considering Legal Issues" section in Chapter 12.

You will want to provide yourself ample time to **record practice podcasts**. You will need to become comfortable with your setting and equipment, as well as with recording and editing. Some podcasters recommend breaking your show up into segments divided by musical cues because it makes it easier to edit. If you are doing a lot of talking on your podcast, you may also want time to review and determine your style of speaking and become comfortable with being recorded.

You will also need to **develop a process for producing each podcast program**. Depending on the type of episode you're recording, you may need to do the following:

- Identify your topic.
- Make arrangements with speakers.
- Digitize archival audio material.
- Prepare an outline or script.
- Prepare any images or illustrations to be posted to your blog.
- Prepare show notes and/or a blog post.
- Record the show.
- Edit the show, including converting it and compressing it (if necessary).
- Publish the show.
- Publish a blog post.

Once you have recorded enough podcasts to develop a good rhythm, it's a good idea to **document your process**. Be sure to include the technical specifications you use for recording or producing your digital files and any conventions you have developed for using tags.

Whether or not you are using a blog, you should write show notes or a short summary of the podcast. Include complete names of any guests, titles of books you reference, and other helpful links. In the unlikely event that you later discover you've made an error, you can also use the show notes as a place to post a correction. This short summary will be part of the ***metadata you create for each digital file***. For most podcast files, this metadata takes the form of ID3 tags. These tags are attached to the .mp3 file and describe the podcast. Because they were developed to describe music files, the field names don't always seem logical for podcasts. You will see fields such as the title, artist, year, and genre. Determine what information you'd like these tags to contain before you launch your podcast—it's better for users if the information doesn't change after they've started to subscribe. Use the "Notes" field to supply your show notes or summary. Under "Album" put the title of your podcast series. Use the "Artist" field to supply the author information, such as the name of your institution. "Track number" should be the episode number. The only things that should change with each podcast episode are the title, track number, and notes.

After you are comfortable with the logistics of recording and editing and feel you have produced a few good sample podcasts, it is a good idea to ***get objective feedback***. Find some people who are willing to listen to your samples and provide candid comments. You must be ready to accept their comments and learn from them. Do they find your topics interesting? How is the audio quality? Do they like the delivery of the speakers? Is this a podcast they would subscribe to? You may want to include some volunteers who are not from your local area. Remember that while you may want to target your podcast to a local audience, you may also attract national and even international listeners. It might be helpful to know when you need to define local terms or add more geographic information (such as identifying what state things are in).

Once you have gotten comfortable with the technical and content side of creating your podcasts, you need to ***publish them and make sure that they are easily accessible*** to your users. (Again, the technical details of mounting your podcast on a host server and publishing it vary with the service you are using and are subject to change. As you are planning your implementation, consult recent Web resources for timely information.) You will probably want to create a page on your Web site for your podcast, if you are not using a blog. In addition to linking your podcast from your institution's Web site, you should make sure your podcast is included in the major podcast directories, such as these:

- iTunes (www.apple.com/iTunes)
- Juice (http://juicereceiver.sourceforge.net)
- Podcast Alley (www.podcastalley.com)
- Odeo (http://odeo.com)
- Podcast.com (http://podcast.com)

You may also want to ensure that users can subscribe to your RSS feed directly from your podcast's blog or your Web site. This will allow users to use tools such as Google Reader and Bloglines to subscribe to your podcast.

As you are learning about podcasting and even after you launch your series, you may want to search out and *participate in podcasting communities* or discussion groups to learn about new tools and ways of doing things. As with many Web 2.0 tools, this is an evolving area, and there is always something new.

Final Tips If You Are Considering Podcasting

- Listen to as many podcasts as possible, and carefully consider what you want your content and style to be.
- Consider starting with a short series to develop your skills before launching an ongoing series.
- Practice your podcasting skills, and get independent feedback before going "live."
- Document your process—record what settings you use, how you tag your files, etc.
- Monitor your feedback mechanisms, and respond to the comments.
- Make sure your podcast is listed in as many directories as possible. You may have more potential listeners than you ever imagined!

REFERENCES

Wikipedia. "Podcast." Available: http://en.wikipedia.org/wiki/Podcasting (accessed May 29, 2009).

Wikipedia. "Podsafe." Available: http://en.wikipedia.org/wiki/Podsafe (accessed April 23, 2009).

CHAPTER 5

Using Flickr and Other Image-Sharing Sites

WHAT ARE IMAGE-SHARING SITES?

Image-sharing sites are Web sites that allow users to upload digital images and share them on the Web. Images can be shared with just a restricted circle of people or with the whole world. Once the images are posted, most sites enable users to do things like include them in groups, tag them, comment on them, or save them as "favorites."

Flickr (www.flickr.com) is by far the most popular image-sharing site used by cultural organizations to post and share digitized images from their collections. Because it is so dominant in the field, this chapter will focus on Flickr, using it as an example of the functionalities of image-sharing sites and how they are being used. Among the other image-sharing sites available (although not commonly used by archives) are the following:

- Photobucket.com
- Webshots.com
- Kodakgallery.com
- Shutterfly.com
- Snapfish.com
- Picasa Web Albums (from google.com)

Most archives have the capability to post digitized images on their own Web sites, so the appeal of Flickr is not that it allows images to be posted, but that it provides a ready-made infrastructure that allows users to tag, comment, and interact in other ways with the images. (However, Flickr may also be useful for archives that have limited capabilities to post images; with Flickr, you can make large numbers of images available without having them hosted on your own site.) Although originally intended as a site for people to post their personal photos, Flickr has been embraced by the cultural heritage community and is widely used by libraries, museums, archives, and historical societies because of the low cost and level of expertise needed to post images and because of its enormous public popularity.

Setting Up a Flickr Account

You do not need to have an account to view images on Flickr, but you cannot comment or take advantage of any of the other interactive features of the site unless you sign up. Anyone can set up a basic account with Flickr at no charge, or you can choose to set up a "Pro" account. (As of May 2009, the annual cost of a Pro account is $24.95.) With a free account, although you can upload an unlimited number of images, you can only upload up to 100 MB worth of images per month, and you'll only see the most recent 200 photos displayed. With a Pro account, there are virtually no limitations on how much you can upload or display.

Note that Flickr now allows users to upload and share video as well as still images. Individual video files must be smaller than 150 MB in size, which usually accommodates about 90 seconds worth of video. Users with free accounts are limited to uploading two videos a month; Pro users have no limitations on the number of uploads.

Flickr is owned by Yahoo, and so they require you to have a Yahoo ID in order to establish a Flickr account. Once you have a Yahoo ID, Flickr will guide you through the first steps of establishing your Flickr identity, including choosing your "screen name," uploading a picture to be displayed as your "buddy icon," creating a custom URL address for your Flickr photos, and entering the information to be displayed in your profile. You can come back at any time to modify any of these elements by accessing "Your Account."

Uploading, Organizing, and Creating Metadata for Images

Images can be uploaded into Flickr by a wide variety of means, including using the Flickr-provided "Uploadr" software, using iPhoto or Windows XP plugins, using Flickr's upload Web page, or by e-mail. Images can be uploaded individually or in batches. All the images you have uploaded are known as your "photostream."

After uploading, image metadata (such as the title, description, and tags) can be added or edited, either individually or in batches. Images can also be organized into different kinds of groups. "Sets" are groupings of photos organized around a common theme. (Note that images can be members of more than one set, if you have sets with overlapping themes.) "Collections" are groupings of sets (or other collections) so that images can be organized hierarchically, for example, within broader themes or time periods.

Flickr also permits you to place different kinds of restrictions on your uploaded images, including limitations on who can access the image, an indication of the usage license (or what kinds of copyright restrictions are on the image), and, if necessary, a flag indicating that the image contains adult content. You can also easily "geotag" your images (a geotag is metadata that indicates where the image was taken) by "dropping" them on a map.

Interacting with Other Flickr Users

Although you can just upload your pictures into your photostream and leave it at that, participating in the Flickr community will result in greater use and activity for your images. Flickr provides several ways to make connections with other users and give more opportunities for your images to be accessed.

One way to connect with other users is by developing your circle of "contacts." Flickr users whom you designate as contacts can be given expanded permissions to interact with your images. Your contacts also have easy access to your new uploads, which will either appear on their homepages or by choosing to view "most recent uploads." (Being a contact is a reciprocal arrangement—one party must request and the other must accept the request. This means that each is a contact of the other.)

You may also want to join some of Flickr's many "groups" formed by users. Several groups are formed by and for libraries and archives, such as ArchivesOnFlickr (www.flickr.com/groups/archivesonflickr). Joining a group allows you to participate in the group's discussion board and also add your images to the "group pool." In addition, all Flickr users can interact with each other, without being contacts or members of the same group, by sending messages using "Flickrmail."

Letting People Interact with Your Images

Flickr provides many ways for users to interact with your images, if you choose to let them. All images on Flickr can be designated as a "favorite" by any user—which means they will come up in that user's "My Favorites." This is the only functionality that Flickr mandates all users will have with your images (assuming that you have made those images public). For all other functionalities, you can establish default settings for your account; for example, you define who has the right to add comments, tags, and notes to your images.

Adding comments to an image is just what it sounds like—users write and submit a comment, which is posted below the description of the image. Comments are attributed to the Flickr user who is the author. Adding a "note" is quite different. This functionality allows a user to attach a short comment to a particular location on your image. Notes are visible as boxes when the image is "moused over"; the content of each note is visible only when the cursor on the screen rolls over that particular area of the image. The "notes" feature can be useful for identifying people and objects or providing information about specific parts of an image.

Recently Flickr added a new feature that allows users to create "galleries"—collections of up to 18 images selected from any of the millions of images being shared. These galleries are themselves available for browsing and sharing. While you can choose not to allow your images to be used in galleries, you will probably want to opt in and make sure your images are available. Flickr's goal for the new feature is to allow users to act like curators, creating virtual exhibits around the topics that interest them. You will be able to see which of your images have been included in user galleries and you can choose to remove your image from a user's gallery if you do not wish to have it included. Each gallery and image in a gallery can be accompanied by introductory or "label" text. This is also a feature you may want to explore yourself, perhaps creating virtual exhibits that include images from other collections.

You also can control which categories of users can download or print your images, which is an issue of considerable interest to archives and historical organizations who are concerned with losing revenue if users can obtain high-quality copies of their images. You can set separate controls for who can publish your images in a blog. There are also third-party companies you can partner with who offer additional services—such as producing high-quality prints—for the images in your photostream.

The Flickr Commons

Flickr's prominence and use by archives was greatly enhanced by the launch of the Flickr Commons in 2008, with the Library of Congress as its first member. The Commons was created as a special area of the Flickr community just for cultural heritage organizations with photographic collections (www.flickr.com/commons). The intent is to create a space where Flickr users can easily locate historical photographs and share their knowledge about them. As of March 2009, the Commons had only 23 members—doubtless a small fraction of all the cultural heritage organizations with Flickr accounts. New members are being added but at a relatively slow rate. The Commons shows great potential as a venue for archives and other historical organizations to share their collections, but unless the rate of processing new members greatly increases, it appears it will be many years before it includes the majority of cultural heritage organizations with a presence on Flickr.

HOW CAN YOUR INSTITUTION USE FLICKR?

Flickr's core functionality—the ability to share pictures—allows it to be used for a wide variety of purposes. Almost all archives and historical organizations on Flickr use it to share images of their holdings (including documents, photographs, and artifacts). Some also use Flickr to share current images of their building, staff, or events. Flickr's functionalities for sharing and commenting are ideal for allowing millions of users to locate and comment on images they might not otherwise have discovered (and almost certainly not interacted with) if the images had just been posted on the institution's own Web site.

Sharing Digitized Archival Material

Probably the majority of archives and similar organizations using Flickr are using it to share digitized images of items in their collections—primarily photographs. Flickr was founded to share photographs, and the majority of the people searching it are almost certainly using it to find images of pictures, not images of documents.

Certainly one of the most prominent examples of the effective use of Flickr for sharing images from an institution's collections is the Library of Congress (www.flickr.com/photos/library_of_congress). The Library posted its first two collections on Flickr (totaling 4,615 images) in January 2008, classifying their participation as a "pilot." In the final report on that pilot, they observed the following:

- As of October 23, 2008, there have been 10.4 million views of the photos on Flickr.
- 79% of the 4,615 photos have been made a "favorite" (i.e., are incorporated into personal Flickr collections).
- Over 15,000 Flickr members have chosen to make the Library of Congress a "contact," creating a photostream of Library images on their own accounts.
- For Bain images [George Grantham Bain News Service] placed on Flickr, views/downloads rose approximately 60% for the period January–May 2008, compared to the same time period in 2007. Views/downloads of FSA/OWI [Farm Security Administration/Office of War Information] image files placed on Flickr rose approximately 13%.
- 7,166 comments were left on 2,873 photos by 2,562 unique Flickr accounts.
- 67,176 tags were added by 2,518 unique Flickr accounts.
- 4,548 of the 4,615 photos have at least one community-provided tag.
- Less than 25 instances of user-generated content were removed as inappropriate.
- More than 500 Prints and Photographs Online Catalog (PPOC) records have been enhanced with new information provided by the Flickr Community.
- Average monthly visits to all PPOC Web pages rose 20% over the five-month period of January–May 2008, compared to the same period in 2007. (Springer et al., 2008: iv)

While not every archives will have the kinds of numbers generated by the Library of Congress's participation, many archives would probably agree with this characterization of their Flickr experience from the Library of Congress's report:

This project significantly increased the reach of Library content and demonstrated the many kinds of creative interactions that are possible when people can access collections within their own Web communities. The contribution of additional information to thousands of photographs was invaluable. Performance measures documented in this report illustrate how the project has been successful in achieving the objectives and desired outcomes of the Library's strategic goals. The Flickr project increases awareness of the Library and its collections; sparks creative interaction with collections; provides LC staff with experience with social tagging and Web 2.0 community input; and provides leadership to cultural heritage and government communities. (Springer et al., 2008: iv)

An excellent example of an archives of more typical size and resources making a successful Flickr implementation is the Seattle Municipal Archives (Figure 5-1; www.flickr.com/photos/seattlemunicipalarchives). To date, the SMA has posted 16 sets of images, focused on topics such as "Seattle at Work," "Seattle at Play," "Getting Around," and "Under Construction." Given the lively nature of the photos, it's not surprising that they receive steady use and a large number of comments.

The SMA has taken an active role in promoting their images by adding individual photos (as well as sets) to various group pools. For example, the image of "Helicopter near Skagit Dams, 1952" is in pools for the groups "The Art of Helicopters," "North Cascades," "The Cascades," "Helicopters," and "Crosscut." Another image, of "Dancers from Dorothy Fisher Ballet, 1956," is in the pools for "Seattle Metblogs," "Dance (new rules)," "Dance, dance, dance!," "Dance No Limit," "Seattlest," "Stranger Photos," and "Crosscut." The image of the dancers has been viewed over 360 times, that of the helicopter over 140. In addition to having individual pictures like these added to group pools, the SMA is a member of over 50 groups, most of them related to Seattle or to Washington State.

Eastern Kentucky University Archives provides a good example of hierarchical organization in their photostream (www.flickr.com/photos/ekuarchives). EKU has organized their images into seven collections, which contain 31 sets:

Manuscript Collections (5 sets)
EKU Campus (3 sets)
EKU By Decades (9 sets)
Athletics (8 sets)
EKU Events (2 sets)
Student Organizations (3 sets)
Model Laboratory School (1 set)

Images can be members of more than one set, which facilitates browsing. For example, an image of students can be in both the "Delta Sigma Theta" set (be-

Figure 5-1. Seattle Municipal Archives Image on Flickr

Motorcycles in Pioneer Square, circa 1914

Share This

Item 111181, Fleets and Facilities Department Imagebank Collection (Record Series 0207-01), Seattle Municipal Archives.

Comments

 First Born Matterhorn says:

The four riders in the foreground are riding Excelsior V-Twins, Pre-Schwinn era. This would place the year at no earlier than 1911. Given the style of dress, I'd wager that this photograph was taken no more than a few years from that model's inception.
Posted 8 months ago. (permalink)

 sonek321 pro **says:**

Hooligans!
Posted 8 months ago. (permalink)

 **Stephen Rees** pro **says:**

Hi, I'm an admin for a group called Transportation, and we'd love to have this added to the group!
Posted 8 months ago. (permalink)

 jgodfrey13 pro **says:**

I am an admin for a group call Washington State Motorcycling. I would like to have this added to the Washington State Motorcycling pool.
Great picture
Posted 7 months ago. (permalink)

 snowboarder2k pro **says:**

Earthkiller is just about right. I'd place it at 1911-1916.
Posted 6 months ago. (permalink)

billp3 pro **says:**

Hi, I'm an admin for a group called Veteran Motorcycles, and we'd love to have this added to the group!
Posted 5 months ago. (permalink)

 Uploaded on September 5, 2008 by **Seattle MunicipalArchives**

Seattle MunicipalArchives' photostream

774 uploads

browse

This photo also belongs to:

− Getting Around (Set)

70 items

browse

+ Seattle (Pool)

+ Pacific Northwest (Pool)

+ Seattle Metblogs (Pool)

+ Period Photographs of Transportation (pre-1960) (Pool)

+ Transportation (Pool)

+ Views: 500 (Pool)

+ Favorites: 5 (Pool)

+ Pioneer Square - Seattle (Pool)

+ Seattlest (Pool)

+ Veteran Motorcycles (Pool)

+ Stranger Photos (Pool)

+ Vintage Motorcycle Photos (Old Photographs Only) (Pool)

+ Crosscut (Pool)

+ Photos from 1910-1920 (Pool)

+ Washington State Motorcycling (Pool)

Tags

seattle municipal archives
seattle
pioneer square
pergolas
vintage motorcycles
1910s
transportation

**Interview with Julie Kerssen
Seattle Municipal Archives**

What made you interested in using Flickr to share images?

I occasionally posted images of fun things I found at work to my personal Flickr account. Seeing how much my friends enjoyed these made me think about doing it on a larger scale and more "officially." It seemed like a great way to reach an entirely new audience—namely, Web-savvy young people who might not know we existed. Going where these users already were would allow us not only to be more accessible to them, but also perhaps help shake the "dusty old-fashioned archive" stereotype. It also gave us a venue to show off some of our materials (e.g., ephemera) that didn't fit into our existing online tools and collections. Putting materials on Flickr also increased their visibility to search engines, and the possibility of users contributing information about our images was an additional plus.

What information, tools, and processes did you need to begin?

Since I was already familiar with Flickr from personal use, there wasn't really a learning curve in terms of technology. A workflow developed naturally after the first couple of sets.

How did you determine what images to include?

We came at this from the "set" side—we thought of topics that might make for interesting sets and then found images that fit into them. Most are broad categories—Seattle at Play, Dining Out, Under Construction— but there are also a couple based on item type (maps, postcards). Additionally, we have a "Cabinet of Curiosities" set that's a catch-all for fun and weird things (generally non-photographic) that we come across.

What challenges did you face?

We are a government agency, so some managers and IT staff were concerned about the public records implications of putting our content on a service that we didn't own or control. We argued that putting images on Flickr was the equivalent of including copies of photos in a traveling exhibit, in that we retain full control of the original content, while surrogates are sent out into the world where more people will see them.

What kinds of positive results have you had? (And, any negative ones?)

We've gotten great feedback via comments on our images and e-mail. One commenter said, "I love what you are doing here—bringing the library into the homes and offices of people. I am new to Seattle and have

(cont'd.)

Interview with Julie Kerssen (continued)

much to learn and by far, this is the most incredible set of photos I have seen." Many blogs have featured images from our site, variously calling it "fascinating," "hours-devouring," "charming and delightful," and "a cultural gold mine"; these posts drove still more traffic back to our site. A local alternative weekly used one of our photos in each issue for several months, often in fun ways. Users have contacted us for reproductions of images on the site, as well as permission to use them for everything from e-books to t-shirts to "motivational wallpaper." Additionally, links from our images have driven hundreds of visitors to our institutional Web site, especially to our online exhibits.

About how much time does it take?

When I'm coming up with a new set, I spend an hour or two searching our database for relevant images. I save them all in one place, and then post a handful of them at a time, which only takes 5–10 minutes. This has worked well in terms of workflow, as I can do the more time-intensive database searches when I have the leisure to do so. This then gives me a pool from which to do quick uploads on an almost-daily basis (thus keeping the people who subscribe to our RSS feed happy). If I come across something neat in the course of processing or reference work, I'll do a quick scan and post it, which again only takes 5–10 minutes.

What advice would you give an organization wanting to do something similar?

Keep all your content private until you've worked out the kinks in how you want to present it. When you do go live, let people know—people won't necessarily find you unless you spread the word that you're out there. Flickr's group pools are a great tool in that they allow you to reach people who you already know are interested in a topic (e.g., streetcars, the Space Needle). Also, many blogs have associated Flickr pools; images from the pool will often automatically show up on the blog's home page, and blog writers will often search their pool for images to feature in their posts, giving them even more exposure. Neighborhood blogs are an especially good target for us, as everyone loves to see old photos of the old drugstore or streetcar stop down the block from where they live.

---

cause the students were members of that organization) and the "1980s" set (because that's when the photo was taken.

In addition to sharing what you know about your collections via Flickr, you can also use it to ask for new information from other Flickr users. The Kalamazoo College Archives is taking this approach with its Flickr account.

They have uploaded only one set into their photostream: "Unidentified Study Abroad Photographs" (www.flickr.com/photos/kalamazoocollegearchives). In the description of the set, they say:

> Please help the Kalamazoo College Archives identify this group of photographs! According to our records, we know they were taken during Study Abroad experiences in the past, but we often don't know where the photographs were taken, who is in them, who the photographer was, or what date the photos were taken. Please leave a comment or make a note on any photo you know more about! Thank you! (Kalamazoo College Archives, accessed 2009)

Once you have posted your images on Flickr you can create links back to them from your Web site, essentially using Flickr as a way to store and manage copies of your digital images. Some archives also go back and update finding aids and other reference materials to include links to relevant images, sets, or collections on Flickr.

Sharing Current Photographs of Your Organization

Although sharing digitized historical content seems to be the most common use of Flickr among archives and organizations with historical collections, some are also using it to share photographs of their present-day activities. This kind of use can help give the public a sense of the archives as a living, breathing organization rather than just a collection of old documents and photos.

The photostream of the Idaho Historical Society (www.flickr.com/photos/idahohistory), for example, consists of three sets: pictures from a public program ("Pioneer Cemetery Tour 2008"), pictures of their building and staff ("Idaho State Historical Society's Public Archives and Research Library Introduction and Welcome!!"), and a sampling of images from their collections ("Historic Idaho"). This is a good example of using a relatively small number of images to convey a general impression of an institution and its collections.

The Special Collections Research Center (SCRC) in the Earl Gregg Swem Library at the College of William and Mary (www.flickr.com/photos/scr) has taken a similar approach, dividing its photostream into collections for exhibits, artifacts, William and Mary events, and "miscellaneous." Some of the more interesting aspects of the SCRC's use of Flickr are its inclusion of images that document current campus and archives activities. For example, included is a set of images that document reactions on campus to a controversial event—the sudden resignation of college president Gene Nichol in 2008. The images in this set show protests, posters, and sit-ins. The SCRC is using this Flickr set as an opportunity to solicit donations as well:

> The photos and videos here are from events and locations on campus after his resignation. The Special Collections Research Center continues to document events related to the term of President Nichol and his resignation. Those interested in assisting with the documentation should contact the department at [. . .]. (Special Collections Research Center, 2008)

Included in the "Exhibits" collection are images of conservators working on a World War I–era memorial flag (see Figure 5-2; www.flickr.com/photos/scrc/3370127269/) in preparation for an exhibition—giving some "behind the

Figure 5-2. College of William and Mary Image on Flickr

Swem Library staff preparing a WWI Gold Star flag for exhibit

Swem Library staff are preparing this WWI Gold Star flag for display as part of an exhibit that will open in Swem Library in the coming weeks. The flag is part of the University Archives Artifact Collection.

The WWI Gold Star flag has a red background with a white field in the middle that includes 294 blue stars and 16 gold stars. The gold stars represent the alumni and former students of the College of William and Mary who died during the war, although there were actually more than 16 who died during the war. The flag measures 5' x 7.5'. Acc. 1989.149.

Interview with Amy Schindler **Special Collections Research Center** **The College of William and Mary**

What made you interested in using Flickr to share images?

My interest in using Flickr to share content from and about the Special Collections Research Center (SCRC) in Swem Library stemmed from experimenting with it at another repository as well as my own use for my personal images. I was interested in Flickr as an outreach tool to share images from events, exhibits, and scenes in the repository. Flickr was the most obvious tool for sharing current events with the world. Our later decision to make images of artifacts available was partly driven by the fact that we did not have a reliable online digital content option.

What information, tools, and processes did you need to begin?

We had only the bare minimum resources when we began using Flickr: personal digital cameras that belonged to staff, a computer, and some basic ideas for tags to use. After finding a certain level of success with this effort and deciding to continue using Flickr to share (and find new) content, policy formation came after implementation.

How did you determine what images to include?

After our first foray into Flickr to share an image of an artifact with an interested archivist at another institution, it was a matter of capturing and selecting photos of SCRC exhibits and events. For most events, we avoid using images that focus primarily on the people in them, but instead add images that are about the event, the exhibit, the crowd, etc.

We also include images of SCRC, library, and campus scenes in part initially because I was new to the university and exploring it for myself. We also of course had in mind alumni who had not visited campus recently and might find the images of the recently remodeled library and new buildings on campus of interest.

Within a few months we also began adding images of selected artifacts that students inventorying the collection found interesting. When a project to re-house all of the artifacts in the SCRC was begun it was decided that each object would be photographed, and so we wanted to share those images with the public as well. Flickr provided a simple way to do so, which explains why you will find dozens of t-shirts in our photostream.

What challenges did you face?

A challenge for the department has been making our photos on Flickr as relevant and interesting as possible to our diverse internal and external

(cont'd.)

Interview with Amy Schindler (continued)

audiences. When we began using Flickr, we were not certain how it would be used by the department nor how we would (or if we could) garner interest from users. We were fortunate to have the luxury of freedom to try different approaches to the type of content added to our photostream without unreasonable pressure or challenges to the usefulness of Flickr specifically or sharing content online through similar Web sites generally.

What kinds of positive results have you had? (And, any negative ones?)

One of my favorite things remains when someone—usually an alumnus or current student—comes across the Flickr account and writes about it on their blog. It is a thrill when someone who has never had reason to use or interact with the SCRC in the past discovers us and gets an inkling that there is more to the department than stereotypes about dusty books and collections.

Using Flickr has also allowed us to share exhibits with alumni who had donated material that we then used in an exhibit. Flickr provides an easy way for us to share the exhibit with people thousands of miles away, which they can then send to their family and friends. Who wouldn't like to see photos of people enjoying an exhibit opening that featured something you donated to the repository?

I honestly cannot think of any negative results.

About how much time does it take?

One of the great things about Flickr is that it can take as much or as little time as you are able to give to the effort. If you are just looking to upload images from an event without adding a great deal of individual description, Flickr's batch uploading makes that relatively simple, and you could add a fair amount of content in just a few minutes.

What advice would you give an organization wanting to do something similar?

While it is important to establish guiding principles before you begin using Flickr for your repository, I strongly believe we should always remain flexible and open to new and evolving practices.

I do recommend that repositories spend a bit of time joining Flickr groups whose members will be interested in your content whether it be by geographic area, subject area of your collection, or type of institution. While we selectively post images to the university's and library's photo

(cont'd.)

Interview with Amy Schindler (*continued*)

pools, we also look for other groups related to specific batches of images. For instance, when we posted images of staff preparing a World War I gold star flag for exhibit, we joined Flickr groups related to WWI and flags so that we could post those photos to the group in an effort to get the image in front of those with a particular interest in the subject matter.

---

scenes" views of the exhibit. Photos also document a visit that a "Flat Stanley" made to the archives—spending some time in the old card catalog, helping process collections, and using the online database.

The archives blogger Linda Clark Benedict used a combination of blogging and posting images to Flickr to help document the move of Hobart and William Smith Archives in the summer of 2008. She wrote short blog posts describing the current phase of the project (on her blog "Alone in the Archives" available at www.lcb48.wordpress.com) and posted images to her own Flickr account (www.flickr.com/photos/28191070@N07). The images remain on her Flickr account, divided into sets for the "Old" archives, the intermediate archives, and the "New" archives. This technique allowed her audience to follow the progress of the move at the time and leaves a record of the moving process for future audiences.

WHAT DOES IT TAKE TO BE ACTIVE ON FLICKR?

As stated earlier, ***starting a Flickr account*** can be easy and free. There is no reason you can't start with a free account and upgrade to a Pro account as you begin to add more images and become more active. Here are some things to remember when you are setting up your account:

- Choose a screen name that clearly identifies your institution. Try to avoid acronyms—they may not be as well known as you think! If you use an acronym, be sure to provide the complete name of your institution prominently in your profile and elsewhere on your account.
- Upload a picture to use as your "buddy icon." If you do not upload a picture, a generic, unhappy-looking face will be displayed as your icon. Many institutions use a picture of one of their buildings or an image of their logo.

- Take the time to share useful information in your profile. Provide a brief description of your institution, including where it is located (city, state, and possibly country). Include additional information about your mission and holdings to give users a sense of who you are. Be sure to include a link to your Web site. Your images may get hundreds or thousands of hits—you want to maximize this outreach opportunity.
- Carefully review and select the "Privacy & Permissions" that apply to the images posted by your account. This is the section where you decide what people can do with the images you post—including options like tagging.

Either before of after you set up your account, you need to *decide what images* you want to upload. As illustrated by the examples in the previous section, there are many ways to approach posting images on Flickr. You may choose to include groups like these:

- Images that demonstrate the kinds of material in your collections, taking representative images from many collections
- One or two whole collections (or selections from one or two collections)
- Images on popular or relevant topics (as the North Carolina State Archives did when it created sets for subjects like tobacco farming, liquor stills, and the Wright brothers)
- Images that show what your building and facilities look like or what your special events or exhibitions are like (as the Idaho Historical Society and the College of William and Mary's Special Collections and Research Center did)
- Images that you'd like help in identifying (this is a popular use with colleges and universities, looking for help from alumni with old pictures of campus life)
- Images from your collections that are far removed from what people might expect to find in your repository (as did Dickinson College Archives with pictures of 1920s Alaska and 1890s Germany)

Whatever you choose to include, *think about the copyright status* of the works. If you have a signed donor agreement that transfers copyright of the images to your institution, then you are probably fine. (A problem could arise if the person who donated the materials was not authorized to transfer the copyright.) For other materials in your collection, it may be difficult to know for certain if the copyright for the images is still held by someone. These are so-called "orphan works." Most archives seem to be taking the commonsense approach that they will post images and then remove them if someone raises a copyright issue. As described in the "Considering Legal Issues" section in Chapter 12, the Society of American Archivists has recently published a very useful guide to "best practices regarding reasonable efforts to identify and locate rights holders" for orphan works (Society of American Archivists, 2009: 1). This new document provides a clear discussion of the issues involved and is something you should definitely consult.

When you have selected your images, you can ***upload them*** using either Flickr's online upload tool or download their uploader application. Once the images are in Flickr, you can ***add and edit the metadata*** (i.e., descriptive information) for the images in the batch.

- Whenever possible, provide a descriptive title for each photo. Using its numerical identifier may be easier for you, but it is not appealing to users. If you decide not to provide a descriptive title, you should provide some kind of identifying information in the description below the image.
- If you use accession numbers or some other form of unique identifiers for your holdings, include that number in the description. This is especially important if you have created or changed the title for the image.
- Provide as much contextual information for each image as possible. This includes anything you know about the creation or use of the image, but most important the name of the collection or series the image is a part of. You may even choose to include a hyperlink to the finding aid for the collection or the description of the collection in your online catalog.
- Provide your contact information in the metadata for every image. You may assume that people will be willing to click one more time to locate it on your profile or on the page for the set, but that may not be the case. Make it easy for your potential users to find you. Include a link to your Web site or your e-mail address (or both) in every description.

An essential part of the metadata for images on Flickr is their tags. You should ***invest time in proper tagging*** of your images to ensure that they are found by as many users as possible. While users have the option to search all the text you provide, some will choose the option of searching only your tag information. Although you can add general tags for all your images at once when you are uploading them, it's important to go back and consider adding additional tags for each image.

When adding tags, remember that if you put a space between two words they will be turned into two separate tags. If you want two words to appear together as one phrase in your tags, put them between quotation marks. In thinking about what tags to add for each photo, consider adding tags such as these:

- Place names
- Names of people in the photo
- Date or date ranges (for example, "1910s")
- Name of activity or objects in the image
- Format of the image (for example, "carte de visite" or "aerial photograph")
- Terms like "archives," "old photo," or "historical," which are sometimes used by people looking for old materials

You should also *consider geotagging your images*. Geotagging means creating or attaching a tag to your image that identifies where it was taken. Flickr makes this easy for you by allowing you to drop images on to a map. Geotagging your images provides yet another way for users to discover them— by simply browsing a map.

As you are planning what images and groups of images to upload, decide how to *organize your images into sets and collections*. Even if you just have one general group of images that is not very large, you should still create a collection for them rather than just present users with your photostream. For large groups of images, it is best to separate them into multiple smaller groups. (An image can be a member of more than one set, so you can create sets that have overlapping content.) Make sure that all your sets and collections have descriptive names that easily communicate what is in the grouping. In addition, make sure that, at the set level, you provide some kind of introduction or description of the set so that people have a clear idea what is in it. Again, it is a good idea to repeat your organization's Web address and contact information on the main page for each set.

Once you have made sure that all the information about your institution and your images is as complete and professional as possible, it's time to begin making contacts within Flickr. One good way to do this is to *look for appropriate groups* to join. You can find a group (or several groups) on virtually any topic in Flickr. Consider joining groups for archives (or libraries, or whatever is most appropriate for your institution), groups for your geographic region, groups that focus on the topics in your images, or groups for people who post "old photos." Once you've joined some groups, add some appropriate images to their group pool. A group pool is like a set of images to which group members can contribute; it does not include all the images in members' photostreams, only ones that members specifically add to the pool.

After you've established your presence on Flickr, there is no way of knowing how long it will take users to find your images or how active they will be once they find them. But when people do begin interacting with your images, you should *monitor user activity* and interact with them. For example, you should do the following:

- Monitor the comments you receive on your images, and respond to as many as you can. You can consider even just saying "thanks" occasionally when someone says they like one of your photos.
- Respond to requests made by administrators of groups, often via a comment, to add a photo to a group. Again, this is a great way to get your image into a place where more people will be likely to see it.
- Monitor the tags people add to your images. You may find that someone has added a tag to one image that would be useful for others.
- Check in, occasionally, on the discussion boards of any groups you have joined. These are good places for learning what Flickr users are looking for and getting ideas for what to do next.

Depending on your level of interest, you may want to apply to *be a member of the Flickr Commons*. As discussed earlier, membership in the Commons draws additional public attention to your images and conveys a certain prestige. However, all members of the Commons must sign a terms of service agreement with Yahoo, and all images posted in the Commons must have "no known copyright restrictions." Flickr also requires that all images posted to the Commons be open for all users to tag and add notes. You should weigh the implications of complying with these requirements against the potential benefits that Commons membership might provide.

Interview with Katrina Harkness and Joshua Youngblood
State Library & Archives of Florida

What made you interested in becoming a member of the Flickr Commons?

The Florida Photographic Collection is a nationally and internationally recognized component of the State Archives of Florida and contains over a million images which are used regularly by book publishers, TV stations, and film makers.

Still, the Photographic Collection felt like a hidden, undiscovered treasure. The number of photographs made searching difficult for any but the most determined researcher. If only there were a way to let Floridians and the world know that we have images of important people and events in Florida history and also a little of the unexpected: flying machines, ostrich racing, mastodon fossils, mermaids, and the largest light bulb in the world.

What information, tools, and processes did you need to begin?

The first and most important step for participation was consultation with the Commons team, from initial discussions about what our institution could and should offer to strategies for organizing our content and planning updates. Since we have been placing digital images and the accompanying records online for several years, the technology learning curve was not that steep. After receiving approval from the Florida Department of State, we developed disclaimers and information for the Florida Memory page based on the models established by other Commons institutions.

How did you determine what to include?

The Florida Photographic Collection as a whole is composed of hundreds of smaller collections. Some collections are the work of individual photographers, and some are the work of institutions such as the Department of Commerce or the Department of Environmental Protection. We decided to work within this existing framework and highlight the images that best represented these collections. We began with self-standing collections, picking collections that were historically interesting, emblematic of Florida, and underutilized. We then added selections from two of the largest collections in the Archives, the Department of Commerce and the Florida Folklife Program. Both collections contain numerous unique, fascinating, and quirky images, but both are so large that browsing the resources can be daunting.

(cont'd.)

Interview with Katrina Harkness and Joshua Youngblood (*continued*)

What challenges did you face?

As a state institution, adapting our traditional communication structure to the Web 2.0 culture has been challenging. Having institutions such as the Library of Congress and the Smithsonian as models has helped tremendously.

What kinds of positive results have you had? (And, any negative ones?)

Being part of the Commons has meant being part of a community of people who are passionate about photographs, history, and contributing to public knowledge. Accessing millions of potential cataloguers and researchers—and volunteer ones at that—is very exciting.

We experienced a steady rise in visits to the Archives' photos since the Flickr release, and the feedback from the Commons viewers has been overwhelmingly positive and very gratifying. Some previously unknown information about specific photos has been provided by Flickr viewers, and we have been adding that information when appropriate to the catalog entries.

We get to see very personal reactions to the photographs that we never got from Web statistics. We've had comments and tags in Spanish, Italian, Portuguese, and Japanese. People have recognized family members, childhood friends, favorite places, or seen intimate glimpses of their own towns in a different era.

About how much time does it take?

Working with the Commons team to work out the logistics for our participation and initial launch took about four months. It can take an hour or two a day responding to questions and preparing new batch releases.

What advice would you give an organization wanting to use something similar?

The opportunity to contribute unique historical resources from your institution to an international dialogue is worth the time commitment.

Final Tips If You Are Considering Using Flickr
• Make sure you clearly identify your institution, its location, and mission.
• Provide as much descriptive metadata for each image as you can.
• Always provide contextual information for the images and contact information for your repository so that people can learn more about your collections.
• Set your preferences so that users can add tags and notes to your images.
• Task someone to monitor your Flickr account to answer messages, respond to comments, and monitor new tags and notes.
• Participate in the Flickr community by making contacts and joining groups.

REFERENCES

Kalamazoo College Archives. "Unidentified Study Abroad Photographs." Flickr. Available: www.flickr.com/photos/kalamazoocollegearchives/sets/721576046539 71934 (accessed May 29, 2009).

Society of American Archivists. 2009. "Orphan Works: Statement of Best Practices." Available: http://archivists.org/standards/OWBP-V4.pdf (accessed July 27, 2009).

Special Collections Research Center. "Campus Reaction to the Resignation of President Gene Nichol." Swem Library, College of William and Mary (2008). Flickr. Available: www.flickr.com/photos/scrc/sets/72157603901798511 (accessed May 29, 2009).

Springer, Michelle, Beth Dulabahn, Phil Michel, Barbara Natanson, David Reser, David Woodward, and Helena Zinkham. 2008. "For the Common Good: The Library of Congress Flickr Pilot Project." Washington, DC: The Library of Congress (October 30). Available: www.loc.gov/rr/print/flickr_report_final.pdf (accessed April 30, 2009).

CHAPTER 6

Using YouTube and Other Video-Sharing Sites

WHAT ARE VIDEO-SHARING SITES?

One of the most popular aspects of Web 2.0 has been the rise of video-sharing sites, which allow anyone with an account to post and share digitized videos of any kind. The most popular of these is YouTube (www.youtube.com), which has become almost synonymous with video sharing. Like Flickr, YouTube started as a site targeted primarily at people sharing their own personal content on the Web—in YouTube's case the content is digital videos rather than photos. Unlike Flickr, which by creating the Commons has sought recognition for its partnership with cultural heritage organizations (as discussed in Chapter 5), YouTube's reputation as a site known mostly for humorous videos has been slow to change. Perhaps because of the nature of video, YouTube has often been associated with controversy—for example, as a site with pirated commercial content or videos that broadcast embarrassing behavior to the world. However, while YouTube may still be thought of by many as the site to go to when you want to see videos of skateboarding dogs, it has also gained recognition as a site with more serious content as well. During the political primaries and the 2008 Presidential election, YouTube was the site where individuals and the candidates themselves shared campaign-related videos. YouTube's use as a venue for sharing more serious-minded videos has continued, and, like Flickr, YouTube has become a place where most major libraries, museums, and archives feel it is desirable to have a presence.

For a time it appeared that Google Video (http://video.google.com) was making an effort to attract cultural-heritage partners and to do with videos what the Google Books project had planned for library holdings—digitize them and make Google a source of digitized historical content as well as the primary search engine. Google Video formed a partnership with the National Archives and Records Administration and digitized some of its video holdings (http://video.google.com/nara.html), but apparently they did not pursue other similar projects. In January 2009, Google Video announced that it would no longer accept any uploaded video and would concentrate entirely on its search capabilities so that it would not compete with YouTube (which Google had acquired in 2006).

While dozens of other sites are available, none has significant participation from archives or similar organizations, with the exception of Vimeo (www.vimeo.com). Vimeo has differentiated itself from YouTube by offering upload of video in high definition, which until recently YouTube did not support. Vimeo also does not limit video uploads by length, only by file size. If you have a free account, you are limited to 500 MB of uploads per week; with a paid "Plus" account you can upload up to 5 GB per week, with a limit of 1 GB per file. (All YouTube uploads must be smaller than 1 GB in size and ten minutes or shorter in length.) Given its dominance, this chapter will focus on the services provided by YouTube, but most video-sharing sites provide similar functionalities and the principles should be applicable to virtually all video-sharing services.

Setting Up Accounts and Channels

As with Flickr, you don't need an account to watch videos on YouTube or the other video-sharing sites, but you do need one to post videos, comment, or use any of the site's features. To establish an account on YouTube, you are required to create a user name, provide your country, postal code, date of birth, and gender, and agree to the terms of service. When you create your account, you receive a warning that if you upload material for which you are not the copyright holder, your account will be deleted. (There is no provision for the "fair use" of materials.)

Once you have established an account, YouTube allows you to customize your profile, add a picture, link to a Web site, and share other information about yourself. Every YouTube user with an account has a profile and by default also has a "channel." Channels are just ways of referring to all of the information about what you create on YouTube. For example, the page for your channel will show your favorite videos, the subscriptions you have, your recent activity, any playlists you've created, your "friends," and, of course, the videos that you have uploaded to your account. The page for your channel also provides ways for people to get in touch with you, including sending a message via YouTube or adding a comment to your channel page. Some features of your channel page can be customized; for example, you can set what categories of users can comment on your channel and to whom those comments will be displayed, as well as other privacy settings. You can also customize features about your channel site's appearance, such as the background colors and what appears on the page.

Finding Videos

The options provided for finding videos on video-sharing sites are generally limited to searching or browsing. Sites like YouTube support keyword searching of video metadata and browsing of available videos by broad topics, such as comedy, education, and sports. The YouTube homepage also prominently features popular videos and videos that are being "watched now" as well as "featured" videos, whose creators pay to have them featured on the site. Based on your activity, YouTube can also offer videos it thinks you will like and also videos that are located "near you" (based on your zip code). When you are on the page for a particular video, YouTube provides you with a choice of "related videos" and the option to see more videos by the creator of the one you're watching.

Whereas Flickr has attempted to create, in the Commons, a portion of the site that is "roped off" as a place where you can go for content created by cultural heritage organizations, YouTube has not yet created this kind of section on its site. You can browse a list of available channels, but at the moment there is no similar browse or search function of YouTube's "groups."

Interacting with and Organizing Videos

When you are on the page for an individual video, you can express your opinion of it in several ways. You can write a comment about it, you can rate it by assigning it a level of one through five stars, you can add it as a "favorite," or you can express concerns about its content by "flagging it." You can also create and upload a "video response," which will be posted on your channel but linked to the video you're responding to. YouTube also makes it easy for you to share the video, with quick links allowing you to easily post it to social networks such as MySpace, Facebook, and Twitter and also send to an e-mail or instant message with a link to the video. If you want to be notified when other YouTube users post a new video, you can subscribe to their channels.

YouTube and other video-sharing sites provide tools for organizing your favorite videos, as well as for sharing them with others. On YouTube, making a video a "favorite" is not only a way of telling others you like it but it also automatically adds the video to the list of "your favorites." All of your favorite videos appear in one continuous list, which can be cumbersome to navigate. To help, YouTube provides the option to create "playlists" of videos, which allows you to organize your favorites into separate groups; your playlists can be shared with others and are available on the page for your channel. If you want to make a note of a video you want to watch later, you can add it to your "quicklist."

Interacting with Other Users

As mentioned, YouTube and other sites also provide ways to interact with other users. You can engage in public dialogue about a specific video by participating in a discussion via the comments feature or by posting a video response. If you would prefer not to post your comments publicly, you can also send a private message directly to any other YouTube user.

YouTube allows you to invite another user to become your "friend." If the invitation is accepted, the other user will automatically be added to your list of contacts. You can manage your list of contacts by creating separate lists for different contact types, giving you an easy way to send interesting videos to different groups of people. You can also set different privacy settings for your various contact lists, allowing you to make the videos you upload visible only to members of specific lists. In addition to your YouTube "friends," your contact list will also include the e-mails of people with whom you've shared videos.

You can participate in conversations on YouTube by joining or creating a "group." A group allows YouTube users interested in a particular topic or group of topics to have public discussions and post relevant videos to their group page. Either the creator or members of a group can add videos, invite other members to join, begin and participate in conversations, or add comments about the posted videos.

Uploading and Creating Metadata for Your Videos

Once you have an account on a video-sharing site, you can begin to upload and share your own video content. (Again, although this process is similar for most video-sharing sites, only the specifics of YouTube will be discussed here. For some insights into uploading video with Vimeo, see the sidebar interview with the State Archives of Michigan later in this chapter.) Although YouTube states

Interview with Mark E. Harvey **Archives of Michigan**

What made you interested in using YouTube and Vimeo to share digitized video?

As the new Seeking Michigan Web site developed on paper, we thought it's not enough to build a great site and sit back and wait for people to find it. This led us to viewing social media as part of an overall syndication plan. Flickr, Twitter, Ning, WordPress, Facebook, and YouTube/Vimeo quickly became the tools we would use to advertise the site. Frankly, YouTube and Vimeo became more than just a syndication tool. Vimeo, in particular, allows upload of full-length movies (HD too). It is much cheaper to use Vimeo (as opposed to CONTENTdm) as a delivery tool for video, and we tap into new user groups. We understand YouTube is where everyone REALLY is, so we put up clips there and point them to the full version on Vimeo. (One of our films had almost 500,000 views in two months.)

What information, tools, and processes did you need to begin?

We already had a catalog of films with metadata and descriptions. The 16-mm films had to be converted to a master DV tape and DVDs and then ripped as MP4s. This was a nominal cost. I believe we did 40 film titles for $1,200 with a local vendor. Then it was a matter of putting the MP4 file into iMovie, adding a bumper with the Archives ownership information, and re-outputting the file. Vimeo is a couple of click operations and the film is online. We have an unlimited account with Vimeo for $60 per year, which allows us to upload 5 GB per week (about five films per week).

How did you determine what to include?

We began with our most popular films that deal with wildlife, hunting, fishing, and tourism. These are touchstones for anyone familiar with Michigan. Plus, we already had good control and descriptive information.

What challenges did you face?

I think we still face the challenge of giving the films context. We are promoting them as general interest but also to educators. The YouTube/Vimeo debate lingers. Most users are on YouTube, but I must admit, we're not willing to sacrifice the user experience just to be where everyone is viewing—that speaks to the challenge of going out and meeting your audience.

(cont'd.)

Interview with Mark E. Harvey *(continued)*
What kinds of positive results have you had? (And, any negative ones?) Our film on the Snow Motor machine [see Figure 6-1; http://vimeo.com/2638558] has been wildly popular (maybe even viral). It has generated newspaper articles as far away as Utah and Montana. We made contact with a person who had the original patent papers and we have received a few reproduction orders from our Vimeo account.
About how much time does it take? Conversion of 40 films: 1 week from vendor; upload: 1–2 hours per film.
What advice would you give an organization wanting to use something similar? Again, in the metadata of every film we point users back to the Seeking Michigan Web site (www.seekingmichigan.org). The advantage of these video-sharing sites is syndication but also creating a presence where the public is engaged in media. When the next new Vimeo/YouTube site comes up and people shift to it, so will we.

that it can accept "almost any" video format, they recommend that you upload your video as H.264, MPEG-2, or MPEG-4 files. Your files must be smaller than 1 GB, and your video must be under ten minutes in length. Additional technical specifications and recommendations are provided on the YouTube site.

Uploading your video is accomplished by simply pressing the "upload" button, available on any YouTube page. After you identify which file (or files) to upload, and you have confirmed that it has successfully uploaded, you will be prompted to provide information about the video, such as the title, description, tags, and categories. Once you have uploaded a video, you cannot re-upload another version of it and still retain any of the information associated with the original—such as comments, ratings, or "favorites"—so you should make sure the video you're uploading is your final version.

HOW CAN YOUR INSTITUTION USE VIDEO-SHARING SITES?

Archives and historical organizations are using YouTube and similar sites much as they are using Flickr—to share original content that they have created

Figure 6-1. Vimeo Page for Seeking Michigan's Video "Armstead Snow Motors"

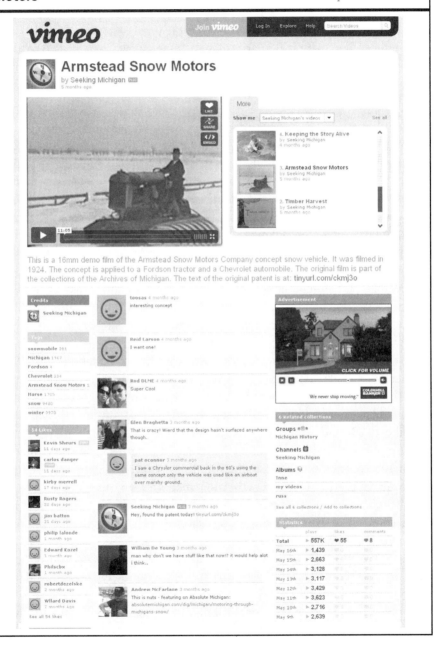

and to share digitized materials from their collections. Because digitizing film is a more complex process than creating scanned images, there seem to be fewer examples of institutions sharing materials from their collections on YouTube than there are on Flickr. However, the inherent ability for video to tell a story better than mere still images or audio alone means that those institutions creating their own videos and posting them are able to share more information in more depth than through some other forms of Web 2.0 communication.

Sharing Digitized Historical Content

Many archives, special collections, museums, and other kinds of historical organizations have collections that include some video content, although for many of them it is a small fraction of their total holdings. Information stored in a video format presents many challenges to its custodians and potential users. Film can be an unstable medium for storing information, subject to deterioration if not properly stored. Unlike still images, film or video content requires the right type of player or projector to access it, and many collections that hold videos do not necessarily continue to maintain the type of machines necessary to view them. Older machines (as well as older films and videos) are subject to breakages that are expensive and difficult to fix. And yet, for all its problems, video content can be a very compelling way to give researchers a view into earlier times. For these reasons—both the positive and the negative—film and video content are ideal candidates for digitization and distribution via the Web.

Some of the most prominent historical organizations presenting content from their collections on YouTube are ones that have large film and video collections. The British Film Institute (www.youtube.com/user/BFIfilms) has posted over 220 videos on YouTube. The BFI has created playlists for some of the films it has uploaded, including the remarkable series "The Open Road—A Cinematic Postcard of Britain in the 1920s," which contains film shot using an experimental early color process that documents a road trip taken in 1924 from Land's End, at the eastern tip of Cornwall, to John O'Groats, at the northern tip of Scotland. The BFI has posted 51 short videos from the collection on YouTube (and created a map using GoogleEarth that shows the path of the trip).

The Library of Congress has so far focused its YouTube contribution on making available examples of very early films, including those produced by the Edison Companies and Westinghouse Works (www.youtube.com/user/ LibraryOfCongress). The National Library of Scotland (see Figure 6-2; www .youtube.com/user/NLofScotland) has contributed films that show the variety

Figure 6-2. National Library of Scotland Channel on YouTube

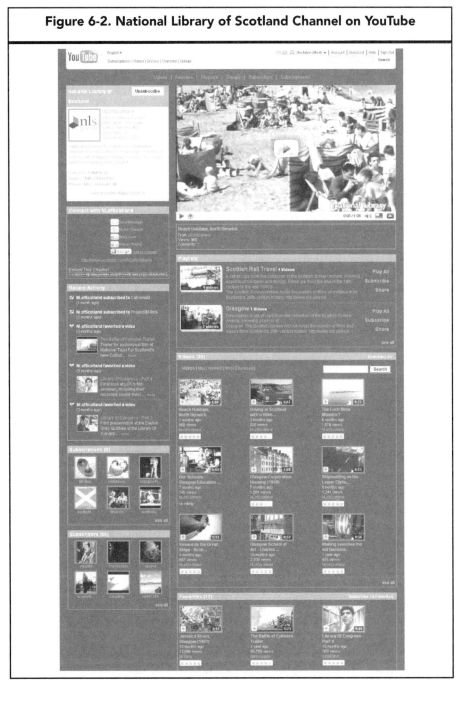

Interview with Ann Cameron, Gill Hamilton, and James Toon
National Library of Scotland

What made you interested in using YouTube to share digitized video?

The initial interest in YouTube was as a result of a broader development activity to expose and promote National Library of Scotland's collections to Web 2.0 services with the intention to engage with a wider audience as part of the Library's "widening access" strategy. The Library's Scottish Screen Archive was the most obvious contender for exploiting YouTube, as it hosts a collection of films and videos, some of which had recently been digitised as part of an ongoing digitisation programme. YouTube seemed quick, easy, and fun, so we thought "let's have a go."

What information, tools, and processes did you need to begin?

After setting up an account on YouTube, staff at the Scottish Screen Archive (SSA) used the YouTube video loader to load short clips in Flash Video format. They also used the descriptive metadata from their database to populate the YouTube title, description, and tag fields. Copyright information from the SSA database was also used to assist in the selection of clips.

How did you determine what to include?

We only considered film and video that was already encoded to Flash Video (as a result of our digitisation programmes). Thereafter, the deciding factor was material we knew was copyright Scottish Screen Archive or Out of Copyright material. We steered clear of material held in third party copyright and personal family home movie-type footage. We tried to include material that would make an interesting "playlist."

What challenges did you face?

The perception that we can upload everything we have digitised onto the Web, whether that be on the NLS Web site or YouTube. (Demand always outstrips practical reality!!).

  We had to impose some sort of structure onto the data we published on YouTube to indicate a clip was part of a longer film, and that film was part of a National Collection. We also had to have some sort of quality to the metadata we published. We faced resourcing issues, mostly in terms of staff time. We also had concerns regarding quality, given that we supplied Flash Video (a compressed format of lower quality than the original film/video) to YouTube, which then further compressed the video.

(cont'd.)

Interview with Ann Cameron, Gill Hamilton, and James Toon
(continued)

What kinds of positive results have you had? (And, any negative ones?)

Positive: It is great to see NLS with a presence on YouTube, and we know from our statistics that new users are coming to the Library's Web site via such Internet sites. We are therefore extending access to our collections and services beyond the Library.

We are raising awareness and promoting our work on YouTube and other Web 2.0 services (Flickr and Facebook) through professional seminars and conferences. A seminar we presented (Web 2.0 Cataloguing & Indexing Group, Scotland) led to further interesting posts on blogs including Lorcan Dempsey at OCLC.

It has enabled us to connect with other archives and channels on YouTube and has allowed us to experiment a little with how we present ourselves online.

Negative: We have had an instance with breach of copyright on YouTube where another channel uploaded material illegally. We followed procedures YouTube had in place to ask the Channel owner to take the film down. All in all it was a painless enough process though it required a bit of "form filling" on our part. The films were taken down in due course.

We also had a couple of comments that could have been interpreted as derogatory or offensive so we chose to remove these from YouTube.

How much time does it take?

Longer than you think! Using our current processes it takes approximately one minute to upload the video clip and approximately half an hour to add and modify the descriptive metadata appropriately. Our approach to date has been somewhat ad-hoc, and we have not yet taken time to explore if it's possible to automate the process of adding videos and associated data to YouTube.

I would suggest for every clip uploaded to date (circa one minute) in practice this has taken around half an hour to input metadata and upload. We have just been using YouTube as a small pilot. There would be larger staff and resource implications of going bigger with it which we have not considered at present.

(cont'd.)

Interview with Ann Cameron, Gill Hamilton, and James Toon
(continued)

What advice would you give an organization wanting to use something similar?

- Think carefully about why you are using YouTube. YouTube is free and available to all; however, does this agree or conflict with your organisation's strategy (e.g., income generation vs. free access).

- Read the small print! YouTube videos can be enabled so that they can be embedded in other Web sites and applications. If you wish to maintain close control over re-use and re-purposing of your videos then you may not want to make this option available to viewers of your videos.

- Make sure you have the rights or have cleared rights to publish on YouTube. It's possible that if the original agreements pre-date the Web/Web 2.0 then it may be difficult to establish if you have the rights to publish on YouTube without seeking further clarification.

- Be aware that a minority of people will probably illegally use tools to download the material you upload.

- Make sure you have some material ready to upload, and if you don't, do budget for getting the content encoded.

- Remember you have no control over the mechanisms of the site or the way your data is compressed, etc. Even in the time we have been using YouTube, the site has changed the way an upload is performed, meaning the film appears online before metadata is completed about it, and also the aspect ratio of the film has been changed without our control. YouTube is concerned with visual content, it really is not fussed about the quality of the images presented or the way they are presented.

- Track usage of your content by gathering the statistics generated on YouTube and also through use of other tools such as Google Analytics (to track referral traffic from YouTube to your Web site).

- Consider preparing a policy for use of Web 2.0 services, but don't let development of this policy get in the way of making your content immediately available.

- Enjoy using it and interacting with other channels and users!

of their holdings from the early and mid-twentieth century—including a short film that some think shows the elusive Loch Ness monster.

YouTube isn't just for national archives and collections—colleges and universities have also posted selections of digitized historical film. Iowa State University (www.youtube.com/user/ISUSpecialCollection), for example, has 114 videos currently available, most of them digitized versions of 16-mm films produced by Iowa State University and WOI-TV, a local television channel. The Woodrow Wilson Presidential Library (www.youtube.com/user/WWPL StauntonVA) uses YouTube to make available very early films of President Wilson, helping bring a distant historical figure to life for new generations. The Archive of American Television (www.youtube.com/user/TVLEGENDS) has posted almost 2,000 videos, each of which is all or part of an oral history interview with a significant figure in the history of television.

Sharing Videos You Created

In addition to sharing digitized historical content, some archives and historical organizations are creating their own videos and sharing them on sites like YouTube. The technical complexity and quality of these videos varies, from rather simple to quite sophisticated. However, the goal for all of them is the same—to communicate information about their collections or institution in a dynamic and interesting way. The content of the videos ranges from simple overviews of collections to videos that highlight special aspects of the collections or historical events.

Some archives are creating videos that serve as introductions to their collections. Purdue University Archives (www.youtube.com/user/PUarchives) has created two simple videos, "Griffin's Gold" (see Figure 6-3) and "Forgotten Faces and Faded Memories," that highlight their mission and collections, using primarily still photographs with some video excerpts, overlaid with a narrative giving context for the images. The library of the University of Maryland, Baltimore County (www.youtube.com/user/umbclibrary) has posted two notable videos on YouTube: "Visiting Special Collections" and "Special Collections Overview," as part of its series of videos that introduce various aspects of the library. The "Visiting Special Collections" video could serve as a model for other archives in creating videos that walk researchers through the process of using the archives and outline policies and procedures.

The State Records Authority of New South Wales includes on its channel (www.youtube.com/user/AlanVentress) a mixture of different types of videos—including a professional interview first broadcast on television, videos of

Figure 6-3. "Griffin's Gold" on Purdue University Archives YouTube Channel

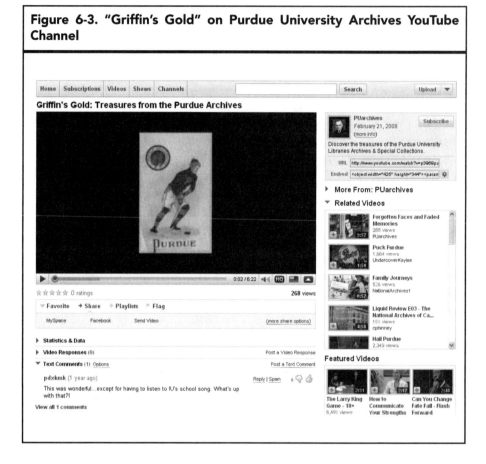

talks shot with a handheld camera, and videos about the collections made specifically for YouTube. One video in particular, "New South Wales Railway Refreshment Rooms," provides almost a virtual exhibit of images, with a slideshow of images (taken from the archives' digital collections) described in the voiceover narration.

Capitalizing on a popular subject, the National Archives of the United Kingdom has created six videos for its channel (www.youtube.com/user/NationalArchives08) that discuss the release of information in its "UFO Files." Of these, three videos comprise a single audio podcast lecture (broken up because of YouTube's running time limit of ten minutes), which is accompanied by animated slides. This model, which is similar to the "virtual exhibition" video discussed in the preceding paragraph, shows ways to share information

Interview with David Hovde
The Virginia Kelly Karnes Archives
and Special Collections Research Center
Purdue University Library

What made your institution interested in creating videos for YouTube?

The origin of "Forgotten Faces and Faded Memories" was an idea of mine for an in-house "how-we-do-it-good-in-my-department" program for the Purdue University Libraries. It quickly evolved into a video. I wanted it initially to be an instructional and promotional tool attached to our Web site and something we could use for programs given to alumni, donor, and community groups. The idea of putting it on YouTube made it that much more transportable and accessible to students. The "Griffin's Gold" video was, from the beginning, a promotional and instructional tool, again to use for both students and donors.

What information, tools, and processes did you need to begin?

I first needed to address questions about my audience, the message and mission of the video, and what skill sets and technologies were available in-house. I then came up with the idea and made a list of images I wanted to use to tell the story. I created a story board and a script outline. I made a light table and used a digital camera for the artifacts in "Griffin's Gold." We used a ZOOM Corp. digital H4 Handy Recorder and Adobe Premier Elements software.

The good thing about YouTube is the time limit. That forces you to be brief and to the point.

How did you determine what information to include?

I am the instruction person in the Archives and have used many of the objects in the classes that I teach. I made a list of all the different types of material we have in the collection and then tried to find a good example of each. I wanted to tell the story of the collection and the story of our mission.

What challenges did you face?

Juggling various priorities and work flow was the biggest issue. One of our team was a graduate student who was nearing the end of her program. Other challenges included building a light table and getting used to the H4 Handy Recorder and Adobe Premier Elements software.

(cont'd.)

Interview with David Hovde *(continued)*
What kinds of positive results have you had? (And, any negative ones?) Everything has been compliments, except one who didn't like our choice of music. We couldn't help that. It was in the original film. I send the link to "Griffin's Gold" to faculty before their students come to an instruction session so they get an idea of what we have, and they uniformly appreciate it. "Forgotten Faces and Faded Memories" is featured on the Lone Arrangers Web site: http://lonearrangers.ning.com. It's an honor to be promoted like that and have a colleague find it useful.
About how much time does it take? The script writing took a few days initially, and then it was edited and re-written a few times. It was further edited during the recording process. The audio recording took three hours at most. Some lines were read six to ten times. The camera time was about three to four hours. Choosing the film clips and the oral history clip took two to three hours. The software time was about 40 hours for each video at most.
What advice would you give an organization wanting to use something similar? You should have an idea of why you are doing it. Is it for instruction, promotion, or both? What is your goal? How long of a shelf life will the video have? Who is your audience? Give the creators a free rein, and don't impose deadlines that stifle creativity and quality.

about your collections on YouTube without actually filming new video content or digitizing archival film or video holdings.

Among the most sophisticated content on the archives-related channels on YouTube is that created by the George Eastman House (www.youtube.com/user/GeorgeEastmanHouse). This is a repurposing of their award-winning video podcast (in 2009 they received the highest award in the podcast category from the American Association of Museums' Muse Awards). The Eastman House series has very high technical quality and diverse content, ranging from an introduction to photo conservation, to discussions of the work of individual photographers (such as Ansel Adams and Lewis Hines), to a discussion of the Lunar Orbiter Camera that took pictures of the surface of the moon.

The University of Manitoba's Archives and Special Collections provides proof that you don't have to post a lot of videos to make a YouTube splash. It has posted only one video, but the video has been viewed over 73,000 times. "T.G. Hamilton's Photos of Ectoplasm" (www.youtube.com/watch?v=

W0HncGNBCqY) incorporates still photographs from the Hamilton Family Fund documenting psychic phenomena that occurred in their home between 1918 and 1945. The four-minute-long video is a slide show of images showing telekinesis, trance states, ectoplasm, and other psychic phenomena. The format is very basic, with simple captions and an appropriately eerie soundtrack, but it is the oddly compelling images that make this video stand out.

WHAT DOES IT TAKE TO BE SUCCESSFUL WITH VIDEO SHARING?

Before starting a YouTube, Vimeo, or other video-sharing presence for your institution, you should first *determine what archival content you have to share*. Consider the volume, format, and content of your film and video materials, as well as your ability to digitize the nondigital content. You may already have plans to digitize some of this content, or you may be hoping to use the opportunity to share it on a site like YouTube as a catalyst for obtaining funding to do digitization. If you have not already done so, you might want to do an inventory and preservation assessment of your film and video collections. (For example, when the materials were accessioned, the actual content may not have been verified against the description provided. For film in particular, the condition may either be too damaged to digitize or at the point where digitization is critical to ensure future access.)

After you are confident you know the content and condition of the archival material you have available to share, *consider what kind of presence you want*. Several different models were described in the previous section, and you can no doubt find many others. Some institutions share only historical content, while others have a mixture of historical and new content. Some organizations upload videos on an ongoing basis, while others just publish new content occasionally. You should also consider what audience you are most interested in attracting. Do you want to share material that is primarily about your own institution's history or about the local area (as Iowa State University has done), or do you want to post a video that may attract people who have no previous interest in your collections (as the University of Manitoba Archives did)?

As with the other Web 2.0 tools, you should *explore what similar organizations are doing* to inform and inspire your own implementation strategy. Assess what you like and don't like about the way other organizations present themselves on their account (or channel) pages and what you think about their mix of content and the individual videos they have shared.

You should also ***think about creating new content*** for your video-sharing channel. While you may not have the capabilities to film something new (as the University of Maryland, Baltimore County did in their "Visiting Special Collections" video), you might be able to create a video by working with other content. Taking as examples the virtual exhibit created by the State Records Authority of New South Wales and the video that Purdue University Archives created based on materials in their collections, you can create your own animated slide presentations or slide shows of images and screenshots accompanied by an audio track. This is a lower tech way to make existing content more dynamic and bringing it to a new audience.

Whether you are contemplating using archival materials or creating new content, it is important to ***consider any possible copyright issues*** you might encounter. If you are creating entirely new content, you should not have anything to worry about. But if you are reusing archival video, film, images, or audio, you will need to examine what rights you have for the materials, as well as how much of the material you might want to reuse. Some large media corporations have been aggressively targeting use of their content on YouTube, so you might want to be particularly cautious about using any material that was originally created for commercial purposes. YouTube has created a page of Copyright Tips (www.youtube.com/t/howto_copyright) that may be useful. However, if you have concerns about copyright issues, you may want to consult with your legal counsel (as discussed in Chapter 12).

While you are still in your planning stages, you also need to ***decide which video-sharing site to use***—or whether you want to post content on more than one site. At the moment, YouTube is the dominant site, and some archives are using Vimeo, but this is a rapidly changing market, and you should explore it for yourself. Look at the site policies regarding size limitations for uploading, and assess if they meet your needs. Explore the site layout and page design, as well as the options available for sharing and commenting on videos. You should be aware that some schools and companies block access to sites like YouTube and Vimeo on their systems. If you want to make sure your videos are accessible in schools, explore educational video-sharing sites like TeacherTube (http://teachertube.com). All of these, in addition to the site's popularity, should be factors in your decision making.

When you are ready to ***start your account***, you need to consider the same kinds of issues discussed in establishing accounts in other Web 2.0 tools, including the following:

- Choose a name to identify your channel or account that clearly identifies your institution. (For example, you probably do not want to use your personal name or a nickname if the account really represents your institution.)
- Upload the image or logo for your account that represents your organization.
- Fully flesh out the information in your profile. Although the account profile on YouTube is set up to describe individuals, use it to share information about your institution, such as your mission, Web address, and contact information.
- Carefully review the privacy settings for your account in general (and for your uploads, when you make them). You probably want to maximize the way users can share and interact with your videos, but you may have reasons to choose other more limiting settings.
- Look at the choices available for customizing your channel or account page. You may have the option to upload a picture to be used in the background, customize colors, and select what information is displayed and how it is organized. If your organization has a strongly established graphic identity, you may want to spend more time making your page reflect that.

Either before or after you create your account, you will need to **create videos to share**. Whether you are making a video from digitized archival material or creating a new video, this will be the most challenging part of your implementation. The process for creating videos is complex and varies greatly depending on what kind of content you want to include. It is not possible to include all the information you would need in an introductory book like this one. After you have decided what kind of video you want to create, look for recent information on the Web or through your library to help you learn about the best way to produce your final product. If you see good examples of videos created by other archives or historical organizations on video-sharing sites, contact them and ask for their advice. They will probably have many specific lessons learned to share with you.

It is relatively easy to **upload your videos** to video-sharing sites. In YouTube you can upload videos one at a time, or utilize their Uploader application to upload up to ten videos at once. You can choose to **enter the appropriate metadata** for your video, such as the title, description, tags, and category, before you upload or after. Uploading may take a few minutes, and your video may not be accepted if it does not conform to the site's requirements.

On YouTube videos are represented by "thumbnails," or small images of one screenshot that represent the video. After your video has been successfully uploaded, YouTube will automatically create three representative video thumbnails for it. You can view these and select the one you prefer by accessing the "My Videos" section of your account. Select the video you are interested in, and select the "Video Still" option under "Edit Video Info." In this section you will be able to select the thumbnail you prefer, as well as edit other information about your video, such as its tags and description.

Just as YouTube users can create "playlists" of the videos they like, you can ***create playlists of the videos on your channel***. Users can subscribe either to your whole channel or to individual playlists. Each playlist will have its own homepage, where you can display a short description.

As with other Web 2.0 tools, it's important to ***monitor comments*** you receive on your channel and videos. The comments you receive may call for you to provide more context for the video or perhaps add to or correct existing information. It's also useful to know how people are responding to your content. Other users of the service may send you messages, so you should always monitor that message account as well and respond appropriately.

Final Tips If You Are Considering Video Sharing

- Research the policies and functionalities of different video-sharing sites carefully before deciding where to set up your account. You might find that the most popular site is not the one that best meets your needs.
- Make sure everyone in your organization understands that once you post video publicly, it is essentially out of your control.
- Consider creating your own videos to introduce or highlight your collections.
- Talk to others who have created the kind of videos you want to produce, and ask for their advice and suggestions.
- Make sure your profile or channel page clearly conveys information about your institution.
- Consider copyright issues for the materials you plan to upload.
- Give your videos descriptive titles and tags so that more people will find them.

CHAPTER 7

Using Twitter (Microblogging)

WHAT IS MICROBLOGGING AND WHAT IS TWITTER?

Microblogging, as it sounds, is blogging on a very small scale. Microbloggers publish extremely short updates or messages. The platform provided by Twitter (www.twitter.com) has quickly risen to dominate this field, and the verb "to twitter" (or "to tweet") has entered the public vocabulary, becoming popularly synonymous with microblogging. Other microblogging sites include these:

- Plurk (www.plurk.com)
- Identi.ca (http://identi.ca)
- Jaiku (www.jaiku.com)
- Laconia (http://laconi.ca/trac)

In addition, recent changes to the Facebook homepage interface have made Facebook status and other kinds of updates act much more like microblogging (see Chapter 9).

However, Twitter is by far the most popular microblogging platform with the public and therefore with cultural institutions like museums, libraries, and archives. This chapter will describe Twitter's functionalities and uses, from which you may extrapolate how other microblogging services might be used.

Setting Up a Twitter Account

You can look at the content being created by people on Twitter without having an account, including accessing the pages of people who have open accounts and searching all "tweets." However to "follow" someone or to participate yourself, you must have an account. Currently there is no cost to be on Twitter, although that, like most other things related to Web 2.0 sites, is subject to change.

To establish an account on Twitter, you need to create a short Username and provide a longer "full name." Your Username is limited to 15 characters and must be unique—in other words, you cannot duplicate a name taken by another Twitter user. You will also need to provide an e-mail (which is not publicly displayed) and create a password. This is the only information you need to create an account.

However, once your account is established, you may add information to your profile, such as specifying your geographic location and providing a link to your Web site. You also have 160 characters in which to describe yourself (your "bio"). You can also upload a picture to represent your account; this image will be displayed alongside your updates. If you do not upload a picture, a generic image will display.

You can change the background and colors to customize how your profile page displays. One option is to upload an image of your own, which can display as one large background image or with multiple tiled copies (later in this chapter, Figure 7-2 shows a page with one large background image).

When you are accessing your account information, you can also choose to "protect" your updates. This means that you must approve any requests to "follow" you and that your updates will not appear in the "public timeline" that Twitter creates of all tweets by Twitter users. This also means your tweets will not appear in any search results.

Creating "Tweets," Following and Being Followed on Twitter

The messages you publish on Twitter, sometimes called "tweets," may not be longer than 140 characters. Tweets are often just short statements about what people are doing or how they are feeling. People and organizations on Twitter also use it to share news about current events and to point followers to items of interest on the Web. Once a message is published, it cannot be edited. Messages can be deleted (although, depending on how quickly you delete it, the message may have already been seen by anyone following you).

While anyone may see your Twitter messages if they look at your Twitter homepage or discover them via a search (unless you have "protected" them), the point of Twitter is to subscribe to the messages of the users you care about by "following" them. When you are following someone, the updates will automatically appear when you access Twitter. In turn, people who are interested in the content you are producing will "follow" you. As mentioned, those users who have elected to "protect" their tweets (signaled by a padlock symbol next to their Username) must approve any requests to be followed. Some Twitter users feel that if someone follows you, that you are obligated to follow them in return; there is no hard-and-fast convention regarding this practice, however.

Some Twitter Conventions

Twitter users are addressed by adding "@" before their Usernames. Conversations between Twitter users (sometimes among more than two users) are conducted by prefacing a message with "@[username]." (See Figure 7-1 later in this chapter for examples of some of these conventions.) Exchanges such as these are public and so can be viewed by other Twitter users or discovered via a Twitter search. It is also possible to send a "direct message," which will be private between two users. However, it is only possible to send a direct message to someone who is following you.

One of the most popular Twitter conventions is the "re-tweet"—a message that repeats a message sent by someone else. This is signaled by adding "RT @[username]" to the beginning of the copied message. Twitter has recently announced that it will soon begin to formally support re-tweeting, incorporating a new feature that will allow you to re-tweet a message by simply clicking on it. It appears that this new feature will not allow you to edit or add anything to the re-tweeted message, but Twitter has stated that users will still be able to re-tweet manually, and so continue to add editorial comments. This new feature may also make it easier to track which of your messages are being re-circulated.

People on Twitter commonly use tags to identify content in their tweets—specifically, they use "hashtags," or tags preceded by the hash or "#" symbol. Because of the character limits of Twitter, hashtags are often abbreviations. There are no rules or conventions for creating hashtags; if you add "#" in front of something, it becomes a hashtag. Usually, Twitter users who want to share information, such as people sharing information about a conference, will come to a consensus on what hashtag they will all add to their tweets. Using a common hashtag allows you to find all relevant tweets in a single search.

Accessing Twitter

Twitter can be accessed through the Web interface (at twitter.com) or via a variety of third-party interfaces (such as Tweetdeck [www.tweetdeck.com] and

Twhirl [www.twhirl.org]) that allow users to manage the flow of messages from the people they follow. Many people send and receive tweets via their mobile phones. You can also use instant messaging services, such as AIM, Google Talk, iChat, or LiveJournal chat to access Twitter.

People who are not on Twitter can also subscribe to your updates through the RSS feed Twitter automatically generates for your account. If you want to set up a search (for all tweets that contain references to your organization, for example) and get regular updates on new tweets that meet your search criteria, you can also set up an RSS feed for your search results. If you want to set up an RSS feed for a search, bear in the mind that Twitter users frequently use abbreviations and shorthand in order to fit information into the 140-character limits. You may need to spend some time refining your search criteria to make sure you know how people may be referring to your organization.

HOW CAN YOUR INSTITUTION USE TWITTER?

Many media reports on the popularity of Twitter convey the impression that people use it primarily to convey trivial information about their daily lives. However, for many people and organizations, Twitter has evolved into an efficient platform for conveying news and short pieces of information directly to interested people. The power of the networks of popular Twitter users and their followers can be seen in the reach of re-tweeted information. Often links to interesting items on the Web or news stories are passed from user to user, migrating through networks of Twitter users in a "viral" fashion.

Providing News about Your Institution

Many large archives and historical organizations have embraced Twitter as another way to communicate news and establish connections with their audiences. Organizations such as the Library of Congress (@librarycongress), the Smithsonian Institution (@smithsonian), the Internet Archive (@internetarchive), and the New-York Historical Society (@NYHistory) use Twitter regularly. As you might expect, the larger organizations, such as the Library of Congress and the Smithsonian, are more active Twitter users. They mix updates about events and exhibitions with references to news stories about their institutions and links to quirky or interesting stories on the Web. For example, a Library of Congress tweet asked "How do fortunes get inside fortune cookies?" and provided a link to an article created by the Library's Science Reference Services that explains the process.

Interview with Matt Raymond
The Library of Congress

What made you interested in using Twitter?

I've had a personal interest in social media for a long time. As soon as I got to the Library, I immediately got plugged in with a group of people who believe in social media as strongly as I do in order to get some of these things off the ground.

What information, tools, and processes did you need to begin?

To be honest, Twitter was one of those things that took some convincing for me to do. A colleague got me interested in trying out a personal feed, at a time when Twitter was far less the force it is today, in preparation for a possible Library feed. So probably the most important thing was for me to get used to it and have my eyes opened to the possibilities.

How did you determine what information to include?

It's basically up to me. Press releases and events announcements via Twitterfeed were an easy call. In terms of the tweets themselves, I sometimes get good suggestions from other staff. I keep my ears open in hallways and meeting rooms for interesting tidbits. I also subscribe to all the Library's RSS feeds, so I can cull from there.

What challenges did you face?

Very few, actually. Twitter is one of the few sites where we, as a government entity, didn't have to negotiate altered terms of service to meet our unique needs. A broader issue was ensuring that the Library as a whole was comfortable with where we wanted to go with social media. It wasn't a tough sell, but we still wanted to present a thoughtful business case for it.

What kinds of positive results have you had? (And, any negative ones?)

It's very personally gratifying for me to watch the results. First is the sheer number of subscribers—more than 4,000 as of this moment—which is pretty huge for a government entity. That's thousands of people who want to know what the Library is up to almost minute-to-minute. Another benefit is that it actually drives a good amount of traffic to our Web site, and it helps uncover some hidden gems for people. I assume it's having some benefit for attendance at our exhibits and other programs, but I don't have numbers to back that up.

(cont'd.)

Interview with Matt Raymond *(continued)*
The only negative I can think of is a couple of tweets that had some ramifications for others here that I didn't think about at the time, but nothing major.
About how much time does it take? It's hard to say exactly, but it FEELS like very little. I keep it open in my browser all day, so whenever I'm at my desk and something looks tweetable, it takes only a few seconds. Plus, our account is on several other devices, so I can even tweet from home at midnight if I want to.
What advice would you give an organization wanting to use something similar? Do it! Your customers use it, and they crave any information you can give them. Plus, it's become a bit cliché, but I really do see it as adding transparency to government. In a way, we owe it to taxpayers to be as open as possible. But go into it with your eyes open in terms of policy, resources and doing it in a way that respects the conventions and practices of the community.

These large institutions, like their smaller counterparts, generally adopt an informal, conversational tone in their tweets. They almost convey a sense of making their followers "insiders" and so are performing more than just a simple outreach function. An example of a tweet that combines news with a sense of an institution with a personality is this one from the Lyndon Baines Johnson Library's Twitter account (@lbjnow):

> Sci fi fest tonight CANCELLED due to weather. That pesky rain—good for wildflowers Lady Bird loved, but bad for outdoor movies.
> (sent 10:17 AM Mar 27th from Web)

For smaller organizations, such as the Johnson Library, Twitter can be a way of both keeping in touch with established audiences and reaching out to new ones by promoting their institution via this new platform. Among the smaller archives on Twitter are these:

- East Texas Research Center (@ETRC_archives)
- Nova Scotia Archives (@NS_Archives)
- Binghamton University, Special Collections and Archives (@buspecialcollec)

- Special Collections Research Center, College of William & Mary (@SwemSCRC)
- Deseronto Archives (@DesorontoArch)
- Jewish Women's Archive (@jwanonline)
- The University of Texas at San Antonio (@UTSAYesterday)

Some of these organizations feature a link to a document or picture of the day in their tweets. Some accounts include a mixture of "official" information with tweets that discuss what the person responsible for the account is doing. In this regard, they are using Twitter much like other archives use traditional blogs—to provide a sense of what is happening at the institution. Some organizations, like the Nova Scotia Archives (see Figure 7-1; http://twitter.com/NS_Archives), make a point of engaging in conversation with other Twitter users about the content of their tweets. Others post updates but do not participate in much two-way dialogue.

Innovative Uses for Twitter

In addition to these conventional uses of Twitter, there are a few users who are taking Twitter's extremely limited functionalities in creative directions.

One way to create a different voice for your Twitter account is to literally give it a different voice—that of an inanimate object. The "bio" for the Tenement Museum's Twitter account (@tenementmuseum) says: "I'm a 5 story brick walk up, built in 1863. A museum takes care of me now (I'm lucky!)" The Tenement Museum's Twitter postings are largely written from the point of view of the building but still provide the usual news about the events of the organization.

An approach with less charm but equal value was being explored by the Wiltshire and Swindon Archives (@wsadocuments), which was including in its Twitter account only messages that described the documents that had been pulled for researchers. Each message provided the unique identifier for the document and a short description. This gave the account's followers insight into the holdings of the archives and also allowed this information to be discoverable by those searching Twitter (for example, for those searching on geographic terms, document types, or family names). This account seems to have gone inactive.

Figure 7-1. Nova Scotia Archives Twitter Feed

NS_Archives

✓Following

@hikethehighland Ingonish is one of my favourite places on earth! I've gone on many great hikes, there. http://twurl.nl/v8qenz

2 minutes ago from web

@ourvalley Thank you so much! We have some lovely shots of the Valley http://twurl.nl/45xibn

4 minutes ago from web in reply to ourvalley

@untitleddesign Wow, great shot! Really looked like you stepped back into the 50s. Where was this?

21 minutes ago from web in reply to untitleddesign

@untitleddesign Me too! I love the little convertible right outside the theatre... pretty unique looking.

27 minutes ago from web in reply to untitleddesign

@christinacopp I agree! The Oxford looks as though it hasn't changed at all... the rest of Quinpool is another story :)

30 minutes ago from web in reply to christinacopp

@CynatNovaScotia Two shots of the Halifax Farmers Market (1886 & 1953) http://twurl.nl/n8lwkv http://twurl.nl/j4mqo7

32 minutes ago from web in reply to CynatNovaScotia

1957 shot of the Oxford Theatre in Halifax http://twurl.nl/pywtp8 The lovely Sophia Loren starred in "Boy on a Dolphin"

35 minutes ago from web

RT @ns_museum Osprey is up! I can see the eggs! http://museum.gov.ns.ca/mnh...

about 20 hours ago from web

@eastern_shore Unique name! Do you know the meaning?

about 21 hours ago from web in reply to eastern_shore

**Interview with Lauren Oostveen
Nova Scotia Archives**

What made you interested in using Twitter?
I come from a background in public relations and have been interested in social media for quite some time. I've been using a personal Twitter account for over two years, and when I came to work at Nova Scotia Archives & Records Management I immediately saw the value that Twitter would bring. We have such a wealth of content on our Web site (www.gov.ns.ca/nsarm), and Twitter gave us a new way to share that content and reach out to our researchers, Web site users, and anyone with an interest in history!

What information, tools, and processes did you need to begin?
Having already familiarized myself with Twitter, I didn't need a whole lot of background information to begin. I use Tweetdeck because it's much easier to "follow the conversation" versus simply refreshing the Web site and trying to keep up.

How did you determine what information to include?
I sometimes follow a "this day in history" format when I have the photos to back it up, but most of the time I simply look for photos or documents that will inspire a conversation with my followers. I try to include as much content from around the province of Nova Scotia as possible rather than just keeping it centric to Halifax (where I'm from), which can be tough, sometimes. Something else I like to do is to support other archives/libraries/museums initiatives by "re-tweeting" some of their tweets, especially if they are from Nova Scotia or Eastern Canada.

What challenges did you face?
The number one challenge that Twitter provides is simply keeping up with the conversation, especially as our number of followers grows. I don't want to miss the opportunity to share something or answer a question. Another challenge would be measuring our success, as Twitter is a (relatively) new business tool and doesn't quite fit in to the usual standards for measurement.

What kinds of positive results have you had? (And, any negative ones?)
Many people have responded so well to this feature, and in my mind these are people who would normally never surf onto our Web site or come into the archives to do research. It's an easy way for them to access our province's history, and they like the engagement that we provide

(cont'd.)

Interview with Lauren Oostveen (continued)
them. More people are familiar with us, our products, and have made it known that they wholeheartedly support what we do.
About how much time does it take? I have Tweetdeck running all the time with a search keyed in for "ns_archives," so anytime anyone mentions us I see it pop up. I try to do one update in the morning and one in the afternoon from Monday to Friday and reply to any queries that follow. Not counting the time I spend monitoring, the actual update process takes only a couple of hours for a week's work.
What advice would you give an organization wanting to use something similar? Don't just "dump links" and hope for a response. Try and engage your followers in a conversation . . . that's what Twitter is for! Give your tweets personality, rather than hiding behind your institution, and have fun with it!

One Twitter user noted some similarities between 140-character messages captured by this modern tool and the short entries recorded in an early twentieth-century diary. David Griner, a social media strategist, describes how the Twitter account for @genny_spencer (see Figure 7-2) came about:

> Late last year, my family found a line-a-day diary maintained by my great-aunt from 1937 to 1941. She was in her early teens, living on a small farm in rural Illinois with her two brothers, one of which was my grandfather.
>
> It's a fascinating account of life in a bygone era, a time when my family's only connections to the world were schoolhouse chatter and a neighbor's radio. Looking at the terse journal, my sister quipped, "This is the Twitter of the 1930s." We glanced at each other and almost immediately began planning the Twitter account that would become Twitter.com/Genny_Spencer. (Griner, 2009)

A typical entry in Genny Spencer's diary (and so her Twitter account) reads something like "Daddy painted on Mr. Williams' barn. Herbert A. missed school to-day sick. -March 22, 1937" or "I went to school in the rain. Norman or Kerby didn't go. -April 5, 1937." This approach, like the picture or document of the day, gives followers regular archival content rather than just administrative information.

Figure 7-2. Genny Spencer Twitter Page

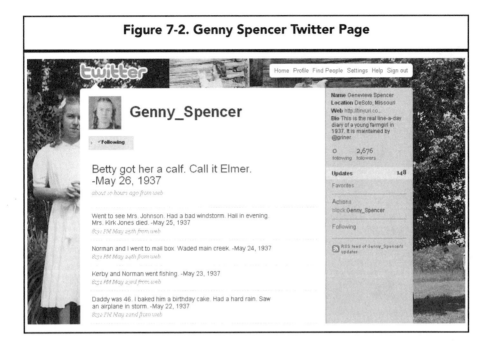

The Genny Spencer diary has inspired others to tweet diary or historic materials. The University of Texas at San Antonio is sharing the diaries of James Redford, Sr. (@RedfordDiaries), who moved from Canada to Texas in 1877 and homesteaded 160 acres. As noted in Chapter 3, the Orwell Diaries blog also has a Twitter feed (@orwelldiaries), which provides excerpts from the latest diary entry and a link to the complete entry on the blog.

Another innovative approach is being explored on TwHistory (www.twhistory.com), a collaborative volunteer effort to provide insight into historical events by tweeting diary and other information to represent the perspectives of different people involved in the event. Their current project revolves around the Battle of Gettysburg; they are "following" 11 "characters," all of whom have their own Twitter account, providing information based on the people's own writings (see Figure 7-3).

This approach of creating tweets out of historical materials was put to a more lucrative use by the National Trust for Scotland to raise money for the Robert Burns Birthplace Museum. Over the weekend prior to the celebration of the 250th anniversary of Scottish poet Robert Burns's birth, for every donation made, a line of Burns' poetry was tweeted (via @ayrshirebard) and the donor

Figure 7-3. Tweeting History's "Battle of Gettysburg"

Tweeting History

The Road to Gettysburg

Rev. A. D. Betts *about 10 hours ago*
Meet Chaplains. Bro. Stradly preaches for me at night.

Louis Leon *about 10 hours ago*
Rested. I went to see my brother Morris, who belongs to Dowles' Brigade, 44th Georgia Regiment. Did not see him, as he was on picket.

John Pardington *about 19 hours ago*
They have had a Pretty hard time of it. By accounts a good many of them were sun struck so you can form some Idea how hot it is down here.

John Pardington *about 19 hours ago*
Our Regiment has not come in yet from the Recognacene they went on. We expect them back today or tomorrow.

Charles Wainwright *about 22 hours ago*
...my doctor reported 30 of them physically unfit for artillery service, which report was sent up to corps HQ. I eventually got my men.

Charles Wainwright *about 22 hours ago*
Robinson is not happy about the batteries being taken from him. He sent over 35 men to help. I had them examined by my little doctor...

Louis Leon *05:32 PM May 25, 2009*
Resumed our march this morning at 6. Got six miles and halted. We pitched our camp here on a hill two miles from Fredericksburg.

Rev. A. D. Betts *05:31 PM May 25, 2009*
Examine 2 candidates for Missionary Baptist Church. Rev. J.H. Colton, Chaplain 53rd Regiment spends night. He had been my classmate 3 years.

Charles Wainwright *05:07 PM May 25, 2009*
But there is only one man in whom this army has confidence, and there is no chance of his ever again having command.

publicly thanked on Twitter. These donations were also made via Twitter (using PayPal).

WHAT DOES IT TAKE TO BE ACTIVE ON TWITTER?

As described earlier, creating a Twitter account and posting individual tweets is comparatively easy. As with most Web 2.0 tools, it is essential before diving into Twitter to *identify what you want to do*. While setting up an account may be easy, a good Twitter presence is a consistent Twitter presence. Being consistent does not mean being prolific, it means establishing a pattern so that users know what kinds of information they can expect. Here are some suggestions for how you might use your Twitter updates:

- To make administrative announcements (including weather-related closings and cancellations)
- To make announcements and send reminders about upcoming public programs
- As another vehicle for promoting information on your blog (for example, by linking to a "document of the day" post)
- As a means of promoting other kinds of information on your Web site (such as images of documents or photographs)
- To share brief "today in history" information
- To promote local events that are not sponsored by your institution
- To share first person accounts of what is happening in the archives (for example, that you are working on a new exhibit or that a school group visited, etc.)
- To share "finds" that you've made while processing (such as fun quotes from documents or unusual artifacts)

It is a good idea to *establish a personal Twitter* account before establishing an organizational account. This allows you to follow other archives, museums, and historical societies to get ideas for your institutions' account. It will also allow you to get a feel for how Twitter works.

Establish who will be responsible for providing the content and actually managing the account. Depending on what kind of information you want to include, more than one person may be responsible for gathering the information for your tweets, and you may choose to give more than one person access to the account. Regardless of who is involved, responsibilities need to be clear.

Part of establishing a professional Twitter presence for your archives is to *create an account with a clear identification*. Select a Username (within the 15 character limit) that people will immediately associate with your organization. Provide complete information on your profile page—your location, Web site, and a useful "bio" section. Before selecting the image to upload to identify your account, take a look at what other institutions have done. Both the Library of Congress and the Smithsonian Institution use versions of their logo. If your logo will not work effectively at the small scale required by Twitter, you may consider using all or part of an image from your collections (as the Nova Scotia Archives and Deseronto Archives have done). You also have the option for uploading an image to use as the background on your profile page; many archives also use images from their collections here too.

Most people on Twitter don't just publish their own tweets; they also follow people and engage in conversations. You can make your own decisions about who your institution wants to follow, but you should make an effort to *engage with your Twitter community*. When people direct comments or questions to you, whether you are following them or not, you should respond to them. (You can easily see all comments directed at you by clicking on the "@[your Username]" option at the right of the Twitter interface). You might want to locate other local organizations that are twittering and follow them. You might want your archives to follow other archives or historical organizations on Twitter. You can begin slowly, but you should try to connect your Twitter presence with those of people or organizations that you feel are appropriate for your organization.

While you can't rely on any commercial Web 2.0 service to preserve your data (as will be discussed in Chapter 12), Twitter is particularly ephemeral. Twitter makes no guarantees about how long you will be able to access your tweets (or anyone else's). If you want to maintain a record of your Twitter feed, including any responses people have sent to you ("@" tweets) or direct messages, you *must export your tweets* into something else. While this is a changing field and you should explore the options that you have available, many people are using Tweetake (http://tweetake.com), Tweetbackup (http://tweetbackup.com), and "The Archivist" (http://flotzam.com/archivist) to preserve their Twitter contributions.

As with many Web 2.0 applications, new services are constantly emerging to help you manage your Twitter account, and it is always a good idea to *keep up to date on what is available*. You might want to explore options such as Tweetdeck or Twhirl, which provide a more user-friendly interface for using Twitter. If you are producing tweets on a regular basis, you might want to consider using a service such as "Tweetlater" (www.tweetlater.com), which allows you to prepare tweets, schedule them, and then have the service post them on your account according to your schedule.

Final Tips If You Are Considering Using Twitter

- Study organizations and people on Twitter so that you understand the culture.
- Make it easy for people to know who you are.
- Have a plan for what kind of content to include in your tweets.
- Decide what kind of "voice" you want to have—and having a personality is welcome on Twitter!
- Consider using Twitter for something a bit different—like tweeting content from your collections (like diaries or letters) or setting up a Twitter collaboration (like TwHistory's "Battle of Gettysburg").
- Interact with your followers and fans.

REFERENCES

Griner, David. 2009. "A Daily Diary of Depression-Era Life, Told on Twitter." The Social Path (January 28). Available: www.thesocialpath.com/2009/01/twitter-from-1937.html (accessed April 7, 2009).

CHAPTER 8

Using Wikis

WHAT IS A WIKI?

A wiki is a Web site that allows many people to contribute by editing content and adding pages, working collaboratively to create an information resource. The term "wiki" originated with the first wiki software, WikiWikiWeb, created by Ward Cunningham in 1994, incorporating "wiki," the Hawaiian word for "fast" (Wikipedia, accessed 2009).

Today, because of the enormous popularity of Wikipedia (http://wikipedia .org), almost everyone with access to the Web has used a wiki. Wikipedia has contributed to the growth of wiki adoption in another way—by making its software freely available to the public. MediaWiki (www.mediawiki.org), the software developed for use by Wikipedia, can be downloaded and used by anyone to create a wiki. To use MediaWiki you must have a server to host the software, but there are also many commercial sites that allow you to create and host a wiki for free on their site (in exchange for allowing advertisements to appear on the wiki site). You also have the option of having a site without advertisements for a fee. Among the most popular wiki host sites are these:

- PBworks (formerly PBwiki) (www.pbworks.com)
- Wetpaint (www.wetpaint.com)
- Google Sites (http://sites.google.com)
- Socialtext (www.socialtext.net)
- Wikispaces (www.wikispaces.com)

Although the technology is easy to use, wikis are one of the less popular Web 2.0 tools among archives and historical organizations. Unlike sites such as Flickr, YouTube, and Facebook, creating a wiki requires a considerable commitment of time to create a rich information resource, attract contributors, and encourage participation. Creating and maintaining a successful wiki takes sustained effort from a community—big or small—of participants. While it may be a challenge, if you are successful in building an engaged community of followers and contributors for your wiki, you will have expanded your institution's base of supporters. People who see value in and contribute to your wiki are potentially another group of people who can advocate for your institution and testify as to its value.

Another challenge of implementing a wiki is that, although wiki software is a powerful tool, it is also one that may be somewhat intimidating to novice users. Unlike tools such as blogs, Flickr, and Facebook, the chances of people becoming familiar with using wiki software for personal reasons are somewhat slim—unless they have edited or contributed to Wikipedia. Thus, although editing a wiki really just involves using simple HTML codes and a simple text editor, it is something that most people need to spend some time learning how to do. Most will find this small investment of time to be well worth it.

A wiki is essentially a Web site—complete with a hierarchical structure, navigation, and multiple pages and links—but one that can be built without any technical expertise. Wiki software gives people with subject area expertise the freedom to create their own resources without an IT intermediary. Creating a Web site as a wiki also means that it can grow organically according to the interests of the community by people merely creating pages for new topics. If there is interest to support it, users can make the site as broad or as deep as they want to.

What Wiki Web Sites Look Like to Users

From a user's perspective, reading and navigating information that is displayed in a wiki is not significantly different from using any other Web site. A site created with wiki software will have a hierarchical structure and generally an option for seeing a listing of all the pages (also called "articles") or subjects (also called "categories") on the site. What is different about a wiki is that users can usually access information about the creation of the pages themselves. For each wiki page there will be an option to view the "page history" (see Figure 8-1; http://yourarchives.nationalarchives.gov.uk/index.php?title=France&action=history). (This functionality may also be called simply "history" or "updates"; the terms used vary from software to software.) Clicking this option will show you a listing of what was changed, at what time, and by which user. The "what" may include a brief summary provider by the user, such as "27 words added" or

Figure 8-1. Example of a Page History from The National Archives of the United Kingdom's "Your Archives" Wiki

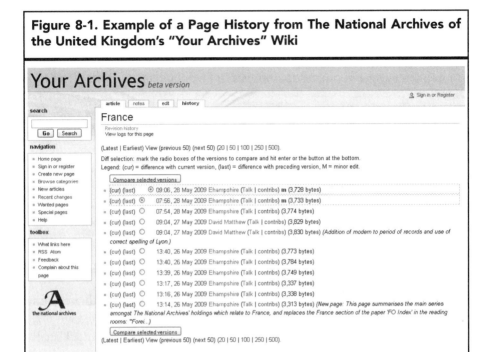

"changing image." The timestamp for the change and the name of the user who made it are automatically captured by the wiki software. Most wikis also allow you to compare different versions of the page so that you can see exactly what was changed. Administrators can even replace the page with an earlier version before a particular change or changes were made.

Wiki pages usually have the option to view (or participate in, for registered users) a discussion about the content of the page. This option may have a label such as "talk," "notes," or "discussion." Options such as these are supposed to be used to discuss the actual text on the page, not the subject matter the page addresses, but, depending on how actively monitored the wiki is, this may or may not be enforced.

Unlike typical Web pages, wiki pages may have an indication about the reliability or completeness of the information provided. Some wikis use features that can tag entries as needing review or additional information. These flags can serve two functions: they assist readers in assessing the accuracy of the information, and they assist wiki contributors by flagging what work the page needs. For example, the "Summary of Afghan Wars" page on the Your Archives wiki (created by the U.K. National Archives) has a banner at the top that reads: "This article or section does not contain sufficient references to *verifiable* archival or published sources. Sources for this information should be cited or unverifiable material may be *removed*" (The National Archives, accessed 2009).

In addition to these kinds of warnings on individual pages, many wikis that are open to the public to edit will have some kind of statement on their homepages indicating that not all the information in the wiki has been reviewed or verified. There has been much discussion around the issue of whether or not public wikis, particularly Wikipedia, provide reliable information, but most sophisticated users know the information provided in a publicly created wiki may not be entirely accurate. Nevertheless, wikis generally provide a good starting point for research or simple reference.

Contributing to a Wiki

Contributing to a wiki—whether by adding new information, editing existing information, or participating in a discussion—is relatively easy. Most wikis require you to register and create an account before you can contribute. Usually the information requested is very basic—often just a Username, password, and an e-mail address. You may also have to agree to a set of terms and conditions of use before completing your registration, depending on the requirements of the wiki's administrator.

Note that some wikis, including Wikipedia, allow you to edit a page anonymously—although you will be identified publicly by your IP address. While you may feel more comfortable editing anonymously, some wiki communities, including many users on Wikipedia, are suspicious of anonymous users and their contributions. If you want to become a trusted member of a wiki community, it is best to register and create an account. This also ensures that your IP address will be kept private.

Once you have registered and logged in, you are usually free to edit any information in the wiki (although some wikis lock down the essential hierarchical arrangement of the wiki or the homepage, for example, so that users cannot change its major elements). You should also be aware that some wiki administrators (including those on Wikipedia) can choose to lock down individual wiki pages if they think there is controversy or they see a large number of edits happening in a short time frame. This can happen on pages that involve political figures or that relate to controversial topics.

HOW CAN YOUR INSTITUTION USE A WIKI?

The wikis that archives and historical organizations have created seem to fall into two distinct categories based on who the primary group of contributors is expected to be. The first category is composed of wikis whose expected contributors are primarily the staff of the creating organization; the second category includes wikis whose expected—or hoped-for—contributors are members of the general public. Both types of wikis are open to the public to view, and in most cases the public can contribute to either type of wiki.

Wikis Created Primarily by Internal Contributors

Many archives use wiki software to create Web resources that describe their own holdings or institution. Perhaps not surprisingly, these types of wikis are often created and contributed to almost exclusively by the organization's own staff. (In some cases the wiki may even be "locked down," preventing members of the public from editing or contributing content.) This type of use seems particularly popular among colleges and universities to create wikis describing their institution's history. For example, the YouMass wiki (www.library.umass .edu/spcoll/youmass/doku.php) describes itself on its homepage as follows:

> Intended as a comprehensive online encyclopedia of the University of Massachusetts Amherst, YouMass documents the lives and activities of the campus community, its departments, programs, faculty, staff, and students. At its heart, YouMass is a collaboration between the Du Bois Library's Department of Special Collections and University Archives (SCUA) and the campus community, and we encourage members of the community to help us tell your stories, document your organizations, and share information about who you are and what you do. (University of Massachusetts, Amherst, accessed 2009)

Similar examples are the Drew University wiki (http://wiki.drew.edu/Special:Allpages) and the SCRC wiki (http://scrc.swem.wm.edu/wiki) at the College of William and Mary; both were designed as resources on campus history and were started and are maintained by their university's Archives and Special Collections departments.

The Montana Historical Society uses PBWorks to support the Montana History Wiki (see Figure 8-2; http://montanahistorywiki.pbworks.com). This

⌂ **Montana History Wiki**

VIEW   ▸

FrontPage

last edited by 🧑 Roberta   1 wk ago   🕙 Page history

Welcome to the Montana Historical Society Research Center's

Montana History Wiki

The Montana History Wiki is a collection of information to help guide researchers to the resources available through the Montana Historical Society Research Center. It is designed to assist researchers in finding the best resource for their projects or topics. The wiki also contains collaborative projects designed to meet the needs of particular groups. Users should note that the Montana History Wiki is not open for editing. However, if you have comments or would like to add content please e-mail your comments to mhslibrary@mt.gov

Select a category below to get started or use the **search box** in the upper right-hand corner. For more tips, please visit the Help Page.

Subject Guides	Indexes
A list of suggested resources for both topical and biographical subjects avaliable at MHS	Various indexes used as tools to access information
Montana Newspapers	**Montana Facts**
Index of microfilm and hardcopy holdings at MHS	"Quick" but reliable information about Montana history
Monthly Features 2009	**Contributions from the Public**
Online exhibits highlighting the Research Center's collections	A forum for public contributions to Montana history

New Additions to the Research Center Catalog
A list of materials recently catalogued, including new books, archival collections and photographs

COLLABORATIVE PROJECTS

Lewis and Clark County History Project

Montana County History

Vigilante Parade Resources

**Interview with Molly Kruckenberg
Montana Historical Society**

What made your institution interested in creating a wiki?

Each year the reference staff in the MHS Research Center answer thousands of telephone calls and e-mails requesting information about Montana history. The staff found that they were repeatedly looking up the same information for patrons. At the same time several staff were exploring Web 2.0 applications and their relevance to the library and archives profession. Staff members suggested creating a wiki as a place to store this type of information, as an easier and more functional alternative than adding information to our agency Web site.

What information, tools, and processes did you need to begin?

Our initial information need included what exactly a wiki was and how to create one. Once we determined that a wiki was the tool that fit our needs, we explored the software options available for creating wikis. Based upon our research and financial considerations, we settled upon PBwiki as an affordable and easy to use solution.

How did you determine what information to include?

Deciding upon the information to be included in the Montana History Wiki has probably been the most challenging part of this project. Initially staff members developed lists of possible topics for inclusion on the wiki. We focused at first on ready reference information. Since then we have developed a standing committee and a set of guidelines to direct the growth of the wiki. We did decide not to make the Montana History Wiki open for public editing, primarily as a way to control the accuracy of the information available. Our guidelines emphasize citing the source of our information whenever possible.

What challenges did/do you face?

The biggest challenge we face is keeping the Montana History Wiki limited to its intended purpose and content. Our wiki is designed to assist researchers in finding the best resource for their projects or topics. It is not designed as a place to display digital content or to provide a comprehensive examination of topics. Other challenges would include dedicating staff time to making software updates and to adding and editing the information.

(cont'd.)

Interview with Molly Kruckenberg (*continued*)
What kinds of positive results have you had? (And, any negative ones?)
The most remarkable feedback we have is that, on average, over 500 people visit the Montana History Wiki weekly. We have also had positive feedback on the wiki from a number of sources, particularly from Montana libraries involved in AskMontana, a free online service for information and research help provided by librarians. The librarians participating in AskMontana refer to the wiki regularly. Equally as important, MHS staff report that they use the wiki, particularly our indexes, regularly in their reference work. We have not had any negative feedback.
About how much time does it take?
The amount of time varies depending upon how many new projects are underway. I would estimate that the five staff involved in the Montana History Wiki spend one hour or less per week on adding and editing content and any software issues that arise. Because we do not allow public editing, there is no work involved in monitoring contributions.
What advice would you give an organization wanting to use something similar?
My advice would be to determine exactly what you want your wiki to be before creating it. We found that this, in particular, has helped us to keep the Montana History Wiki from becoming something that we did not intend it to be. Additionally, limiting the wiki to only staff as contributors has saved time in reviewing publicly added comments.

site is designed to provide an easily accessible and updatable resource for reference information. As Zoe Ann Stoltz, the Society's Reference Historian, describes:

> A good share of the info found on the wiki is not available elsewhere. For example, it is the only online index for our microfilmed newspapers and thousands of vertical files. It also provides a forum for trivia and facts which are often needed in the research center and by our patrons. Since its inception, it has taken on a life of its own as colleagues recognize its versatility and potential. The Lewis and Clark History project is a good example of this. It was done in collaboration with the county library to assist

young researchers. Staff decided that this project would not supply "quick information/answers," but rather help younger students in locating sources and encouraging the research process. (Stoltz, 2009)

Although it is not open to the public to edit, there is a section on the wiki for public contributions on relevant history topics.

The Montana History Wiki illustrates how a wiki can be used to complement or augment the information provided via an institution's Web site. This may be an appealing option for many organizations. Often the logistics of adding new information to organizational Web sites—particularly complicated information such as indexes—may be a bit of a nightmare. In smaller organizations, for example, the Web site may have been created or managed by a volunteer, or the person responsible for Web matters may have only basic Web skills. Larger organizations may have created layers of bureaucracy or restrictive policies that discourage Web updates. Creating a wiki independent of the organizational Web site provides a relatively easy and quick way to make resources available on the Web.

A model that's more narrowly defined is a wiki organized around a person or topic that is particularly relevant for an institution's community. A good example of this is the DuBoisopedia (www.library.umass.edu/spcoll/duboisopedia/doku.php) created by the Special Collections and University Archives of the University of Massachusetts, Amherst. As home to the W.E.B. DuBois Papers, UMass Amherst has become a center for scholarship on DuBois, and the wiki is a natural extension of their outreach efforts. The site is constructed like an encyclopedia, with articles on key people, events, places, and topics related to DuBois. Although open to the public for contribution, the main contributors so far have been the archives staff.

The Coroner Case File Documentation Wiki (see Figure 8-3; http://coronercasefile.pbworks.com), produced by students and staff of the University of Pittsburgh's Archives Service Center, was created primarily to serve the needs of a group of students processing a specific collection but now remains available as resource for the public. The wiki served as a common place to share logistical information about how to process the Allegheny County Coroner case files and also as a place for workers to share information about what they were finding in the records. Although the processing project has been completed, the wiki lives on as a supplement to the traditional finding aid and as a document about the process of making the case files available to the public.

Figure 8-3. Page in the Allegheny County Coroner Case File Documentation Wiki

Wikis Targeted at Public Contributors

Like the Allegheny County Coroner Case File Documentation Wiki, the Archives New Zealand Audio Visual Wiki serves both an internal and external function (www.audiovisual.archives.govt.nz/wiki). Designed to facilitate sharing and updating information about the archives' National Film Unit Collection among Archives New Zealand's six distributed locations, the wiki is also open to the public for their contributions. This is an interesting model for opening up a part of an institution's catalog for additions, corrections, and comments.

Another example of an archives making a subset of records available for the public to build on is Chinese-Canadians: Profiles from a Community, a wiki-based project developed by the Vancouver Public Library in partnership with

Interview with David Smith
Archives New Zealand

What made you interested in implementing this wiki?

Our initial interest in using a wiki emerged at the annual National Digital Forum held here in 2006 which had a focus on Web 2.0 and its relationship to the cultural heritage sector. We were also fortunate to have had a talented programmer working at Archives New Zealand at the time.

The idea of having a space in a database for the public to edit and make contributions appealed, as well as the ease for us to maintain, monitor, and add new information. This meant we could move away from our existing audio visual search aid.

The way collections were described meant that although every separate element of any particular film, for example, master negative, combined print, was listed, it was only as a title with some technical details. For researching actual content a supplemental search aid called Firstref, a giant list of descriptive information in a Microsoft Word file, was needed. This file was available only in the reading rooms of Archives New Zealand's four offices in Auckland, Wellington, Christchurch, and Dunedin, and each time films were preserved and new access copies made, all four sites had to be updated.

When we looked at improving access to the audio visual collection we toyed with the idea of doing something with HTML or Java to add search functionality, but the size of the original document, three and a half megabytes, made this difficult. Our programmer suggested using a wiki as the database as he knew how to set it up, create the look, and add some of the specific elements we needed from an archival perspective into the programme.

What information, tools, and processes did you need to begin?

We started by consulting with other staff. This work crossed over between two sections within Archives New Zealand; the Archives Management team, who list, describe, and care for the collections, and Access Services, who make the material available to the public. This was important because we didn't want to create two places to search for audiovisual records. As *Archway*, Archives New Zealand's main search tool, only lists the title and technical detail level, having another database with descriptive information for film content was ideal.

Our programmer created the wiki and managed to migrate the information from the giant Microsoft Word file into a spreadsheet format we could use. This task was not as simple as it sounds. Inconsistencies in

(cont'd.)

Interview with David Smith (*continued*)

data entry meant the data required some manipulation before they could be imported into the wiki. Once these problems were ironed out, our programmer placed the wiki on an off-line server for us to work on.

How did you determine what content to include?

The New Zealand National Film Unit (NFU) collection, which Archives New Zealand preserves and makes accessible, was the obvious choice. The collection covers a set time period (1941–1989), is under Crown copyright, and is also the highest use collection we hold. Searching other collections remains with *Archway*.

What challenges did you face?

The main challenge was that the raw data for the wiki was "dirty" because of the complex export process from the Word file. Cleaning the data is still on-going and can sometimes mean that easy searches don't work as they should.

Another challenge, from an archival perspective, was the possibility of important contextual and technical information being changed either by mistake or maliciously. We got around this by creating two spaces within each page, an edit section which was editable by the public and a no-edit section which was only editable by the administrator. This meant that important contextual, technical, and archival information relating to a record could not be publicly altered, but the description field could be. This is quite unusual for wikis as ours is not 100 percent open, but it does allow us to preserve the contextual information for each film.

Another big challenge has been spam. This started off as relatively small scale and then exploded. To help solve the problem we added additional security via a random text generator that had to be filled in prior to completing the edit process. This is not ideal as unfortunately it can put people off making edits, but the spam level was unmanageable.

What kinds of positive results have you had? (And, any negative ones?)

The results are mostly positive. People are happy to search the NFU collection themselves, and this has taken some pressure off our Access archivists from doing the research on their behalf. We have also started to add Flash video versions of our films to the site. This has been a popular move as the collection is now accessible to people outside of New Zealand's big cities and overseas. The new accessibility has been good for promoting our audio visual collection which was often overlooked.

(cont'd.)

Interview with David Smith (continued)

While some believe archival description should be left to professional archivists, our perspective is that there is no reason the two approaches cannot work hand-in-hand. The public can have different interests and perspectives on how to describe the same piece of film as a professional cataloguer would, and this extends the information we have about the collection. For example, a train enthusiast can have almost encyclopedic knowledge of a particular type of train. How they describe the footage would be completely different from a cataloguer using a set of subject terms. Engagement with an audio visual record is no longer just the public sitting down and viewing a film. These tools make it possible to interact in new and interesting ways.

About how much time does it take?

It didn't take that long to set up, although the ongoing maintenance does need someone to own it.

What advice would you give an organization wanting to use something similar?

Have a good programmer to set it up. Open source is a good approach, but the downside is the lack of support and an assumption that you have some knowledge and ability with programming.

And don't be disappointed if you do not get a response on the scale of the Wikipedia! Wikis can be quite intimidating things to work on from the public's perspective; if you don't think your audience will really like using a wiki, I suggest considering user tagging, which can work really well.

Most importantly know your audience. If they are not "tech-savvy" they may not feel comfortable working with a wiki.

Library and Archives Canada (http://ccgwiki.vpl.ca/index.php/ccg_wiki). In this case, the LAC has made available via the wiki basic information about Canada's earliest Chinese citizens:

In 1885, the federal government imposed a head tax on Chinese immigrants, the amount of which was raised in 1900 and again in 1903, creating a major financial obstacle to would-be immigrants from China. The head tax was followed in 1923 by comprehensive legislation designed to exclude Chinese people from entering the country and regulate those already living there. Under Section 18 of the Chinese Immigration Act, all

Chinese in Canada were required to register, including those born in Canada to parents of Chinese origin.

As a result of this registration, a listing of Canadian-born Chinese was produced. The *Chinese Immigration List* forms the basis of this wiki. The core is separate profiles corresponding to each of the first 461 individuals listed in the *Chinese Immigration List.* (Vancouver Public Library and Library and Archives Canada, accessed 2009)

The wiki seeks to expand upon the extremely limited facts known about these 461 people, as well as share relevant links and advice about how to effectively conduct research on Chinese-Canadian history. This site provides a model for using a wiki to promote and make accessible a set of records that is of vital interest to one particular community, as well as for providing background information and resources to help members of that community locate and expand on the information in the records.

The National Archives of the United Kingdom took a somewhat different approach in their Your Archives wiki (http://yourarchives.nationalarchives .gov.uk). Rather than incorporating a part of their catalog or a subset of records into their wiki, they encourage contributions on all aspects of their holdings, as well as information about historical collections in other repositories. Using Your Archives, anyone can do the following:

- Add information that expands on the archives' existing online catalogue
- Publish transcriptions of the archives' online documents
- Contribute information to the National Register of Archives (a list of archival collections relating to British history)
- Expand or update one of the National Archives Research Guides
- Create new articles to supplement the Research Guides
- Collaborate on research projects
- Add one of the "wanted pages"
- Contribute by expanding on existing "short pages or stubs" (only a title or a line or two of text)
- Help maintain the wiki by taking on a task from a list of "housekeeping categories" (in which "moderators and users have identified articles which could be improved by merging duplicate articles, expanding abbreviations, adding sources, and expanding on the content, etc.") (The National Archives, accessed 2009)

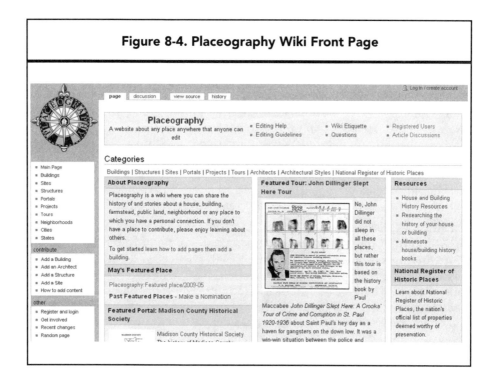

Figure 8-4. Placeography Wiki Front Page

While many of the articles in the Your Archives wiki are about locations, in their Placeography wiki (see Figure 8-4), the Minnesota Historical Society created a "place" just for places (www.placeography.org/index.php/Main_Page). Their wiki is open for anyone to "share the history of and stories about a house, building, farmstead, public land, neighborhood or any place to which you have a personal connection" (Minnesota Historical Society, accessed 2009). Although currently populated largely by information about places in Minnesota, Placeography is intended to capture stories and pictures about places across the United States. The site also supports and encourages "projects":

> "Project" pages are ways to organize information on this site. It may have real world connections, as in "Right on Lake Street" which is a project page that was created in conjunction with an exhibit at the Minnesota Historical Society, or it could be like the "McGowan House Project" which is just an attempt to chronicle the changes to houses built using the same house plan from 1946–47. (Minnesota Historical Society, accessed 2009)

Interview with Tracey Baker
Minnesota Historical Society

What made your organization decide to start the Placeography wiki?

The MHS Library teaches a class called "Whose House Was This?" emphasizing skills and collections for researching the history of buildings. We were interested in seeing the results of the participants' research and that of other library researchers with similar research interests. Preserving buildings and historic places is also an important mission of the Minnesota Historical Society and its partner organizations throughout the state. Our Enterprise Technology (IT) staff had an interest in developing a wiki, and the Library had the content and research skills knowledge to be partners in this endeavor.

What information, tools, and processes did you need to begin?

The Enterprise Technology staff worked with MediaWiki software and developed semantic Web forms to aid in creating and linking content. The Library already had online tutorials, handouts, and class materials on research sources and techniques as well as extensive collections of research materials. We assisted with determining the data fields, pull-down menus, rules of conduct, and instructions for use.

How did you determine what content to include?

Ultimately, our contributors and partners will determine the content that makes up Placeography. However, to get things going and create model entries, we worked with an intern to add the first entries which focused on Minnesota properties associated with famous individuals. We also incorporated content created for other projects, such as the Right on Lake Street Project, which had been an exhibit at our museum, and the John Dillinger Slept Here Tour, which utilized information from a book published by MHS Press. More recently our interns and volunteers have created entries for state institutions for which MHS holds government records and for the 87 Minnesota county courthouses. MHS holds court records for all counties in the state.

What challenges did you face?

On the technical side we've had challenges at times in the site crashing and in installing the latest semantic form versions. Attracting individual contributors and partner organizations has also been somewhat challenging. There is more of a learning curve to uploading images and creating links in wiki format than in some other social software. Most of our contributors come with knowledge of research and their community but limited

(cont'd.)

Interview with Tracey Baker *(continued)*
technical skills. It has been most difficult to enlist volunteers with semantic Web and wiki programming skills.
What kinds of positive results have you had? (And, any negative ones?) We're very pleased to have over 1,300 entries on Placeography, not only from Minnesota but also from places as distant as Utah and Kentucky. Contributors have added memories, links to other sites and sources, additional architectural and historical information to existing entries as well as creating new entries. We've been contacted by local media and featured on a radio program and television news program and Web site as well as in the print media.
About how much time does it take? In the development stages both the Enterprise Technology and Library staff spent many hours doing development of the site, adding content, and reaching out to contributors. Now the Library staff spends minimal time, perhaps one hour per week, supervising volunteers and interns and promoting Placeography in its classes and presentations to library and archives groups. In addition, our IT staff spends about five hours per week sustaining the wiki—including welcoming new contributors, answering questions, removing spam, and updating the software.
What advice would you give an organization wanting to use something similar? First determine the interest, need, and audience for your product. Talk with interested parties within your own organization as well as those in the larger community. Enlist partners who can contribute time and content. Make sure that they have the training and support to succeed. Highlight the work of individual and partner contributors in a prominent place on your Web site. Creating a wiki takes serious time and resources to get it going and manage the community (if one is desired).

WHAT DOES IT TAKE TO START A WIKI AND KEEP IT GOING?

The most critical part of creating a successful wiki is to *define what your wiki is for*. Before you spend any time thinking about software or logistics, be sure you have solid answers for these questions:

- Why do you need this new information product?
- What do you hope to achieve by creating it?
- Who will be the main contributors?
- What value will this create for the public? For staff?
- What will motivate people to become involved?

If you expect staff to be the primary contributors, work to *make sure they see value in it* for themselves and for the public. If contributing information to the wiki will be an added job responsibility, and if staff are not motivated, they may be slow to contribute and your wiki will wither.

If you want to attract public participation, *think carefully about what kinds of contributions you want and how you could attract them*. Do you want people contributing scholarly or historical information? Do you want personal reminiscences or stories? How big is the potential pool of contributors? Do you have a good way to reach them? Will this wiki serve a need that's not currently being met?

Once you have a clear definition for your wiki and a supportive staff environment and you understand who your public audience is and how you can reach them, *scope the workload* involved in supporting the wiki. Make sure you include all phases—creation, launch, and lifetime maintenance. It is usually a good idea to *define clear roles and responsibilities* (such as administrator, content provider, reviewer, monitor, and approver) for the wiki, and make sure these are accommodated in staff job assignments. If adding to, monitoring, or promoting the wiki is something that is "extra," there is a good chance it may not get done in a timely manner.

It's important to consider these kinds of issues up front, because a wiki, like a blog, requires continuous investment of effort over time. A wiki that shows evidence that it hasn't been updated recently and doesn't have a lot of contributors does not reflect well on its sponsor. If regular visitors stop seeing new content, they will probably stop visiting.

When you are ready to consider your actual implementation, *explore your software and hosting options*. Like starting a blog, starting a wiki can be very easy. If you use one of the commercial sites that provides both software and hosting, all you usually have to do is to register and find a name for your wiki that's not already taken. Within minutes, you have a wiki. Starting a wiki using MediaWiki or other software that requires you to install it on a server is much more complicated, and you might not want to attempt it unless you are confident about your technical skills or have access to people who can assist you. On the other hand, using software like MediaWiki enables you to have more control over the "look and feel" of your wiki. You may want to find some archives, historical societies, or libraries that have implemented wikis and talk to them about their experiences with their software before making your final decision.

Once you have signed up for your hosted wiki software or successfully installed your own, you now need to *determine how your wiki will be structured*. A complicated hierarchy is not necessary, and you can make changes as the site grows, but it's a good idea to have a sense of what your major content areas will be and how they relate to each other. Once you have decided on your wiki's general structure, you can *begin populating the wiki* by creating new pages, linking them to each other, and assigning tags or subjects. As you do this, you should try to structure the content of your pages consistently, which will allow users to find things more quickly.

As with a blog, picking a template or creating a consistent graphic identity is necessary to *create an identity for your wiki*. You may have had to finalize your wiki's name when you registered your site (if you are using hosted software), but you still need to think about what information and images you want to include on your opening page. The typeface you select, color scheme, page layout, and other options are an important part of how your users will perceive your site. You might consider using a consistent logo or tagline on each page.

Before your site goes public you also need to *determine your policies and controls for the wiki*. How much freedom do you want to give public users to contribute to the site? Will you let users contribute who have not registered on the site? Do you want to have a set of terms and conditions all users must agree to? Do you want to approve all changes before they "go live"? How do you want to handle inappropriate content? When would you want to lock down an individual page? You should be able to set controls such as these in the administrative area of your wiki. This is another area you might want to discuss with people at other institutions who have some experience administering a wiki. Your initial policies probably won't account for everything, but it is a good idea to have thought about these kinds of issues before they arise.

Once you are satisfied with the way the site looks, have entered the information you want to start with, and have determined your policies and implemented your controls, it's time to *open the site up to the public*. (Make sure that, before you make the site public, you have finalized the terms and conditions of use that people must agree to, if appropriate.) You may want to begin with an announcement to the appropriate communities and distribute the news through your regular communications channels. Or you may want to begin with a "soft roll out" by telling a few key users who may begin to enter data and use the wiki, as well as spread the word informally. After gaining some experience in moderating the wiki and observing how users contribute to it, you may want to make some changes or improvements and then announce it to the public.

Now that your wiki is in operational mode, someone will need to *moderate the site*, reviewing the content that people are contributing in order to watch for things like vandalism or "edit wars" (i.e., spats between contributors who keep removing each other's edits). In keeping with your policies, the moderator may need to contact users to warn them about inappropriate behavior or even ban users who are vandalizing pages. The moderator should also give encouraging feedback to contributors and participate in discussions. The use and growth pattern of the wiki should also be monitored to see whether users are expanding some areas more than others or whether key areas are being neglected. Factors such as these should be taken into account as staff *add new content to the wiki*. Even if you have an enthusiastic contributor base, you should still add new content or content areas to the wiki periodically both to show your institution's commitment and to give your users new material to build on.

Final Tips If You Are Considering Creating a Wiki

- Have a clear definition of your wiki's subject.
- Know who you expect your contributors to be.
- Understand what will motivate your contributors and emphasize it.
- Train key personnel in how to manage and edit the wiki.
- Make appropriate contact information easy to locate.
- Be prepared to populate the wiki with rich content, both before and after roll out, to make it interesting for visitors.

REFERENCES

Minnesota Historical Society. "Homepage." Placeography. Available: www .placeography.org/index.php/Main_Page (accessed May 3, 2009).

———. "Projects." Placeography. Available: www.placeography.org/index.php/ Category:Projects (accessed May 3, 2009).

The National Archives. "Summary of Afghan Wars." Your Archives. Available: http://yourarchives.nationalarchives.gov.uk/index.php?title=Summary_of_Afghan_wars (accessed May 4, 2009).

————. "What Can I Contribute?" Your Archives. Available: http://yourarchives.nationalarchives.gov.uk/index.php?title=Help:What_can_I_contribute%3F (accessed May 3, 2009).

Stoltz, Zoe Ann. E-mail to the author. May 4, 2009.

University of Massachusetts, Amherst. "YouMass." Available: www.library.umass.edu/spcoll/youmass/doku.php (accessed May 3, 2009).

Vancouver Public Library and Library and Archives Canada. "Chinese-Canadians: Profiles from a Community: Project Overview." Available: http://ccgwiki.vpl.ca/index.php/ccg_wiki/User_Resources:Project_Overview (accessed May 3, 2009).

Wikipedia. "Wiki." Available: http://en.wikipedia.org/wiki/Wiki (accessed May 1, 2009).

CHAPTER 9

Using Facebook and Other Social Networking Services

WHAT ARE SOCIAL NETWORKING SERVICES?

Wikipedia defines a "social network service" as one that:

> focuses on building online communities of people who share interests and/or activities, or who are interested in exploring the interests and activities of others. Most social network services are web based and provide a variety of ways for users to interact, such as e-mail and instant messaging services. (Wikipedia, accessed 2009)

Most Web 2.0 tools, such as Twitter and Flickr, have social networking capabilities in that they allow users to create connections and groups for those with common interests. What distinguishes the dominant social networking sites, like Facebook and MySpace, is that their only purpose is to connect people. Because they are dedicated only to social networking, they support the creation and sharing of information on a huge scale. While the initial purpose of many services was purely social, today most social networking services include official corporate and nonprofit marketing efforts along with the traditional social functions. Facebook, like blogging and wiki sites, provides a relatively easy way to create a Web presence for your institution—in this case, a presence in a "place" with millions of potential visitors.

Although other social networking sites, such as Friendster.com, MySpace.com, and Bebo.com, were earlier arrivals on the Web, it is Facebook (www.Facebook.com) that is currently by far the most popular among potential users of archives and so virtually the only social networking site being commonly used by archives and similar historical organizations. Therefore, this chapter will discuss the specifics of using Facebook, although the goals and strategies outlined should be applicable in other social networks.

Readers should note that Facebook's interface and business model are subject to change, and the information provided here reflects how Facebook operates in the spring of 2009. Earlier this year Facebook made significant changes to the way both personal profiles and "pages" function. Currently, membership in Facebook is free (although there have been rumors in the press that Facebook may begin to charge for membership). There have also been reports that changes are on the way that would make all information on Facebook public, rather than private, by default. Like most Web 2.0 businesses, the services Facebook provides and how it supports them are open to change in response to corporate strategy and perceived user needs.

Types of Facebook Accounts

To access any information on Facebook, you must have an account. The predominant way to join Facebook is to establish an individual account or a "profile." To establish a profile, all you need to provide is your name, a valid e-mail address, your gender, and your date of birth and agree to Facebook's terms of service. Facebook's policy is that profiles can be held only by individuals (not businesses or organizations). With a Facebook profile, however, you can establish groups and create "pages" for your organization (groups and pages are defined later in this chapter). In addition to individual profiles, Facebook has a different account option for bands, celebrities, and businesses that provides them with a page as their central Facebook presence rather than the profile page provided for individuals

Establishing Your Facebook Presence

Once you have signed up for an individual profile with Facebook, you can populate it with as much or as little information as you want. You can upload a picture that will be associated with your profile. You can provide "status updates"—short messages that usually describe what you are doing or thinking. You can join one or more "networks" based on your current employment, current or past educational affiliation, or geographic location. You can look for groups to join or pages for people or organizations to become a "fan" of. You can take quizzes, play games, rate movies, or enjoy hundreds of similar activities.

One of the first things most people do after joining Facebook is to look for friends. You can find potential friends through the networks you join or by allowing Facebook to access your e-mail address book to tell you which of your contacts have Facebook accounts. You can also search the names of Facebook members to find people you know. To make someone your friend on Facebook, you click on "Add as Friend," which sends a "friend request" to that person. The person has the option to accept or ignore your friend request or to send you a message. Once you have one or more friends, Facebook will suggest other people you may know, based on who your friends are friends with.

Public and Private Information on Facebook

Facebook has recently changed the way some of its privacy settings work, and it appears this area will be evolving for some time. One of the first things you should do after opening your personal Facebook account is to become familiar with the options under "Privacy Settings." In this area you can select whether the information you share on Facebook will be publicly available (including to non-Facebook users, and so to anyone on the Web), available to your friends and people in your networks, or available to only your friends. You may also want to take a look under the "Application Settings" tab and make sure you are comfortable with the kind of access Facebook applications will have to your data.

Once you have friends, you will notice that information about what they are doing on Facebook will show up in your "news feed" (the page that loads automatically when you log in). You will see things such as their status updates (and all the comments others have made on their updates), information for sites they have posted a link to, the results of quizzes they have taken, comments they have made on other people's status updates, and pictures they have posted. Likewise, almost every action you take on Facebook (except sending and receiving messages and activities with "secret" groups) may show up in the news feeds of your friends (and more widely than that if you have selected this option in your privacy settings).

Facebook Groups

Any Facebook member can create a "group" around any topic. Until recently, Facebook groups could not be accessed by non-Facebook members, but that has changed, and now any Facebook group that is "open" can be seen by anyone on the Web. To create a group, all you need to supply is a title, a description, and a "type" (such as Business, Common Interest, or Just for Fun). You can also choose to upload an image to use as a profile picture for the group, as well as supply additional information about the group, such as a link to an external Web site and contact information (see Figure 9-1; www.facebook.com/search/ ?q=iowa+state+special+collections+&init=quick#/group.php?gid=6210484802).

When you create a group, you become its administrator, with the power to define the functionalities on the group page and the access rights required to join the group or post information. Groups may be open to everyone, closed, or "secret." Your name will be publicly displayed as the administrator of the group (along with anyone else to whom you grant administrator privileges). As the administrator, you also have the ability to send messages to all group members.

Figure 9-1. Facebook Group Created by the Special Collections Department, Iowa State University Library (Top Section of Screenshot)

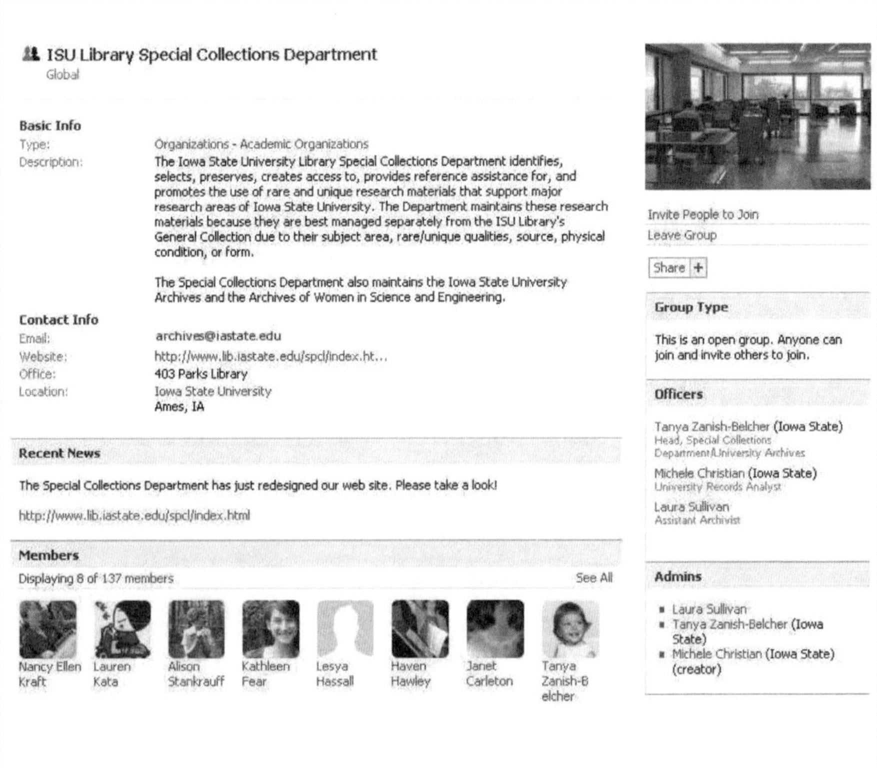

ISU Library Special Collections Department
Global

Basic Info

Type: Organizations - Academic Organizations

Description: The Iowa State University Library Special Collections Department identifies, selects, preserves, creates access to, provides reference assistance for, and promotes the use of rare and unique research materials that support major research areas of Iowa State University. The Department maintains these research materials because they are best managed separately from the ISU Library's General Collection due to their subject area, rare/unique qualities, source, physical condition, or form.

The Special Collections Department also maintains the Iowa State University Archives and the Archives of Women in Science and Engineering.

Contact Info

Email: archives@iastate.edu

Website: http://www.lib.iastate.edu/spcl/index.ht...

Office: 403 Parks Library

Location: Iowa State University
Ames, IA

Invite People to Join

Leave Group

Share +

Group Type

This is an open group. Anyone can join and invite others to join.

Officers

Tanya Zanish-Belcher (Iowa State)
Head, Special Collections Department/University Archives

Michele Christian (Iowa State)
University Records Analyst

Laura Sullivan
Assistant Archivist

Recent News

The Special Collections Department has just redesigned our web site. Please take a look!

http://www.lib.iastate.edu/spcl/index.html

Members

Displaying 8 of 137 members

See All

Nancy Ellen Kraft | Lauren Kata | Alison Stankrauff | Kathleen Fear | Lesya Hassall | Haven Hawley | Janet Carleton | Tanya Zanish-Belcher

Admins

- Laura Sullivan
- Tanya Zanish-Belcher (Iowa State)
- Michele Christian (Iowa State) (creator)

After you have created a group, you have the option to send invitations to join it to your Facebook friends as well as to the e-mail addresses of non-Facebook members. The fact that you have created or joined a group will also appear in the news feeds of your friends (unless the group is "secret"). When your friends join your group the fact that they have done so will show up in the news feeds of their friends, providing a "viral" means of spreading the word about your new group. People may also find your group by searching Facebook.

There is an incredibly wide variety of groups on Facebook, ranging from serious groups formed to support political candidates or issues, to groups for members of professional or social organizations, to groups formed to show support for sports teams, to groups formed to support informal organizations like book clubs.

Facebook Pages

Like groups, Facebook pages (sometimes referred to as "fan pages") are a way for you to show public support for an issue or organization and associate with other Facebook members with similar opinions (see Figure 9-2). Pages, however, are designed as a way for an organization to establish a presence in Facebook to share information with its "fans." (While you *join* a group, you *become a fan* of a page.)

Like groups, Facebook pages are now publicly available on the Web rather than just being accessible to Facebook members. This change has, of course, greatly increased the value of Facebook pages for organizational outreach. Now when you add videos, pictures, links, and other content to your institution's Facebook page you are essentially building a public Web site.

Facebook's policy is that pages can only be created to represent real people and organizations and that they may only be created by an official representative of the topic of the page. Organizations such as colleges, universities, professional organizations (like the Society of American Archivists), and many archives and historical societies (like the National Archives of Australia, the Ohio Historical Society, and many others) have created Facebook pages to share information and interact with the public on Facebook.

Despite Facebook's policy, any Facebook member can create a page for any topic, although you must certify that you are authorized to create the page. (Presumably, that authorization is only verified if someone lodges a complaint with Facebook.) Just as when you create a group, when you create a page you have the option for entering only basic information or more extensive profile

Figure 9-2. Facebook Page Created by the University of Wisconsin–Eau Claire Special Collections & Archives

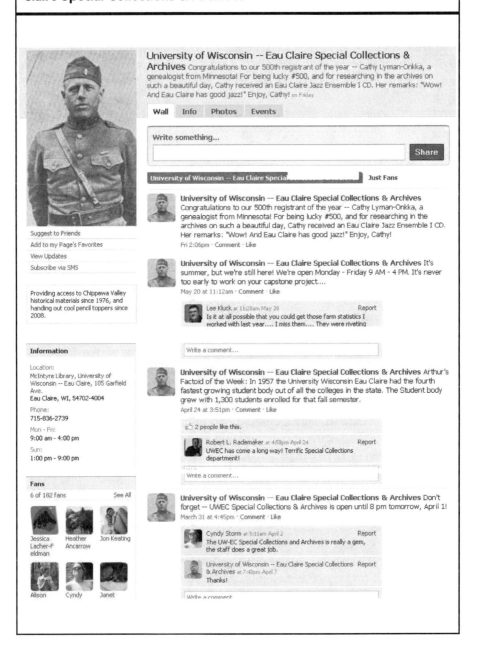

information about the subject of your page. You can upload a profile picture for the page and create status updates for the page, which will be displayed on the page much as your news feed is displayed on your personal profile page.

As with groups, the creator of a page is also its default administrator. Unlike groups, the fact that you are the administrator does not appear anywhere on the page. As the administrator, you have the option to define what capabilities you want to use and define what rights your fans have to add information to the page. You can also make your page more sophisticated by adding applications. (Applications can't be added to groups.) Applications are discussed later, but, in brief, they are tools that can be used to import data (for example, from a blog or Flickr account) or functionalities (like adding readers' locations to a map) into Facebook.

Like personal profiles, when you write a status update for your page, that information will show up in the news feeds of all the fans of your page. This means that pages are somewhat more powerful than groups as a way of connecting with followers of an organization (because there is no equivalent functionality that pushes information from a group out to members' news feeds). Groups have one advantage over pages in communicating with members, however. Group administrators can send a "message" to all the members of the group. Messages show up in a Facebook member's inbox, and they may also receive an e-mail alerting them to the Facebook message. This is a more proactive (and permanent) way of communicating, because a status update appearing in a news feed may only appear for a short amount of time. In keeping with their more serious intent, Facebook allows page administrators to see a wide range of metrics about the page's fans and page views.

Common Capabilities of Groups and Pages

Groups and pages have many similar capabilities, and for both it is up to the administrator to define which of these functionalities are available and the extent to which group members or fans may contribute. Both groups and pages can allow you to create and participate in discussion topics on a discussion board. It is possible to post images, videos, notes, and links to both groups and pages. (See Figure 9-3 for examples of how these appear in a group.)

Either a group or a page (as well as any Facebook member) can create an "event." The creator of an event defines the essential information about the event and can then invite people from their own network of friends and group members or page fans (whichever is appropriate) to the event. Once an event has been created, you can see the status of all those invited (planning on attend-

---

Figure 9-3. Facebook Group Created by the Special Collections Department, Iowa State University Library (Middle Section of Screenshot)

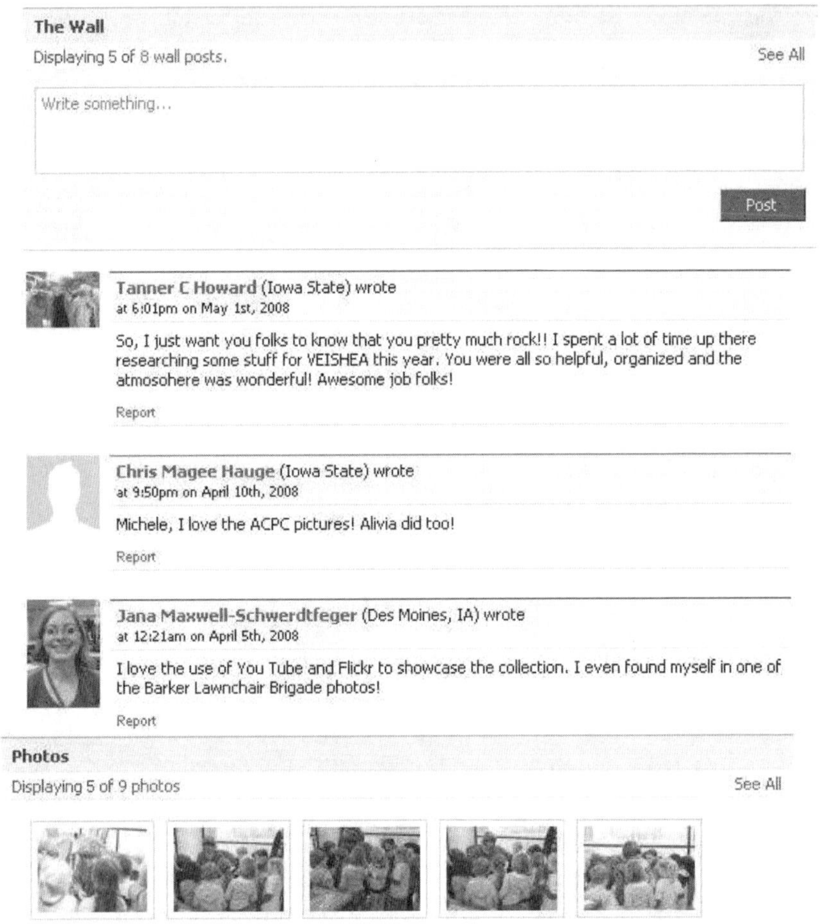

The Wall

Displaying 5 of 8 wall posts.   See All

Write something...

                                                                                                    Post

Tanner C Howard (Iowa State) wrote
at 6:01pm on May 1st, 2008

So, I just want you folks to know that you pretty much rock!! I spent a lot of time up there researching some stuff for VEISHEA this year. You were all so helpful, organized and the atmosohere was wonderful! Awesome job folks!

Report

Chris Magee Hauge (Iowa State) wrote
at 9:50pm on April 10th, 2008

Michele, I love the ACPC pictures! Alivia did too!

Report

Jana Maxwell-Schwerdtfeger (Des Moines, IA) wrote
at 12:21am on April 5th, 2008

I love the use of You Tube and Flickr to showcase the collection. I even found myself in one of the Barker Lawnchair Brigade photos!

Report

Photos

Displaying 5 of 9 photos   See All ing, declined invitation, and not yet replied). Pages for events have the same basic functionalities as groups and regular pages—people can write on the event's wall, as well as post images, video, and links.

HOW CAN YOUR INSTITUTION USE FACEBOOK?

Probably most archives and historical organizations establish a presence in a social network such as Facebook without having clear goals. For most, the goal is often just to "be there" and this is not a bad goal to start with. Given its enormous user base—and especially now that Facebook groups and pages are accessible to nonmembers as well—using Facebook for general outreach is a smart idea. For a relatively small amount of effort, your institution can be found by millions of Facebook users and you can create a public Web site for sharing links, pictures, videos, and other information too.

Providing General Information

Both groups and pages allow you to share essential information about your institution, such as the address, contact information, and Web site address. The space provided for this kind of information is limited for groups. Pages provide more space on a separate "Info" tab, and you can add an "Extended Information" application that allows you to expand even further. Both groups and pages allow you to upload a profile image to be displayed; most archives use their logo, an image of the building or reading room, or an image of an interesting object from their collections.

In some ways, groups are slightly better than pages at displaying this kind of basic information prominently (see Figure 9-1). For example, groups have an automatic functionality for listing "officers" on the right sidebar and for displaying "recent news" near the top of the page.

Sharing Content and News

Sharing pictures, video, links, and events are basic Facebook functions that are supported for both pages and groups. Pages can be configured so the fans may add pictures and tag people in pictures, but they cannot add video or events (although they can post pictures, video, and links to the wall, if permitted). Groups can be configured so that either all members or only administrators can add pictures, video, and links. Most archives with either a group or a page use

Interview with Michele Christian
Iowa State University Library Special Collections Department

What made you interested in creating a Facebook group for your archives?

In the fall of 2007, we decided to start a Facebook group for the Department in order to connect with Iowa State University students and outside researchers. We chose to start a group rather than a page to encourage our members to be more interactive and feel like a part of the Department.

What information, tools, and processes did you need to begin?

In order to start our Facebook group, the only thing we had to do was to join Facebook. Our Department is flexible in regards to trying new technologies to encourage access, so we just started it to see if we could do this and what kinds of responses we would have. This was an incredibly simple process, and it was easy to see the appeal of Facebook as a way to connect with others.

How did /do you determine what to include?

We decided to keep the site simple in order to easily maintain it. We usually add news items about what we are doing, new collections available for use, and new donations. We also include other interesting items, such as images from a departmental tour given to four year olds or digitized video from our 16-mm film collection. It all depends upon what we think our members would be interested in seeing.

What challenges did you face?

The main challenge we face is the lack of time to update the page with interesting information. With all of the day-to-day activities of the Department, it is hard to remember to update Facebook or to find something unique to add to the page. Sometimes, we do have something to share, and this is a wonderful way to get the word out fast.

What kinds of positive results have you had? (And, any negative ones?)

I believe that we have had positive results in using Facebook. We have over 125 members from around the world. Although we are not as active as I had hoped, I have not noticed any negative results to having a Facebook group. This seems to be a great way to stay in touch with our researchers and other friends. Several people who have used the resources in the Department in the past have found us and decided to join the group. I think this says something positive not only about the Department, but about what Facebook can do for us.   *(cont'd.)*

Interview with Michele Christian (*continued*)

About how much time does it take?

I guess I can say that the amount of time this takes depends upon how much effort you put into it. Unfortunately, I have not had as much time as I would like to devote to our Facebook group. Therefore, I can honestly say that it does not take much time at all. However, I feel that in order to get the most out of Facebook it is important to spend at least a bit of time tending to it. I am hopeful that someday we will be able to be more active.

What advice would you give an organization wanting to use something similar?

The advice I would give to those thinking about using Facebook is to go for it. Making yourself more visible and inviting to all types of potential patrons may result in them having a greater understanding of archives in general and your department in particular. As a profession, we seem to be becoming more proactive in our outreach. Facebook should be utilized as another tool in our arsenal of educating the public. Fad or not, Facebook is one of the most popular methods of interacting with people both locally and globally and should not be dismissed.

---

these capabilities to share pictures and post links and events about things happening at their institutions.

Most archives seem to be using Facebook groups and pages more to promote their current activities than to share information about their historical collections. The images posted are more often images of open houses or exhibits than digitized images from the collections. The Historical Society of Washington, DC, for example, has created four albums on its page: HSW Building, HSW Special Events, Kiplinger Research Center, and Public Programs 2008. Similarly, while some of the links posted to groups and pages do discuss the use of the collections, most of them report on activities of the organization, or they share news stories relevant to the community.

Communicating with Supporters

While sharing general information, content, and news about your institution are all worthwhile goals, the point of Facebook is to be interacting with other users. Not surprisingly, Facebook provides many avenues for connecting and communicating with your friends and supporters.

A major component of any Facebook profile, group, or page is the "wall" (see Figure 9-3). In groups and pages, group members and fans can write on the wall to share their thoughts and share links. In pages, the wall is the primary place where the page owner shares information, and it also automatically shares actions taken by the page owner (such as posting new pictures, adding a link, etc.).

Actions taken on pages—such as writing on the wall and adding pictures—will show up in the news feeds of all the fans of a page. Actions taken in a group—such as writing on the wall and adding pictures—do not show up in the news feeds by group members. In order to know something is taking place in a group, you have to search out that information. This is one of the advantages of a page for pushing information out to your supporters.

In addition to providing the wall as a space for group discussion, Facebook provides a "discussion board" for both groups and pages. Whereas the wall is just one continuous thread of conversation (with the most recent displayed at the top), the discussion board supports separate discussion topics. This feature shows promise for archives to encourage discussion of relevant topics, but it does not seem to be widely used to start discussions, and when attempts are made they rarely get much of a response. This is particularly true on pages, and this may be the result of the lack of visibility for the discussion board in the default layout of pages.

One possible reason that discussion topics do not see much activity is that many Facebook members may see groups and pages more as ways to express their personality or allegiances rather than as areas they want to participate in. In Facebook, joining groups and becoming fans of pages is in some ways like collecting stickers to decorate something—they are a way to express who you are but not much more than that. While some may find this possibility discouraging, Facebook is still an excellent way to increase your institution's visibility and spread information.

Facebook makes it easy for visitors to your page or group to see who your supporters are; both groups and pages prominently display their members/fans on the primary page. This allows visitors to rapidly see how popular you are and what kinds of supporters you have. Members and fans can also spread the word about you by inviting their own friends to join a group or share information about your page with their friends. While having a large group of supporters is no guarantee your Facebook group or page will be an active one, it does mean that more people (and potentially their friends) will be exposed to your content.

The Ohio Historical Society page has added an application that has the potential for use by other archives—the "Reviews" application. This application allows people to write reviews, or testimonials, of the subject of your page. The Ohio Historical Society has so far received five reviews (all of them rating the institution at "five stars"). Reviews such as these are an excellent way of getting spontaneous compliments from users that could be used for marketing and advocacy. The Ohio Historical Society received praise such as the following:

- "It is good to know that there are some truly wonderful people and websites available to acquire all sorts of information that would have been next to impossible to do without all the dedicated people, and of course technology."
- "This is a great place that will draw your attention into the past that has formed our world today."
- "I love the OHS! I just used the African American Experience in Ohio collection last week while working with a student. Our students and I use digitized collections of primary sources quite a bit and yours had some great gems that we would not have had access to otherwise. I'll look forward to staying in the OHS loop on Facebook." (Ohio Historical Society, accessed 2009)

Sharing Information from Other Web 2.0 Sites

One of Facebook's strengths has been the ease with which users can share content from other popular Web 2.0 applications via Facebook. There is a wide variety of easy-to-install applications that you can add to your Facebook page to let it serve as a "dashboard" for most of your other Web 2.0 information streams. (Applications cannot be added to groups.) For example, many archives have added applications to their pages that automatically pull in the latest images added to their Flickr and YouTube accounts. You can also install an application that automatically pulls information from the RSS feed for your institution's blog, and you can specify other RSS feeds to pull in and share on your page as well. Tools such as these could be combined with customized applications that let users search your online catalog from Facebook (already available for some libraries) to create an experience that is in some ways a "light" version of your institution's own Web site.

Interview with Colleen McFarland
Special Collections & University Archives
University of Wisconsin–Eau Claire

What made you interested in creating a Facebook page?

As a university archivist who works with history students quite a bit, I found it difficult to communicate with them as a group. I wanted to make announcements about new collections, extended hours, and archives promotions but didn't have a way to do it until I began using Facebook.

What information, tools, and processes did you need to begin?

When I began, all I had was a basic understanding of Facebook that I acquired by setting up an individual account and using it.

How did you determine what information and features to include?

My goal in implementing Facebook was to help history students "bond" with the archives as a place and as a community. Facebook is merely a tool that helps me realize my larger goal of outreach to a distinct user group. Without a vision of what I wanted to achieve through Facebook, there would have been no point in setting up and maintaining a fan site.

What challenges did you face?

The biggest challenge was figuring out what kind of page to create. I tried both personal pages and group pages, neither of which were a good fit. I then discovered the fan page, which allows page administrators to push content to users through "updates," and that has worked really well. Anybody considering using Facebook as an outreach tool should also realize that Facebook changes its look and feel with some frequency and that one doesn't always have as much control over the pages as one might like.

What kinds of positive results have you had? (And, any negative ones?)

There are students who clearly read the updates and find them useful! For example, students seeking collections to work with will sometimes reference materials I highlighted through a Facebook update. Also, I've been surprised by the number of students who remain "fans" of the archives after they graduate. I've not had any negative experiences.

About how much time does it take?

One to two hours per week to develop content for the site.

(cont'd.)

Interview with Colleen McFarland *(continued)*
What advice would you give an organization wanting to use something similar? Have definitive goals in mind before investing a lot of time into Facebook outreach. Also, be aware that it requires attention at least every week; otherwise the content and the site both go stale.

Creating an Application

Another way to use Facebook to raise awareness about your institution is to create your own application that all Facebook members can use. Recently Albion College's archives has taken advantage of an easily customizable application that allows Facebook users to send each other "gifts" from your collections. The institution creates the "gifts" by adding images and creating captions. People can then "send" and "receive" these gifts (which is a popular Facebook activity). Users of the Albion College Memorabilia application can give gifts such as fraternity paddles, a freshman beanie, "Albion, Dear Albion" (sheet music), or the Faith of Odysseus Sculpture.

These gift applications are a great example of archives entering into the spirit of Facebook—participating in the popular activity of giving and receiving gifts—in a humorous way. Any Facebook member can use these gift applications without being a member of any group or page, and so people don't need to seek out the archives (or even be aware of it) in order to enjoy the gift-giving. Yet by creating these applications, the Albion College archives is subtly promoting its archives to its larger college communities of alumni and staff on Facebook.

As mentioned earlier, some libraries have also created applications that allow users to add to their pages the ability to search individual library catalogs. It does not appear that any archives or special collections has created this kind of application, but this would certainly seem to be an opportunity to create something of great value to add to your institution's Facebook page. (See discussion of widgets in Chapter 10.)

If your institution is a nonprofit organization, you may also consider using the existing "Causes" application to create a way for your supporters to make donations to you via Facebook. Creating your own "cause" will not only allow anyone to make a financial contribution to your organization, but people can also add your cause to their personal profiles and share it with their friends. You can take a look at the Jewish Women's Archive page on Facebook for an example of how one archives is using the Causes application.

Collecting Documentation of Your Community

Depending on your institutional context, Facebook may also be a source for information about new groups or organizations in your community. Some Facebook users, including many college and graduate students, use Facebook extensively to communicate with their peers. For these users, communication on Facebook may have replaced traditional forms of communication, such as hardcopy fliers for events, memos, or minutes. If collecting documentation of community groups is part of your institution's mission, you may need to be active on Facebook in order to learn about new groups and approach them about donating their materials to your archives.

A prime example of this need to be present where the creators of your collections are active took place at the College of William and Mary in 2008 after the unexpected resignation of the university president (see also Chapter 5). Almost immediately after the announcement, student and alumni groups formed in response to the perceived political motivations behind the resignation. Many of these groups were formed and communicated exclusively via Facebook. In order to obtain as complete a record as possible, Amy Schindler, the University Archivist in the Special Collections Research Center, used her personal Facebook account to contact these groups:

> I began visiting the dozens of Facebook groups organized in support, opposition, or apathy to the president and made the decision to contact, via a direct message in Facebook, the individuals who were listed as administrators and officers of groups. I requested material documenting the current events that were happening, but was also able to include a request for material from the previous two years "now or at some point in the future."
> ... My private Facebook message was then posted by some of those individuals to their groups and events and forwarded to friends. Students, faculty, staff, alumni, parents, and members of the public began sending copies of their letters to the president and the Board of Visitors, posters, images, video, artifacts, etc. via Facebook, email, and postal mail. This material now makes up the Nichol Resignation Collection. (Schindler, 2009)

Other organizations are using Facebook more traditionally, as a means of sharing their collecting mission with the Facebook community, and using it to solicit donations of materials. On its Facebook page, the Florida State University Heritage Protocol shares its mission to find materials in private and university hands that document the institutional and social history of the university. The page currently has 121 members and has been successful in spreading the word about the Protocol's mission—resulting in the donation of an alumni scrapbook. The way the donation came about is an illustration of how communication often happens on Facebook. One person joined the Protocol group, meaning that his news feed contained an update that he had joined the group. A friend of his saw the item in the news feed and also joined the group. This second person then "friended" the group's administrator, Eddie Woodward, the Heritage Protocol Archivist, and contacted him about a scrapbook from 1938–40 belonging to his mother, an alumna of a predecessor to Florida State University (Woodward, 2009). Through the social networking functions of Facebook, the Heritage Protocol archives received a donation it would probably not have otherwise received. While cases like this may not be common, they do happen, and they will probably happen more often as more and more people and institutions establish Facebook accounts.

WHAT DOES IT TAKE TO BE ACTIVE ON FACEBOOK?

The first step to being active on Facebook (or any social network) is to *create a personal account*, make some friends, join some groups, become a fan of some pages, and in general spend some time getting a feel for how the network works. In all social networks, it is wise to be cautious in the beginning about how much and what kind of personal information you share. Many people eventually end up with a mixture of friends, coworkers, and colleagues in their pool of "friends" on Facebook. As you add information to your personal profile you should be mindful that although you may start your account only "friending" people you know well, you may later add professional colleagues. It is best not to say anything on Facebook that you would not say in front of a professional colleague.

As you consider creating a group or a page for your institution, you should *explore how groups and pages work*. Although hopefully the basic principles described in this chapter are still valid, Facebook does make changes, including adding new features. In addition to observing the groups and pages you belong to, you should see what information is available in the Facebook "Help" area.

You may want to experiment with creating a group or page of your own to help you learn what is involved. If capturing metrics is important to you, make sure you know what kind of statistics can be captured for each option. (See Chapter 12 for more discussion of metrics.) You can also consider contacting the administrator of an archives group or posting a comment to an archives' page asking for advice. Most people are on Facebook because they are interested in connecting and sharing information with others and so will be happy to help you.

Once you have decided what kind of presence you want (group, page, or something new), spend time to **create your institution's profile** before you make it open to the public. Try several different images as your profile picture to find one that is interesting and memorable. Make sure you provide information about all the ways users can get in touch with you—mailing and street address, telephone number, e-mail, and Web site. Provide a brief explanation of what your institution does. Before you launch your site, you may want to upload images of your facility, images of items from your collections, or a video about your organization to help give visitors a better sense of who you are.

Explore the applications or features you can use for your organization's profile. Again, you can browse through the applications that are available, but you can also look at what applications are being used on other pages, including pages for libraries, museums, and other cultural organizations. If you are using other Web 2.0 tools, such as a blog, Flickr, Twitter, or YouTube, consider using an application to pull that data into your Facebook page to add new content automatically. Adding pictures, video, links, and events makes your profile (and by extension your institution) look active and engaging. You want to create an impression of a place—real or virtual—where users want to visit and come back to.

Once you have decided to make your group or page public, you need to **promote it to your friends (and everyone else you can find)**. In addition to inviting your own friends to join your group or become fans of your page, you can post a link to your new group or page on groups or pages that have a similar audience. Announce your new Facebook presence through your existing communications channels, such as your newsletter, blog, Web site, or Twitter account. Remember that although Facebook groups and pages may be accessed by anyone on the Web, to be a member of a group or a fan of a page, you must be a Facebook member.

Although it is easy to ignore your Facebook presence, you should try to **provide new content on a regular basis**. By writing on your wall, posting new pictures, video, creating events, and adding links, you are not only making the site more interesting for your visitors, you are also creating items that will show up in your followers' news feeds and so be visible to both them and others who may see it in their news feeds.

While you may not get an immediate result, it is worthwhile to *try to interact with your supporters* by giving them opportunities to share their thoughts. You may want to begin by just posting questions on your wall, or you may want to start a new discussion topic on your discussion board. You might consider adding the "Reviews" application to your page and sending an update or doing a wall post inviting people to contribute to it. You can also take advantage of the Facebook functionality that lets you "tag" other Facebook members who appear in the images that you post. Again, when you tag someone, this shows up in their news feed, and your photo will be accessible through their personal profile.

You should also make an effort to *keep up to date* on new tools and features you can add to your page or group. One way to do this is by browsing the pages and groups of other organizations to look for new ideas, tools, and applications. You may also want to *consider making your own application*, if you have the technical expertise. Applications can be fun ways to help your friends, fans, and supporters spread the word about your organization.

Final Tips If You Are Considering Using Facebook

- Create your own personal account, and explore Facebook by creating your own network of friends, groups, and pages.
- Look carefully at the current features of groups, pages, and other Facebook options for your institution.
- Be conscious of your institutional image when you establish your page or group—provide a memorable profile image and complete information about your organization.
- Be sure to incorporate feeds from other Web 2.0 tools that your repository uses to make your page more interesting.
- Add new content on a regular basis.
- Give your visitors things to do on your page—images and video to look at, discussions to participate in, gift applications to use, RSS feeds to read, etc.
- Don't be discouraged if your group or page doesn't have a lot of activity at first. Keep adding content, inviting new people to join, and spreading the word outside of Facebook.

REFERENCES

Ohio Historical Society. "Reviews." Facebook. Available: www.facebook.com/home .php#/pages/columbus-OH/Ohio-Historical-Society/22003234344?v=box_3&view as=616149676 (accessed May 3, 2009).

Schindler, Amy. E-mail to author. April 29, 2009.

Wikipedia. "Social Network Service." Available: http://en.wikipedia.org/wiki/ Social_network_service (accessed April 20, 2009).

Woodward, Eddie. E-mail to author. May 28, 2009.

CHAPTER 10

More 2.0 Tools to Consider

The previous chapters have covered all the Web 2.0 tools most commonly used by archives and other historical organizations, but there are more options in the Web 2.0 "toolbox." This chapter will review four such tools, briefly describing how some archives are using them and giving suggestions for how they might be effectively implemented.

MASHUPS

An essential component of Web 2.0 culture is the reuse of content, often combining it with other content to create something new and original—a mashup. The term probably originated to describe "a song or composition created by blending two or more songs, usually by overlaying the vocal track of one song seamlessly over the music track of another" (Wikipedia, "Mashup [Music]," accessed 2009). While creative recombination of existing artistic works or intellectual products has a long tradition, advances in technology have given rise to new kinds of blended works. The framework that made Web 2.0 possible combined with the availability of information in digital form have brought the ability to "remix" content within the grasp of more people than ever before. It's now possible to combine not just individual songs or works or art, but large sets of data. Mashups are, in some ways, an ideal representation of Web 2.0 culture—merging disparate elements to make a new product that would have been very unlikely to occur before.

What Is a Mashup?

While there are examples of songs, videos, text, and virtually any other creative work available on the Web today that could accurately be called mashups, the term is being used here to discuss what Wikipedia (accessed 2009) classifies "Mashup (Web Application Hybrid)" as:

> a Web application that combines data or functionality from two or more sources into a single integrated application. The term *mashup* implies easy, fast integration, frequently done by access to open APIs and data sources to produce results that were not the original reason for producing the raw source data.

APIs (application programming interfaces) are part of the technical infrastructure that makes the world of Web 2.0 possible. When an application, like Google Maps (http://maps.google.com), makes its API "open," it gives programmers the capability to create other applications or programs that can merge the data and functionalities of Google Maps with something else. An open API is an invitation to programmers to remix and reimagine the data in the application.

Google Maps and Google Earth (http://earth.google.com) are among the most popular applications used in mashups, and their data have been combined with virtually everything, from the locations of happy hours in New York City (www.coovents.com) to images and video of endangered marine animals (www.arkive.org/Earth/ocean.html).

Archives and Historical Organizations Creating Mashups

The overwhelmingly predominant use of mashup technology among archives is to combine information about objects in the collections with geographic data. This combination can make it easier for users to browse collections by looking at a map and seeing markers indicating objects from the collection associated with a particular location. Archives have found many ways to utilize this capability. "Katrina's Jewish Voices" (http://katrina.jwa.org/map), for example, combines Google Maps with geotagged data about the items in the Jewish Women's Archive's collection of materials relating to Hurricane Katrina. The "North Carolina Maps" site offers "historic overlays" (www.lib.unc.edu/dc/ncmaps/interactive/overlay.html) of selected archival maps on top of current road maps or satellite images: "By fading or 'seeing through' the historic maps, users are able to compare the similarities and differences between old and new maps, and to study the changes in North Carolina over time" (North Carolina Maps, accessed 2009).

One of the most acclaimed mashups of archival materials with geographic data was used in the Web site Mapping Our Anzacs (http://mappingouranzacs .naa.gov.au), created by the National Archives of Australia (see Figure 10-1). This site combines Google Maps with the records of more than 350,000 people who served in the Australian Army during World War I. Plotted on the maps is each person's place of birth or enlistment, providing a visualization and means of browsing this large group of data. By clicking on a link to a geographic location, you can see the names of the people associated with that location and then browse their individual records. Although the information contained in the records remains the same, the mashup with the maps makes it easier to see patterns that raise questions:

> Some things are visible at a glance, such as the concentration of the Australian population along the east coast. Others encourage further exploration and discovery. Why did hundreds of soldiers enlist in Egypt? How did people born in Germany come to serve in the Australian armed forces? (National Archives of Australia, accessed 2009)

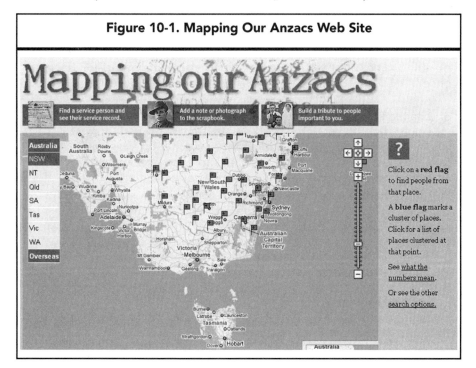

Figure 10-1. Mapping Our Anzacs Web Site

Interview with Tim Sherratt
National Archives of Australia

What made you interested in creating a mashup?

It really started with the records. We hold the records of more than 375,000 World War I service people, identified by their places of birth and enlistment. With war memorials in just about every town across Australia, the connection between local communities and the memory of war remains strong. So we wondered how we could we give the service people in our records back to their communities. Having played around with the Google Maps API the answer seemed obvious—find the places, put them on a map, and let people explore the connections for themselves.

What information, tools, and processes did you need to begin?

The main thing we needed was the confidence to experiment. The process seemed straightforward in principle: first we had to extract the data we needed from the file titles in our collection database, then we had to find the latitude and longitude of each of the place names we extracted, and finally we had to plot these coordinates on a map with links back to details of the service records themselves. Web services, such as those provided by Google Maps, had the potential to do much of the work for us, and we scoured online documentation, user forums, and blog posts for hints. But there were many things we could not know until we actually started. How consistent was our data? How many of the places would we be able to find? How would we be able to display thousands of places at once?

Moving from file titles through to coordinates obviously required a lot of data manipulation, and we used Perl for much of the grunt work. Because our data set was large and variations in spelling and formatting were often unpredictable (including thirteen different spellings of "lieutenant"!), we often had to work by trial and error—seeing what results we obtained and then adjusting our processes accordingly.

Once we had a list of place names in a consistent format we could begin to find latitudes and longitudes through a process known as geocoding. Google's geocoding service was an easy option: it was well documented, reasonably comprehensive and it worked! We fed it our place names through a Perl script, and soon we had a list of coordinates. Of course, many places were not found or returned multiple results, but the basic principle was sound. Our places were no longer just names, but points in space—we could begin making maps.

(cont'd.)

Interview with Tim Sherratt *(continued)*

How did you determine what to include?

What we were creating was an archival finding aid, but one which placed the people, their homes, and their communities up front rather than the systems that control their records. By browsing from a map a user would be able to find the details of a loved one, read a digitised copy of their service record, and then follow a link through to our collection database. These links provide crucial context about the records, but we realised that this project also gave us an opportunity to capture other contexts and meanings. Who were these people? What did they look like? What happened to them after the war? By adding an online "scrapbook" we gave users the chance to enrich the resource by adding notes or photographs about individuals.

This meant we had to deal with three sets of interlinked data: geocoded places, details from our records, and scrapbook posts provided by the public. To bring these all together with limited resources we had to make clever use of what was already out there. Why create our own maps when all you needed to do was write a bit of Java script to embed a Google Map? Why build our own scrapbook application when the blogging service Tumblr provides free accounts and a simple API to manipulate posts? While a substantial amount of custom scripting was required to glue everything together, much of the core functionality was provided by free Web services, available to anyone.

What challenges did you face?

Perhaps the first challenge to overcome was that of imagination. It was difficult for people to understand what the project was until we had a prototype to show them.

The process of handling and cleaning the data at times threatened to overwhelm us. While the geocoding service got us to the point where we could make maps, it also left us with many place names that needed to be manually checked. Often this was the result of misspellings in the original data, or because places either no longer existed or had changed their names. This data cleanup consumed much effort and continues still, though now with the help of our users who regularly point out errors and inconsistencies.

Once we had our coordinates we had to display them on a map without killing anyone's computer. Showing thousands of markers on a Google Map is a challenge to slower Web browsers and can end up hindering navigation. By dividing up our maps, clustering markers, and changing

(cont'd.)

Interview with Tim Sherratt (continued)

the way they were rendered, we managed to greatly improve performance while maintaining the browsing experience. Once again it was trial and error coupled with the advice of the online community that guided us through the roadblocks.

What kinds of positive results have you had? (And, any negative ones?)

From the messages we receive it's clear that Mapping our Anzacs allows people to find records they didn't know existed. Some have met a great-great-uncle for the first time. Others have learned about the war experience of a much-loved grandparent. Local communities have embraced the project, and the scrapbook has developed into a rich and often moving resource. We wanted to give users a new way to explore and interact with our collection, and it seems we have succeeded.

Our users have also become our collaborators, providing corrections and comments that help us improve our data. They have extended the idea of the scrapbook, using it, for example, as a noticeboard for family history research or as a way of creating crosslinks between related resources.

Success brings problems of its own, and the work of moderating the scrapbook and responding to feedback has proved considerable. Issues with performance remain for people on slow connections, and while many are familiar with the Google Maps interface, some find it difficult to navigate. We are planning a number of enhancements based on this feedback and hope to take advantage of the technology as it evolves to improve and extend the interface.

About how much time did it take?

While the project as a whole stretched over about eight months, much of this time was taken up cleaning and processing the data. The development of the interface was completed in under two months.

What advice would you give an organization wanting to use something similar?

Start experimenting. The technology is developing so rapidly that if you spend 12 months planning a project it's likely to be out-of-date even before you start. New Web services and data sources are becoming available every day. Perhaps you could use Open Calais to extract people's names from a collection description or MetaCarta to find the places. You might use the Google Books API to harvest the details of publications

(cont'd.)

Interview with Tim Sherratt (continued)

---

that cite your records. Even if you're not a coder you can use tools like Yahoo Pipes to see what happens when you start to link data and services. Experimentation brings new ideas and possibilities. It's all about making connections.

By providing this visualization, the site allows users to easily understand where all the people described in the records came from—a perspective that would have been almost impossible for any casual user. By creating this kind of visualization, the site encourages users to think about what they might learn from the records.

Several history-related mashups created by archives use digitized versions of one of the most useful resources for historical research—Sanborn fire insurance maps. The site "Beyond Steel" (http://digital.lib.lehigh.edu/beyondsteel), sponsored by a group of historical institutions in Pennsylvania's Lehigh Valley, includes a project that combines geographic data with information about archival materials pertaining to a specific time period:

> The Geographic Information Systems (GIS) project is comprised of the early twentieth-century Sanborn fire insurance maps, Sholes' Directory of the Bethlehems, 1900–1901, 1900–1902 Bethlehem Steel employee lists, a contemporary database of streets, and selected information from the 1900 Census report. The result is a geospatial presentation of turn of the century Bethlehem population and a context for more specialized visualization of workers in the steel industry. (Lehigh University Digital Library, accessed 2009)

While "Beyond Steel" focuses on work, the "Going to the Show" project (http://docsouth.unc.edu/gtts/index.html) documents information related to the experience of going to movies in North Carolina, from the introduction of projected motion pictures in 1896 to the end of the silent film era around 1930. The site overlays Sanborn maps with information such as newspaper ads and articles, postcards of downtown streetscapes, and city directories, providing new context for these collections of ephemera.

Most mashups created by archives associate images of photographs or scanned documents with maps, but the Archival Sound Recordings site (http://sounds.bl.uk/Maps.aspx), created by the British Library, uses maps to support browsing of digitized selections from their diverse collections of sounds. The interactive maps have links that allow you to listen to recordings that capture regional accents and dialects, wildlife and environmental sounds, and world and traditional music.

Although the ability to create mashups may currently be beyond the capabilities of most smaller archives and historical societies, these products are certainly valuable resources for Web exhibitions and encourage new exploration of archival collections. Application developers are making it easier and easier to create tools such as these, and creating a mashup is definitely something you may want to experiment with, as resources allow.

WIDGETS

According to Merriam-Webster, the term "widget" was coined in 1926 and is an alteration of the word "gadget." Originally, a widget was "an unnamed article considered for purposes of hypothetical example" (Merriam-Webster, accessed 2009). The term is also associated with discussions of economics, where it is used to describe a generic product or output in an imaginary scenario. In the late 1990s, the term was adopted to describe a new kind of small, adaptable Web tool.

What Is a Widget?

Wikipedia defines a "Web widget" as a "portable chunk of code that can be installed and executed within any separate HTML-based Web page by an end user without requiring additional compilation" (Wikipedia, "Web Widget," accessed 2009); in practice, a widget is a tool that you can easily add to your Web site that, in turn, imports data or a new functionality from elsewhere. Widgets usually appear as small boxes installed in the sidebar of a Web site or on a homepage. The way widgets can function is limited only by the creativity of Web developers and the availability of online data and applications.

One of the ways widgets work is to share information pulled from another site. Early applications of this feature were widgets that were updated based on time, such as countdown clocks. Many common widgets share snippets of information made available via an RSS feed, for example, showing the latest blog posts or news headlines from another Web site. They can also pull information from a specific user account on another Web site and display it in the widget's window, like the Flickr badge widget (www.flickr.com/badge.gne) that can pull and display on any Web site thumbnail versions of the latest images posted to your Flickr account or one of your groups. Another example is the popular application Library Thing (www.librarything.com), which provides a widget you can add to any Web site that shows people Books from My LibraryThing.

In addition to pulling information and making it available, widgets can also be used to make a small version of a Web application available on your site. Some commonly used widgets of this kind, particularly on archives and library sites, include the following:

- Tools that allow users to subscribe to the RSS feed for the site using tools like Bloglines or Google Reader
- Tools that allow users to tag or share the page using social bookmarking sites such as Digg, Delicious, Reddit, or Google, or share it using social networking sites like Facebook, Twitter, or MySpace (like "Add This" in Figure 1-2 in Chapter 1)
- Tools that allow users to view a map of where a site's readers are located (sometimes called a "Guest Map") and add themselves to the map (often supplied via Frappr Map)
- Tools that allow users to search a library catalog, such as WorldCat or the library catalog of a college or university (see Figure 10-2)
- Tools that provide an opportunity to engage in online chat (see next section) using programs like Meebo
- A search box for Wikipedia (see Figure 10-2)
- Advertisements for relevant books available via Amazon

Google has made it very easy to find widgets (which it calls "gadgets") that can be used on its customizable Google homepage feature, iGoogle (Figure 10-2). Google also provides the capability for you to create simple gadgets for iGoogle, such as ones that share your RSS feed, which you can then make publicly available. There are also services, including Widgetbox (www.widgetbox .com), that provide easy tools for creating widgets that operate outside of iGoogle, including tools that allow you to transform an iGoogle "gadget" into a widget.

Archives and Historical Organizations and Widgets

Perhaps because they sometimes require more advanced programming skills, there are relatively few widgets developed by archives and similar organizations to promote their collections. Some larger institutions, including the Na-

Figure 10-2. A Selection of Gadgets Available on iGoogle

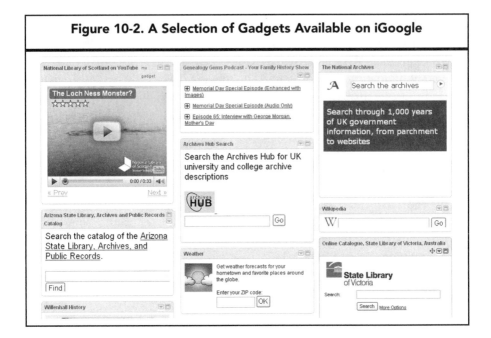

tional Archives and the Archives Hub in Britain, the State Library of Victoria in Australia, and the Arizona State Library's Division of Archives and Public Records, have developed widgets or Google gadgets that allow users to search their online catalogs (as shown in Figure 10-2). These types of widgets would be very useful for other archives, historical societies, educational institutions, libraries, and other kinds of organizations to install on their Web sites if they have users who frequently need to search the collections of the organization that has created the widget. Once a widget like this is installed on, for example, a local historical society's Web site, a user would be able to search the widget-provider's catalog (perhaps the state archives) from the historical society's site. When a user enters a search term in the box provided by the widget, the search results are presented on a new full-sized screen. This benefits both the organization that creates the widget, because it increases access to their catalog, and the organizations that install it, because it increases the resources available via their Web sites.

Widgets that share information from existing RSS feeds can also be useful in promoting an institution, with little additional cost or effort. Using the widget builders mentioned earlier, an institution can create a widget that displays information from its blog or Twitter feed or any other service that has an RSS feed. Ideally, the information being drawn on by the widget would be updated fairly frequently—that is, it would probably not be advisable to have a widget that displayed information from your blog that remained static for weeks at a time. One approach to creating this kind of content is creating an RSS feed (for a blog or Twitter account) that features new content every day—such as "this day in history" or "object of the day."

Another kind of widget that has potential value for historical organizations are those that work with other commercial Web 2.0 sites, such as Flickr badges and similar widgets created for sites like YouTube. These widgets (which are essentially the same as some of the "applications" available in Facebook, described in Chapter 9) allow you to repurpose your existing investment in sharing your collections via other sites. You can install these widgets on your own Web site as a way of reminding visitors that you have information available through these other channels.

Widgets are a diverse category of tools that archives should certainly be aware of and explore. Adding existing widgets for applications the organization is already using (such as Flickr or YouTube) may be a relatively easy way to make your institution's Web site more dynamic and showcase your ongoing Web 2.0 efforts. Creating a new widget from one of your own RSS feeds (such as your blog or your Twitter feed) is another option to consider. You could use this kind of widget on your own Web site and also encourage your friends and supporters to implement it on their sites as a way of spreading the word about your activities. Creating a new widget that would allow users to search your online catalog or finding aids might be a challenging effort but one that has great potential for increasing knowledge and use of your collections.

ONLINE CHAT

Online chat is essentially the act of having a conversation via an exchange of text messages in real time. Many services support online chat along with their other features. For example, Google provides chat as a service for its Gmail subscribers, and Facebook users can chat with any of their friends who happen to be logged in. Other services, such as Google Talk and AIM (AOL Instant Messenger, recently merged with Bebo), focus only on providing online chat services. Chat services have been popular for some time with libraries, which use them to provide another way for remote users to receive reference assistance. Meebo (www.meebo.com) is one of the most popular chat providers among libraries and archives.

How Does Online Chat Work?

Although the details vary among providers, most online chat sessions take place in a small window, which may pop up from the bottom of your screen on sites like Facebook or appear as static content on your site's Web page (see Figure 10-3). Users can see whether you are online and available to chat or not. If you are not available, some services allow users to leave a message in the chat box, which you will see when you log in. If someone you want to chat with is available (that is to say, they are logged in to the chat service), all you need to do is type a message into the box. When you press "enter," your message is sent and published. Once the message has been published, the other person can see it and respond. These kinds of chat sessions are not publicly available; that is, if someone is having a chat session on a Web site, that session is not visible to

Figure 10-3. Sample Chat Session with Earlham College Archives

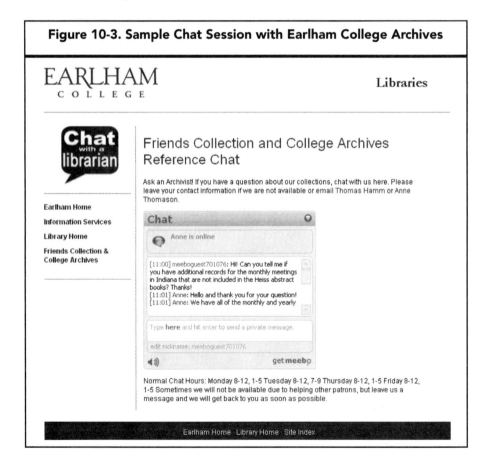

other users. Figure 10-3 shows a sample Meebo chat window and the beginning of a conversation.

Chat sessions are usually limited to two participants. If you want to use chat to have a larger conversation, you will need to move to a "chat room." Some services, like Meebo, also provide this functionality to their users. Chat rooms can be public or private, and the person who created the room also has the power to serve as moderator.

Online Chat in Archives and Historical Organizations

Although chat is not a common feature of many archives or historical societies' Web sites, some are using it successfully. When online chat is available, as the example with Earlham College shows in Figure 10-3, it provides another venue for users to interact with the archivist in real time. Having access to chat may result in users getting a much quicker answer than if they sent an e-mail, since there is no "downtime" between responses. It may also be a useful option for people with hearing or other disabilities.

One challenge in using chat with services like Meebo is that the person asking the question doesn't have an account or any identifying information. So if someone asks a question while the archivist is unavailable and does not leave any contact information, there is no way to contact the user later to provide an answer. Another consideration is that whenever you have set your chat feature "on" (indicating that you are available to chat) you must be available at any time to answer questions, just as if you were at the reference desk. This means if you are also trying to get other work done, you may be interrupted with a question. It is also easy to forget to turn your chat "off" when you leave your desk; having your chat window say that you are available and then letting a question go without a reply can result in frustrated users. While online chat may not offer any technologically complex solutions, it does provide a fast and convenient way for users to get their questions answered, and makes the archivist "available" to users via the Web.

SECOND LIFE

Second Life, like other online virtual environments, seeks to create a virtual world, complete with geography, buildings, businesses, and other institutions, that people can participate in via the Web. Unveiled in 2003 by Linden Lab, Second Life (http://secondlife.com) is the only site of its kind receiving any significant participation by archives and other cultural heritage organizations.

Users of Second Life (referred to as "Residents") appear on the screen as customizable avatars. Everything in Second Life has been created by its Residents. Linden Lab provides only the infrastructure in which the Residents build their own communities and interact with each other.

Although it has similarities to the virtual environments created in some of the sophisticated online game sites, Second Life is not a game. It is a virtual environment that enables people to do things they are unable to do in their "first life," such as attend a faraway meeting with people from around the world, walk through an ancient Egyptian temple, create their own museum, or visit the Sistine Chapel (as shown in Figure 10-4). The ways people use Second Life are as diverse as their "first lives" and are limited only by imagination and the willingness to invest time and resources.

Figure 10-4. Screen Capture of a Visit to a Re-creation of the Sistine Chapel in Second Life

Source: Courtesy of Richard J. Urban

How Does Second Life Work?

To join Second Life, you need to register for an account (which is free) and download the viewer application that lets you access the site. You will be asked to verify that you are over the age of 13. Although a high-speed Internet connection is not required, it does greatly improve the experience, as does having a computer equipped with a more powerful processor and graphics card, and most regular users consider them essential. Once you have an account, you can create and customize your avatar and become a Resident of Second Life. There is no charge to access most of the areas of the site. The Second Life world is organized into "islands," which can be privately owned. Some owners choose to restrict access to their islands, but most are open to anyone. (For example, an island owned by a college or university may limit access to its own campus and alumni community.)

The economy of Second Life runs on its own local currency, the "Linden dollar," which allows you to:

> buy, sell, rent or trade land or goods and services with other users. Virtual goods include buildings, vehicles, devices of all kinds, animations, clothing, skin, hair, jewelry, flora and fauna, and works of art. Services include "camping," wage labor, business management, entertainment and custom content creation (which can be broken up into the following six categories: building, texturing, scripting, animating, art direction, and the position of producer/project funder). (Wikipedia, "Second Life Economy," accessed 2009)

Although Residents can (and some do) spend time and energy outfitting their avatars, the primary costs associated with using Second Life come when you want to build something to establish a permanent presence. There are charges for buying or renting land, as well as for building content. Although people with the right skills can create their own content (such as objects, textures for buildings, and clothing), most users prefer to purchase them, which saves time and takes advantage of others' expertise.

For most people, the real appeal of Second Life doesn't lie in the opportunity to create an avatar or build a virtual structure but in the opportunities it offers to interact with other Residents. In Second Life you can do things like:

- attend a concert (with music streamed in from live or recorded performances),

- visit an art gallery,
- participate in conferences and meetings,
- take a "vacation" by visiting exotic locations (including virtual recreations of historic locations),
- go to a party,
- attend a class, or
- consult a librarian.

As in the real world and everywhere else on the Web, there is "adult content" available in Second Life, and some Residents do take advantage of the anonymity of the site to engage in flirtatious and occasionally lewd behavior. This content is usually limited to certain areas of the site and should not be a significant deterrent to participating, but it is something to be aware of.

Archives and Historical Organizations in Second Life

Although some museums have established an official presence in Second Life (such as the Smithsonian Institution's Latino Virtual Museum), there are almost no archives or historical organizations represented in the site's cultural and information sources. Many more libraries, particularly academic libraries, have set up "branches" in Second Life, where Residents can get reference help from librarians and do things like participate in book discussion groups and attend lectures.

For many archives, creation of a virtual presence in Second Life may require a considerable investment of time and resources for a somewhat limited return. Although the number of people using Second Life is unclear, it certainly appears that the "buzz" around the site has declined in recent years. Unlike many other Web 2.0 tools, such as Flickr and Facebook, Second Life requires users to download software to access it, and it takes some time to figure out how to navigate a new world. Building a "place" in Second Life requires investment of financial resources as well as time, unlike the relatively easy process of setting up accounts in Facebook or Flickr. Second Life's terms of service may have also deterred some institutions from participating (Linden Research, Inc., accessed 2009). For example, copyright for content created in Second Life is granted only to avatars, not to institutions.

Despite these challenges, Second Life does have potential value for archives but probably only to the extent that individual archivists are willing to dedicate their time to a project. Although there are few cultural institutions in Second

---

Interview with Matthew Davies
National Film & Sound Archive (Australia)

What made your institution interested in creating something in Second Life?

I had heard about Second Life from friends who were performing as DJs there. My interest, as Sound Curator at the NFSA, was sparked by the Texas Aussie Music Party.

The 2007 Texas Aussie Music Party was a Second Life event supported by the Australian Music Office in Los Angeles to promote Australian bands at the annual South by Southwest music conference. This innovative approach to promotion of Australian music was also featured in a Second Life Television production, and this struck me as a piece of media that should be archived. Given the NFSA's charge, which includes comprehensive coverage of published Australian music recordings and supporting documentation, it seemed we were the appropriate institution to collect and preserve this material.

I also decided this was something I needed to look at personally, so I registered an account with Second Life. This has led to a small number of acquisitions, mostly machinima (captures of Second Life animations) of music by Australian artists performing in Second Life. I also began experimenting with using Second Life as a platform for dissemination of audiovisual archives. Currently I am developing a small exhibition in support of the NFSA's National Registry of Recorded Sound—the Sounds of Australia. This work is partly for my own interest, but I find it is also useful to share what I am learning with colleagues in the archiving profession as a glimpse into one aspect of our possible future. I've also found that my background in audiovisual media has enabled me to assist colleagues developing Second Life exhibits with some of the technicalities peculiar to a/v.

What information, tools, and processes did you need to begin?

Apart from the essentials of operating the Second Life interface—such as learning to walk—I've had to become familiar with some fairly complex features in Photoshop to create textures for Second Life objects—in particular, the use of alpha channels for transparency in textures. I had never been a chat room user, so there were a set of protocols, abbreviations, and conventions that I had to learn to communicate using Second Life's local chat and Instant Messaging functions—including the ability to interpret hurriedly and badly typed messages (referred to in Second Life as "typonese"). Because I am presenting audiovisual materials in my display,

(cont'd.)

Interview with Matthew Davies *(continued)*
I needed to develop a good understanding of the way Second Life manages streaming media, and some of the underlying streaming technologies such as QuickTime and SHOUTcast. Finally, I am learning the basics of film-making "in world" (machinima) to document some of my Second Life activities in a more conventional form of audiovisual media.
How did you determine what information to include?
Accessibility and low-risk were major factors, so I used a sub-set of digitised content and contextual information already curated for the NFSA Web site.
What challenges did/do you face?
Explaining what I am doing to others in the profession who have no knowledge of virtual worlds is a big challenge, as is finding an appropriate "next step" that connects the possibilities of virtual worlds with the realities of a public cultural institution.
What kinds of positive results have you had? (And, any negative ones?)
• Personal learning—I've gained first-hand experience of the 3D world environment. Second Life is an interesting platform. For me it has really been a great lesson in the power of collaboration. • Networking—Many Second Life users are connected to very interesting projects and activities in a real world that includes creative use of virtual space. • Feasibility testing—I am now more confident in what can be done in a virtual world and roughly how it's done. • Acquiring content—I am working on some specific acquisition outcomes illustrating Second Life music, machinima, and virtual Television. • Limited exposure—On the downside, the audience in Second Life is small, and the site itself has a limited and sometimes negative profile.
About how much time does it take?
You can accomplish a lot in a short time as measured by the "real life" calendar if you spend regular time in Second Life. Getting started is measured in weeks. Getting established is measured in months. A year is a VERY long time. Two years is forever. On an individual level short term it can be very time intensive.
(cont'd.)

Interview with Matthew Davies (*continued*)

What advice would you give an organization wanting to use something similar?

- Second Life probably won't help you achieve your key performance indicators in the short term, but you might learn something.
- If you make photos, machinima, etc., of your Second Life content and link to them via tools like Twitter and YouTube, you can expand your reach beyond the immediate small Second Life audience.
- Second Life is not the future, it is the present, but it tells us something about the future.

Life, there are many cultural resources, and they are there because individual Residents or groups of Residents invested in building them. Archivists, volunteers, or simply "fans" of an archives could, for example, build an exhibit in Second Life of images from an archives' collection, with the permission of the archives but without any institutional involvement. It would also be possible to build collaborative exhibits with contributions from many archives. However, merely making information available in Second Life that people could create elsewhere on the Web does not take advantage of site's inherent capabilities for real-time interaction and the creation of new content that could exist only in Second Life.

Using Second Life to support interaction in real time could include using it to deliver public programming or educational series, as libraries have done for some time. Although these offerings might not attract a large number of attendees, they would probably reach an audience who might not otherwise attend such an event.

Greater potential lies in having archives staff contributing to virtual environments created by others and participating in making information available there. For example, many archives might have something to contribute to sites such as the Land of Lincoln:

> The space will feature area replicas like Lincoln's birthplace, his home in Springfield, and the White House years. The immersive community will be planned and built by librarians, historians, educators, students, and anyone interested in that time period. Individuals will be able to live in the community, open up a period shop, participate in period events such as the Lincoln-Douglas debates, meet characters of the period and experi-

ence the music, art, science, and literature. In addition to reading and hearing lectures about the time, place, and people, attendees will be able to live it. (Alliance Virtual Library, 2007)

Second Life offers the capability to build replicas of historical environments, and for archivists this means an opportunity to interact with the people building and visiting those virtual historical places. Making a significant institutional commitment in Second Life should be considered a long-term investment rather than one that will produce short-term results. However, for archives with staff who have the interest and willingness to invest the time to learn how to successfully navigate Second Life, there are unique opportunities to add value to virtual history-related environments and deliver information in new real-time venues.

REFERENCES

Alliance Virtual Library. "Land of Lincoln in Second Life" (October 24, 2007). Available: http://infoisland.org/2007/10/24/land-of-lincoln-in-second-life (accessed May 11, 2009).

Lehigh University Digital Library. "Beyond Steel: GIS." Available: http://digital.lib .lehigh.edu/beyondsteel/gis (accessed May 7, 2009).

Linden Research, Inc. "Terms of Service." Available: http://secondlife.com/corporate/ tos.php (accessed May 7, 2009).

Merriam-Webster Online. "Widget." Available: www.merriam-webster.com/dictionary/ widget (accessed May 9, 2009).

National Archives of Australia. "About This Site." Available: http://mappingouranzacs .naa.gov.au/about.aspx (accessed May 9, 2009).

North Carolina Maps. "Historic Overlay Maps." Available: www.lib.unc.edu/dc/ ncmaps/interactive/overlay.html (accessed July 8, 2009).

Wikipedia. "Mashup (Music)." Available: http://en.wikipedia.org/wiki/Mashup_ (music) (accessed May 7, 2009).

Wikipedia. "Mashup (Web Application Hybrid)." Available: http://en.wikipedia.org/ wiki/Mashup_(web_application_hybrid) (accessed May 7, 2009).

Wikipedia. "Second Life: Economy." Available: http://en.wikipedia.org/wiki/Second _Life#Land_ownership (accessed May 6, 2009).

Wikipedia. "Web Widget." Available: http://en.wikipedia.org/wiki/Web_widget (accessed May 9, 2009).

CHAPTER 11

Measuring Your Success

An important and often overlooked aspect of implementing a Web 2.0 tool is deciding how to determine whether or not it is successful. You can have a witty and informative Twitter feed with regular updates, but if has only 21 followers, is it a success? What if it has 50, or 100, or 500? If your wiki gets regular updates and use, but it all comes from your own staff, is it a failure?

It is often difficult to translate Web 2.0 efforts into traditional measurement categories. When making the case for Web 2.0 efforts, it is critical to be able to define what these efforts are intended to achieve. While many archives and historical organizations are able to start using these tools without a formal plan as an experiment, when resources are scarce (and even when they are not so scarce), it may be necessary to justify the time and effort needed to keep a Web 2.0 implementation active.

The intent of this chapter is to give you some basic ideas and suggestions regarding evaluation and measurement of your Web 2.0 implementations. It cannot provide you with everything you need to know about incorporating new activities into your existing performance measurement system or how to establish such a system if you do not already have one. Furthermore, the approaches to measurement discussed here are certainly not the only ways to approach this subject. For example, in discussing approaches to measuring and evaluating reference services, Mary Jo Pugh (2005: 258–268) presents two different frameworks that you might find equally valuable. You should also monitor the progress of the Archival Metrics research project (http://archivalmetrics.org) and look at the user-based evaluation toolkits they are developing. Whatever approach you decide to take, the basic steps outlined here—planning for measurement, establishing a baseline, and identifying both tangible outputs and intangible outcomes—should be common to any good program of assessment.

PLAN HOW YOU'RE GOING TO MEASURE BEFORE YOU IMPLEMENT

While it's natural during your planning stages to focus on the technical and content aspects of your Web 2.0 project, it is important to define your goals as well. Often what starts out as a casual experiment can evolve into a serious outreach effort, and, if proper tools to measure this effort are not in place from the beginning, it can be difficult to assess the growth of the project. It's also true, as the saying goes, that "time flies when you're having fun"—you may find that a year has passed since you launched a wiki or a Facebook page, and yet you're not able to articulate what your organization has gained by it or even recall exactly how or why the project was started.

There are two essential ways to measure your Web 2.0 activity: the outputs you have created and the outcomes you have achieved. They measure activity in different ways, but both are important.

Measuring Outputs

The practice of distinguishing between measuring outcomes and outputs was most prominently advanced by the United Way, which used it as a means of assessing the true impact of social services (Laughlin and Wilson, 2008: 9). The United Way provides a library of materials in its Outcome Measurement Resource Network (www.liveunited.org/outcomes), freely available on the Web for those seeking more information on Outcome Measurement. On their site, outputs are defined as:

> the direct products of program activities and usually are measured in terms of the volume of work accomplished—for example, the numbers of classes taught, counseling sessions conducted, educational materials distributed, and participants served. Outputs have little inherent value in themselves. They are important because they are intended to lead to a desired benefit for participants or target populations. (United Way of America, 1996)

These are the traditional kinds of numerical measures that many organizations already include in their annual reporting.

This kind of measurement may seem easy, but it does require some serious analysis. To accurately measure outputs, everyone involved must have the same understanding of how those outputs are defined. For example, if you are measuring how many reference requests are received, you must define what constitutes a reference request, as well as defining ways to categorize requests. If you are measuring the number of accessions processed, you must agree on how you are measuring them—as a simple count of collections or by volume (and if by volume, by what measure?), or both. You must also establish a common understanding of what it means for an accession to be "processed." While such distinctions may seem obvious, when compiling statistics, it's critical to make sure everyone is accounting for their work using the same standards.

Ideally, when considering what data to collect you will be thinking about what use you will make of it rather than just having the goal of collecting data for its own sake. If you are collecting data on your reference requests, do you want to track information such as a category of requestor or purpose of request (family history/genealogy, business, academic research, or personal research, for example)? Do you want to track where the requestor is located? Do you want to know if the requestor is a member of your organization or affiliated with it? Do you want to track how long it took to answer the request? All of these pieces of data (and many more) would be useful to know, but it would be impractical to collect every piece of data that could someday prove useful if you have no real plan for how to use it.

Referring back to your strategic goals and the outcomes you want to achieve can help you determine what outputs you want to measure and what you want to know about them. If one of your strategic goals is to expand your institution's reputation and build a national brand, you may want to track where your reference requests are coming from to help assess your success. If you have a goal to improve the level of service your members receive, you may want to know which requests came from members and how long it took to respond to them.

Measurements of outputs can also be used to demonstrate a need or help you make a case for new activities. For example, in the interview Emma Allen and Joshua Shindler provided about their podcasting activities (see Chapter 4), they observed that:

> In the past few years The National Archives has been moving its focus from an offline to an online organisation to meet our users' expectation that there should be more records, services, and expertise available online. This move is backed up by statistics: for every document viewed on site at Kew, 170 are viewed online. Similarly, while 20 to 100 people at-

tend the regular talks and events at The National Archives in Kew, there are over 5,000 downloads of each talk. (Chapter 4)

Collecting information on your outputs not only should be informed by your strategic plan goal—it can also inform the analysis that supports developing new goals to meet your audiences' evolving needs.

Measuring Outcomes

While outputs are tangible and familiar, outcomes are generally more abstract and difficult to measure and assess. The United Way Web site defines outcomes as:

> benefits or changes for individuals or populations during or after partici- pating in program activities. They are influenced by a program's outputs. Outcomes may relate to behavior, skills, knowledge, attitudes, values, condition, or other attributes. They are what participants know, think, or can do; or how they behave; or what their condition is, that is different following the program. (United Way of America, 1996)

While this definition was clearly written with social services in mind, it is not difficult to translate it for archives and historical organizations. In this con- text, outcomes can be thought of as benefits or changes for our stakeholders: our members, our other audiences, and our institutions. Some possible out- comes from Web 2.0 projects might be an increased public profile for your in- stitution, members who feel more connected to your organization, or greater appreciation for a specific area of your collection.

In thinking about measuring outcomes in relationship to a new Web 2.0 pro- ject, you need to think about what possible outcomes the project could produce. Ideally, you will be able to tie your specific goals for your project into your or- ganization's strategic goals (as discussed in Chapter 2). An excellent example of this is described in the Library of Congress' final report on its Flickr pilot (see Chapter 5). As part of planning and defining the pilot, the Library's team used the institution's strategic goals to inform the objectives for the pilot:

> . . . three objectives supporting the Library's strategic goals to increase Library outreach and improve the user experience, were formalized for a pilot. The relevant strategic goals are listed in Appendix B. The objec- tives were to:

- increase awareness by sharing photographs from the Library's collections with people who enjoy images but might not visit the Library's own Web site;
- gain a better understanding of how social tagging and community input could benefit both the Library and users of the collections;
- gain experience participating in the emergent Web communities that would be interested in the kinds of materials in the Library's collections. (Springer et al., 2008: 4)

At the conclusion of the pilot, the team evaluated its effectiveness on the basis of those objectives.

Although you may have certain goals in mind when planning and implementing a Web 2.0 tool, you should also be open to other possibilities as you see how your tool is actually being used. The Web, particularly Web 2.0, is full of serendipity and unintended consequences. You may find your implementation is a total failure with your target audience but is very successful at achieving a totally unexpected outcome. For example, you may have started a wiki aimed at K–12 teachers and populated it with information about your community, including pages about the development of railroads. Your wiki may have been a flop with teachers but a hit with online railroad enthusiasts, who contributed to and expanded the sections on railroads substantially. While this wasn't what you were aiming for, you would have achieved outcomes like increasing your own knowledge about your collections and cultivating new stakeholders and potential advocates. Be open when it comes to measuring outcomes. While ideally you will achieve what you set out to, sometimes projects can take unexpected turns.

You may also want to consider the overall "impact" of your archival programs, including your Web 2.0 implementations. In a 2008 article, Wendy Duff and Joan Cherry reported on a study examining the impact of orientation sessions the archives provided to students at Yale University. They defined impact as the following:

> The overall effect of *outcomes and conditioning* factors resulting in a *change* in state, attitude or behavior of an individual or group after engagement with the output. (Duff and Cherry, 2008: 500)

While the specific focus on education may not apply to you, the article gives an excellent overview of efforts to measure the impact of archival services and outlines a methodology that might prove useful for other kinds of studies.

ESTABLISHING BASELINE MEASUREMENTS

Establishing causality is difficult when considering outcomes-based measurement. If you are able to determine, for example, that the satisfaction level of your organization's members has increased over the past two years, it may be difficult to determine what factors led to that increase. An important factor in being able to establish which of your outputs contributed to a change in outcomes is being able to clearly state what you have been doing differently. To do this, you need to have baseline measurements—that is, clear measurements and reliable data that document your existing activities.

Ensuring You Can Measure "Before" and "After"

Your institution probably already has systems in place to measure key activities in its major functional areas, such as acquisitions, processing, reference, and outreach. As you are thinking about undertaking new activities, such as using Web 2.0 tools, think about how these might affect your existing processes. For example, if you implement a wiki that provides easy access to commonly used reference materials, you might see a decrease in the time needed to answer some kinds of reference questions. You might also see a change in the number or type of reference questions asked: you may see a decrease in "simple" questions because patrons have better access to reference materials and can answer simple questions themselves, and you might see a corresponding increase in "complex" questions because patrons have access to more background information. Or if you share copies of your most popular photographs on Flickr, you may see either an increase or decrease in the number of orders placed for reproductions of these images; orders might increase if more people became aware of the image and want high-quality copies for publication, but orders might also decrease if fewer people need to order copies for their own personal reference.

By thinking about both why you are measuring an activity and how a new project might affect it, you can assess whether you are collecting the right kind of data to document your future (and perhaps also current) needs. For example, you won't be able to tell whether or not you get fewer "easy" reference questions after you implement a "ready reference" wiki if you did not previously categorize the types of reference questions you received. While it's impossible to anticipate all the ways implementation of a Web 2.0 tool might affect your existing processes, you should be able to identify some possible results. It would also be a good idea to consult with people at other institutions who have implemented the kind of project you're considering. They may be able to give you some indication of what to expect—and what they wished they had been measuring themselves.

Creating Effective Measures of Web 2.0 "Outputs"

Many Web 2.0 tools automatically provide you with ways to measure activity. If you are evaluating different software or service providers for your Web 2.0 implementation, you should take into consideration what statistics they provide. Depending on the tool you are using, you may also need to find other ways to document usage—either because you are using software that doesn't track statistics or because they don't meet your needs. Many institutions install free tools like Google Analytics (www.google.com/analytics) that allow you to collect detailed data about how your site is being used and tools like Feedburner (www.feedburner.google.com) that generate data about your RSS feeds. If you want more granular data about the use of your Web resources, you may want to invest in a fee-based service; the Web site CounterGuide.com (http://counterguide.com) lists a wide variety of both free and fee-based services along with brief reviews. If you have implemented your Web 2.0 project on your own server, you may already have access to basic traffic logging and other kinds of information about your site.

You should also consider how those statistics are compiled. For example, do they allow you to access statistics about use by individual month, or can you access only cumulative statistics about total usage? Although these kinds of distinctions may not determine which tool you select, they should inform what processes you put in place to track the use of your site. If the tool you select provides you with just cumulative statistics about use, for example, you may want to make a note of your numbers at the end of each month so that you can track month-by-month usage. You should also consider how long the tool provides access to your statistics. Some sites may retain data only for periods such as the past three months or six months. In some cases, you may not be able to count on being able to access data for the entire previous year when you're compiling your annual report. You should also consider that sometimes Web 2.0 sites change ownership or format without much warning to their users. To be safe, you may want to copy information into your own records of statistics on a weekly or monthly basis.

What should you be measuring? The answer is different depending on the specifics of your implementation, but in general terms you should think about collecting data that documents the following:

- What you create (number of items you post or share)
- How many people access it (number of hits, downloads, views)
- Number of people who follow your Web 2.0 efforts (subscribers, "fans," contacts, friends, Twitter followers, group members, etc.)
- Number of people who interact with your content (comments, feedback, tagging, replying, re-tweeting, etc.)
- Number of research requests received as a result of your content

In addition to measuring these tangible outputs of your efforts, you may also want to track how much work goes into generating those outputs—things like how much time it takes to create the content and respond to feedback.

You should also consider how you could modify your existing data collection tools to include your Web 2.0 presence. For instance, if you collect information on how your patrons learned about you, you might want to update the list of choices to include things like your blog, Flickr page, or Twitter account. This would not only serve your data collection needs but also would promote your Web 2.0 tools to those who might have been unaware of them. Look for opportunities like this to incorporate your new outreach projects with existing data collection efforts.

Although setting up an online survey of your Web site's users may be a more substantial effort than you're ready for right away, it might be worth while for you to start considering it. Creating a Web survey that asks visitors to answer questions about how they learned about you (giving your Web 2.0 tools as possible answers) is a good way to once again gain information while making people aware of these other resources. Gathering information about your Web 2.0 efforts may not be enough of a driver to get a Web site survey off the ground, but such a survey would collect many other kinds of valuable data. (See discussion of user studies in Chapter 12.) You may be able to partner with others in your institution to gather support for this kind of data collection.

DOCUMENTING EVIDENCE OF YOUR SUCCESS

Some things don't lend themselves to being measured, and success can't necessarily be determined based only on the aggregation of all your outputs. You may process 500 reference requests a year, but one of those requests may result in a significant donation of additional materials, or a pleased board member, or positive coverage in the media, or even in a substantial financial contribution. These results can't be shared through a statistical report at the end of the year.

Capture Compelling Stories

A mention in your annual report that you have a Facebook page with 100 fans may not mean much to your supporters, members, or colleagues. However, sharing comments and stories from your Facebook fans can give those numbers a compelling voice in your report. Stating how many updates you posted to your institution's Twitter account provides a sense of your output, but providing statistics about how many times your updates were "re-tweeted" gives a sense of your influence and the reach of your "tweets." Recording how well your 2.0 efforts are being received gives you a way to share the success of your project beyond the mere numbers.

Many archivists keep a file for things like press clippings, acknowledgements in publications, and particularly meaningful "thank you" notes from patrons. You should make it part of your routine to do the same for your Web 2.0 feedback. When you see a particularly good comment or reference to you, capture it and document it. Things on the Web can be ephemeral—that glowing blog post reviewing your podcast may not be there when you want to access it for your annual report. Take a screen capture or print out the "shout outs" you receive. You may also want to follow up with someone who gives you positive feedback not only to thank them but also to ask if they would like to have their comments shared in your report, newsletter, or other outreach materials. Most people will appreciate the consideration and may even provide you with more information to work with.

Sometimes the Medium Is the Message

Web 2.0 doubters are sometime skeptical of the motives of those who participate, saying that they're just doing it "to be cool." Archives and historical organizations rarely spend much time contemplating how to be cool, but they do think about how to be relevant. Using a Web 2.0 tool doesn't guarantee relevance, but it does show that your organization is ready to try new things and interact with the public in new ways. Creating something like a blog, wiki, or podcast isn't something you should do just to be able to say your institution is doing something "2.0"; you should always have a mission-related goal for starting this kind of new project. At the same time, undertaking an outreach effort using a newer technology does give the effort an added value. Delivering content via a blog rather than through a paper or PDF newsletter makes a difference. Having an RSS feed for your Web site rather than sending out e-mail updates also sends a signal. If you want to project an image of being forward thinking and people centered, then Web 2.0 tools may help to shape that image.

REFERENCES

Duff, Wendy M., and Joan M. Cherry. 2008. "Archival Orientation for Undergraduate Students: An Exploratory Study of Impact." *American Archivist* 71, no. 2 (Fall/Winter): 499–529.

Laughlin, Sara, and Ray W. Wilson. 2008. *The Quality Library*. Chicago: American Library Association.

Pugh, Mary Jo. 2005. *Providing Reference Services for Archives & Manuscripts*. Chicago: Society of American Archivists.

Springer, Michelle, Beth Dulabahn, Phil Michel, Barbara Natanson, David Reser, David Woodward, and Helena Zinkham. 2008. "For the Common Good: The Library of Congress Flickr Pilot Project." Washington, DC: The Library of Congress (October 30). Available: www.loc.gov/rr/print/flickr_report_final.pdf (accessed April 30, 2009).

United Way of America. 1996. "Outcome Measurement: What and Why?" Alexandria, VA: United Way of America. Available: www.liveunited.org/Outcomes/Resources/What/Intro.cfm (accessed May 20, 2009).

CHAPTER 12

Management and Other Considerations

With the knowledge you've gained from the previous chapters, I hope you feel able to develop a plan for what kind of Web 2.0 implementations would work best for your organization. But, in addition to considering how to measure your success (as discussed in the previous chapter), there are other important issues than can affect the success of your project—issues related to planning and managing your project, as well as things you should do to make yourself an engaged Web 2.0 implementer.

PLANNING FOR SUCCESS

Many of the elements that lead to success in a Web 2.0 project have nothing to do with the technology—they are the human elements. Depending on the size and culture of your institution, some of the steps described in this chapter might be very easy for you or very difficult. Some successful Web 2.0 projects have been started by people just "playing around," but eventually these people have to grapple with the kinds of issues described here. Even if you will essentially be doing all these activities yourself, these are still important factors for you to consider as you plan your Web 2.0 implementation.

Getting Institutional Buy-In

Even if your organization does not have a formal process for approving new projects, you need to obtain some kind of approval, however informal, for your Web 2.0 implementation. Just as critical, but harder to define, is making sure you have buy-in from the key people you need to make your project successful.

Again, depending on the size or complexity of your organization and on what you want to do, this may be a large group or a small one. As you think through what your project will require, you should be noting whose approval and cooperation you need. In large organizations, it often helps if your project has a "champion" who will lend authority to your efforts. At a minimum, you will want the person or group who supervises you to be firmly behind your ideas. A grudging approval is better than none at all, but ideally you will have informed and enthusiastic support.

If your project needs to be formally presented to your board or management team, the best preparation you can do is to make sure you have thought through all the requirements, as well as the potential benefits and pitfalls. If your audience is skeptical or if key decision makers are reluctant to venture into this new territory, you may want to have information about successful implementations at organizations similar to yours. You may also want to present statistics and recommendations from other organizations that have done similar projects and prepare mock-up or sample versions of what you want to create to help others visualize your project ideas.

Considering Legal Issues

In gathering your institutional support, you should also think about working with your legal counsel. The main legal issue most Web 2.0 projects need to consider is copyright—both for the materials you may want to use and for the new content you are creating; usually the latter is much simpler to manage than the former. Fortunately, the Society of American Archivists has recently issued a very useful product: "Orphan Works: Statement of Best Practices." This report provides a clear step-by-step description of what "professional archivists consider to be best practices regarding reasonable efforts to identify and locate rights holders" (Society of American Archivists, 2009: 1). It contains examples of what resources to consult in your search, information about the importance of documenting your search, and a flowchart showing the decision process.

The extent to which you need to consult with your institution's lawyers and the amount of support you receive for your project may reflect how risk-averse your organization is. Some institutions are comfortable moving forward without having clearly defined permissions for reuse of materials—for example, using parts of decades-old oral histories in a podcast—while others want to use only materials they are absolutely certain they have rights to publish in a new form. The best preparation you can have for this discussion is a clear understanding of what kinds of material you want to use and what you think their legal status is (as informed by the kind of documented search outlined in the SAA Best Practices document). You should also share with your legal counsel a copy of the terms of service, if applicable, for any Web 2.0 tool you are planning to implement. If your legal counsel refuses to give approval for your use of the material you have in mind or has reservations about the terms of service, you may need to change your plans to build a project around whatever material in your collections your counsel thinks you can safely use or switch to a different Web 2.0 tool. In smaller or less bureaucratic organizations, this kind of formal consultation may not be necessary, but, even so, you should consider at least informing your legal counsel of your plans in order to avoid unpleasant surprises.

You should also research your options for the level of copyright protection you want on the materials you create and share. Many cultural organizations have adopted one of the licenses provided by the Creative Commons (http://creativecommons.org). Creative Commons is a nonprofit corporation that has developed free licenses and other legal tools that can be applied to products on the Web that encourage sharing while reserving some rights. Figure 12-1 (http://creativecommons.org/about/licenses) shows the four different sets of conditions (and their symbols) that are combined in different ways to create the six different Creative Commons licenses. The Creative Commons Web site provides an online tool to help you determine which license is right for you and provides you with a graphic you can post on your site that indicates how people may appropriately share your material.

Figure 12-1. Creative Commons License Conditions and Symbols

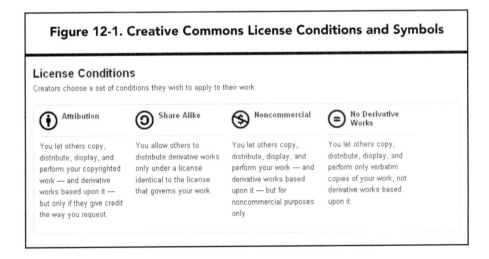

License Conditions

Creators choose a set of conditions they wish to apply to their work.

ⓘ Attribution	⟳ Share Alike	$ Noncommercial	⊜ No Derivative Works
You let others copy, distribute, display, and perform your copyrighted work — and derivative works based upon it — but only if they give credit the way you request.	You allow others to distribute derivative works only under a license identical to the license that governs your work.	You let others copy, distribute, display, and perform your work — and derivative works based upon it — but for noncommercial purposes only.	You let others copy, distribute, display, and perform only verbatim copies of your work, not derivative works based upon it.

Defining Tasks and Assigning Workload

Almost every use of a Web 2.0 tool requires some kind of ongoing attention after you launch it. Blogs and podcasts need to have new content created, edited, and published, and someone needs to follow up on user comments. Wikis need to have new content added and user contributions monitored and responded to, if necessary. Online chat needs to have staff assigned to monitor it. Part of identifying the requirements for your project and planning for its success are identifying all the tasks that need to be done and determining who will do them. (Remember to take into account any reviews or approvals that your content needs before it can be published.)

Once you have identified all the tasks that need to be done and thought about who will do them, have a discussion with the person responsible for defining work assignments. If you want your project to succeed, it is a good idea to have the tasks that support it be a recognized part of people's jobs. If supporting a Web 2.0 project is something "extra" that people do as time allows (and on which they are not evaluated as part of their performance review), there is a good chance the project may fall by the wayside over time. Many Web 2.0 implementations are very promising as they begin, when the project is new and staff and management are excited about it. However, far too many of these projects fail to maintain this momentum, with no new content being added and little attention being paid to site maintenance. Having a Web 2.0 project on the Web that looks as if it has been abandoned for months at a time does not reflect well on your institution.

After you have launched your project and have worked out the kinks in your process, it is a good idea to document that process, particularly any technical aspects. Over time, you may want to shift responsibility for tasks among staff, giving some people a break and others a chance to try something new. By both documenting your process and cross-training your staff, you ensure that your project is not dependent on any one person, which is important for long-term success. Rotating responsibility for your Web 2.0 tasks may mean that more staff feel invested in its success rather than thinking of it as someone else's pet project. Again, in small organizations it may not be possible to shift responsibilities, but you should still document your project and process in case circumstances change.

Creating Policies

Very few people enjoy creating policies, but it is necessary. Many kinds of policies may never need to be consulted unless you have a problem, but when you do have a problem, you benefit greatly from having policies in place that help guide your response. For example, if you publish a blog post or podcast that turns out to be controversial, what are your choices for removing or amending it, and who will make that decision? What are your standards for accepting user-contributed content (such as comments, tags, or contributions to a wiki)? Under what circumstances will you delete content or ask a user to modify it? Under what circumstances would you ban a user from further contributions? A good example of some basic policies about comments on tagging on Flickr was recently posted by the National Archives and Records Administration:

> We welcome your comments on our photographs. Here is some information you should know in advance.
>
> - Our Flickr photostream is moderated and we will only post comments from commenters *over 13 years of age.*
> - We will remove comments that contain abusive, vulgar, offensive, threatening or harassing language, personal attacks of any kind, or offensive terms that target specific individuals or groups.
> - We will remove comments that contain personal information (whether your own or someone else's), including home address, home or cell phone number, or personal e-mail address.
> - We will remove comments that are clearly off-topic, that promote services or products, or that promote or oppose any political party, person campaigning for elected office, or any ballot proposition.
> - Communications made through Flickr's e-mail and messaging system will in no way constitute a legal or official notice or comment to NARA or any official or employee of NARA for any purpose.
> - The content of all comments are released into the public domain unless the commenter clearly states otherwise, so do not submit anything you do not wish to broadcast to the general public.
> - We do not discriminate against any views, but reserve the right not to post or remove comments that do not adhere to these standards.

See our National Archives on Flickr: Frequently Asked Questions (FAQs) for more information. (National Archives and Records Administration, accessed 2009)

A good way to identify what policies you might need is to try to imagine all the problems you might encounter. At a minimum, you should document basic rules about what content needs to be approved and who approves it, as well as how you will handle user feedback (such as the NARA guidelines). This is another area in which you might benefit from talking to people who have some experience with the Web 2.0 tool you're implementing.

Preserving What You Create

Even archivists sometimes overlook planning for the long-term preservation of their own materials, but it's a step you should include in your plans for any Web 2.0 project. Preservation may sound like something that you can put off until later, but, particularly when you are creating data on someone else's servers, if you want to make sure your content is preserved, you need to take responsibility for ensuring your own long-term access.

To plan for preservation you must determine both what you want to preserve and how you will preserve it. Deciding what you want to preserve is essentially conducting the records management process of scheduling and the archival function of appraisal on your own materials. What do you need to preserve in the near-term for practical purposes, and what do you want to keep as a permanent record that documents the function of your organization? Just as when you appraise materials created by others, ideally your decision about what to preserve for the long term will not be affected by the difficulty of implementing your decision. However, when appraising materials in challenging formats many archivists do take long-term preservation and storage issues into account, and you will need to do some research on these issues with regard to your Web 2.0 materials.

To support your decision about what you want to preserve for the long term, consider the different aspects of your implementation—for example, for a blog you might want to preserve the individual posts as text, any images or audio files that accompany the posts, comments from users and your responses, or a screenshot of the blog's page to capture the look and feel of the blog in its template. If you have a wiki, you may have many different pages that are being updated—do you want to try to capture a record of all the changes being made or capture the content at designated intervals? Do you want to preserve conversations in the "talk" section for your pages? Do you want to capture the way the pages look, or are you just interested in the content? Think about how many "parts" your implementation has, how they relate, and what the long-term value is for each.

Once you've identified what you want to save, you need to consider how you will preserve it. The archival profession is still grappling with many issues related to the preservation of electronic information, and discussion of methods for preserving the records of Web 2.0 has only just begun. Moreover, the specifics of preserving Web 2.0 content will vary from tool to tool. If you want to preserve your podcast, for example, you need to research issues related to which audio file format is considered optimal for long-term storage. But if you have a blog that accompanies your podcast (or just a blog), then you need to look into options for preserving the actual Web pages for each post or, depending on your appraisal decision, just the text and any image files. If you're using a tool like Flickr or YouTube, you probably already have a preservation plan for saving the digital images or videos you are sharing. But if you want to preserve user-supplied comments or tags, you will have to learn about your options for downloading them from the site (or you may learn that it is easier to develop your own system of copying and pasting into a document or database on your own system). If you are creating your content on a hosted platform like WetPaint, the system may provide options for backing up your data, but you should consider technical questions such as: can these backups be migrated out of the system; what are the preservation issues of the file format used for the backups; and what data and characteristics are being preserved in the backup?

These issues may sound complicated, and they are. No one has all the answers to these questions yet, but there are many people working on these challenges. When you are considering what to preserve and how to achieve it, do some searching for the latest research and ideas on the Web about what you want to do. As with many other aspects of Web 2.0, the best sources for information are frequently others using the tools, both inside and outside the archival community. For example, for Web 2.0 tools that have large user bases, someone will often come forward to offer preservation services—such as ArchiveIt for blogs and Web sites (www.archive-it.org) or the various services that offer to capture and preserve your Twitter feed. If you are considering options like these for your permanent content, make sure you ask questions about what is required to migrate it out of their system.

If your preservation strategy involves keeping your files—such as text, image, spreadsheet, audio, or video files—on your own servers, make sure they are clearly named and systematically stored and that you have a process for ensuring a reliable backup. If you work in a large organization, backups may be done automatically by your IT department, but in smaller environments it's probably something you need to take responsibility for yourself and work into your regular processes. As with any other collection of electronic records in your care, you need to plan for migrating the files into newer formats to make sure you can continue to access them.

Another topic that is often forgotten is ensuring that you are properly managing and preserving the records created by your project, such as documentation of key decisions, your processes, and policies. If your organization has an established records management program, you should be able to identify what records you need to create and how long you need to maintain them. If you do not have any formal policies in place, you should incorporate simple procedures for creating and preserving important documentation into the overall process for your project.

Learning about Your Users

For several decades now the literature of the archival profession has included calls for studies to help us learn more about who uses our collections, why they use them, and how satisfied they are with the systems and information we provide. These calls for user studies are well founded—for the most part, our knowledge of our users is based on anecdotal evidence and "gut" feelings rather than on hard data.

Conducting your own user studies will help you identify what your users want most from your organization, which can inform planning not only for Web 2.0 projects but also your whole archival program. Most archives and historical societies collect basic information from patrons who register to use their collections, but even this simple way of collecting data leaves out those who make virtual visits. While most of us would agree that we would like to know more about all of our users, planning for this kind of data collection can be intimidating. A 2008 article in *American Archivist* reported the results of a study that identified what kinds of information archivists want to collect about users, how they currently gather user feedback, barriers to conducting formal user studies, and ways they would like to employ standardized tools for user studies (Duff et al., 2008: 144). Not surprisingly, the study found that archivists face "many barriers that often stop them from carrying out these studies: money to hire outside experts, time to conduct user-based evaluation research in-house, and expertise" (Duff et al., 2008: 158).

While conducting formal user studies may be beyond your reach, you can still think of ways to integrate collecting information about your users into your existing processes. For example, you might develop a short survey that's distributed to all reading room visitors and Web site visitors. (You may need to check with your legal counsel, depending on your institutional setting, to verify what information you are allowed to collect without a formal proposal.) In addition to collecting information about who your visitors are, how they learned about you, and the purpose of their visit, you may also want to ask questions about their satisfaction with their experience. This kind of user evaluation data is also relevant to the metrics-gathering process discussed in Chapter 11.

For this activity to be useful, you must allocate time for this information to be correlated and analyzed, and the results should serve as a feedback mechanism for your planning activities. While you will want to ask some of the same questions every year to ensure that you can measure change over time, you should also review your data collection instrument periodically—for example, to add options for your Web 2.0 efforts to a "how did you learn about us" question.

One type of user study involves assessing how well specific products, like Web sites or finding aids, work for users. There have been many reports in the archival literature on this kind of usability testing, including the articles in the *Journal of Archival Organization* discussed in the Appendix, which outline possible methodologies and demonstrate how the results can inform improvements for your products. Commercial sites like Flickr and YouTube conduct their own user testing, of course, but you could conduct tests on products you create, such as wikis or Second Life exhibits. You can also design user tests to study things like the effectiveness of the ways you link back to your Web site from your Web 2.0 material (and vice versa) and the usefulness of the data you provide with online images, videos, or podcasts. Carving out time to conduct these kinds of usability studies and designing and implementing other kinds of user studies may be difficult. However, having reliable data about your users and investigating how they interact with your resources will allow you to create programs and services that are more valued by your current users and may help to attract new users as well.

Publicizing Your Efforts

In thinking about how you want to announce your new project, you should decide if you want to launch it and get some content up (as well as get some feedback from users and experience with the tool) before you make a public announcement. This approach, often referred to as a "soft rollout," allows you more opportunity to work out any problems you may encounter before you have a lot of public attention.

When you are ready to announce your new effort, you should use all the traditional publicity vehicles you have, such as your own institution's newsletter, e-mail list, or Web site, as well as press releases to your usual media contacts. For a Web 2.0 project, you might also consider doing some targeted announcements to other history organizations, libraries, and schools in your area, emphasizing the interactive nature of your project and inviting their contributions.

Different Web 2.0 tools lend themselves to different ways of spreading the word about your project. Sending announcements to relevant listservs and appropriate blogs can help publicize your project to specific groups of potential users. Other tools have their own specialized ways of sharing information—for example, there are special Web directories that list podcast series and Twitter feeds. Again, talking to other people who have been working with the tool you've selected may give you some useful suggestions, and they may also be willing to help promote your efforts.

When you have established a good track record of content, you should consider nominating your project for appropriate awards. You may want to consider awards given by professional organizations like the American Association of Museums, the American Library Association, and the American Association for State and Local History, as well as regional and state organizations. You should also look for awards programs that recognize Web resources on particular subject matter or independent efforts such as the Webbys or the Best Archives on the Web awards. Winning an award is obviously a great way to gain recognition for your project—both with the public and within your own organization. Even if you don't win, having a panel of judges review your nomination still brings your efforts to the attention of a new audience who might not be aware of them.

You should also seek out opportunities to speak about your Web 2.0 project at professional conferences, as well as to contribute articles to professional or subject-related journals. You can also speak about both your project's content and your experiences with Web 2.0 at places like your public library, historical society, schools, or civic groups.

KEEPING YOURSELF IN A "2.0" FRAME OF MIND

The best resource you really have for a successful Web 2.0 implementation is yourself—your own attitude, knowledge, and enthusiasm. It's easy to get bogged down in the details and mechanics of implementing a project or even to become frustrated if working with skeptical colleagues. Here are some final tips to help keep you focused on the many possibilities of Web 2.0 tools:

- It's always a good idea to experiment on your own with a personal account on a new site or tool. You learn how it works and can also build up a network of people to call on for advice.
- Bear in mind that setting expectations for a Web 2.0 project is difficult—some people expect overnight success, and others think no one will ever pay attention. Neither one is probably true, but both are possible.
- Be ready to experiment and be flexible. It's difficult to predict who your audience will be and what content they will like best. Be prepared to adapt once you see the response.
- Don't worry about perfection. Most Web 2.0 audiences realize your content and presentation will not be perfect and that most processes are iterative. Providing engaging content is what's most important.
- Keep looking for new tools, and keep up to date on changes to existing ones.
- Seek out organizations like yours that are doing good work, and network with them to learn from their experience.
- Look for opportunities to collaborate with other institutions—maybe you can join together to create a wiki or podcast, for example. Web 2.0 is about sharing, and most institutions don't have all the expertise or resources on their own.

One of main themes of this book is that Web 2.0 tools are not an end in themselves and should always be used to support your institution's goals. That being said, in these times of tight budgets and shrinking resources, taking advantage of the wealth of free or low-cost tools on the Web can mean a sizable "bang for your buck." In addition, as many of the people who have implemented Web 2.0 tools have said in their interviews, using these tools to share your collections and interact with users can be a lot of fun. I hope your experiences with Web 2.0 will be as positive as theirs.

REFERENCES

Duff, Wendy M., Jean Dryden, Carrie Limkilde, Joan Cherry, and Ellie Bogomazova. 2008. "Archivists' Views of User-Based Evaluations: Benefits, Barriers, and Requirements." *American Archivist* 71, no. 1 (Spring/Summer): 144–166.

National Archives and Records Administration. "Photo Comment and Posting Policy." Available: www.archives.gov/social-media/photo-comment-policy.html (accessed July 9, 2009).

Society of American Archivists. "Orphan Works: Statement of Best Practices" (2009). Available: http://archivists.org/standards/OWBP-V4.pdf (accessed July 27, 2009).

Archives and the Web: Finding the Right Balance

What happens when a profession rooted in the management of tangible items tries to move into a digital world? What happens when organizations with little funding, scarce resources, and limited technical expertise are expected to behave like amazon.com? These are challenges presented by the Web—both 1.0 and 2.0—to archivists and others responsible for historical collections. Web 2.0 has brought some new challenges of its own, but for the most part it has only brought new urgency and complexity to the challenges originally presented by Web 1.0:

- How can we address user expectations?
- How much should be done to preserve traditional archival principles?
- How can we protect copyright while making collections accessible?
- How can we ensure those who lack access to technology are not left behind?
- How can we support having a meaningful presence on the Web and continuing our "real world" functions?

There are no easy answers to these questions. But, as we gain more experience making our collections accessible on the Web and learning how people interact with them, we are gathering more information to guide us as we try to strike the right balance in each of these areas.

For many archives and historical organizations, the most obvious challenge the Web brought was a huge rise in user expectations. People visiting an archives site for the first time (and even some more experienced users) expect—or want—"everything" to be online. Many want a "grab and go" experience, where they type a search term into a Google-like function and get Google-like results, complete with links to digitized documents rather than descriptions of them. Many archivists would like to be able to provide this level of service but lack the time and resources.

In the age of the Web, with a world full of new users, archivists have little chance of making the world change its expectations to meet our traditional practices. The challenge we face is how to adapt our traditional principles, processes, and practices to work toward meeting these new expectations while at the same time addressing the problems of limited resources, backlogs, and scarce support.

One example of these traditional archival principles is the concept of provenance, which dictates that records be kept in separate groupings defined by the person, family, or organization that created them. The preservation of this context—who created the materials or assembled the collection and why—is one of the key differences between archives and other kinds of cultural heritage organizations. Preserving this kind of context is often very challenging, if not impossible, in the digital world. Digital copies of archival materials can be accompanied by information that cites their repository, collection or record group, and series, but for most people who see them on the Web, that information is largely meaningless. Most users do not want to understand the context of the document or image; they just want the information that it contains.

This presents a challenge for archivists—how much effort should we put into preserving provenance or providing context for our collections on the Web if most users neither understand nor want it? If provenance is preserved in the original collection and in the descriptions and finding aids we create, how much does it matter if it is lost when we post images on Flickr? If you assume that anyone doing "serious research" will always access materials in the traditional way and will seek out contextual information, then you might not worry if casual users in Flickr are missing the larger picture. But as more and more students and scholars seek to use materials only on the Web, might they themselves lose sight of the importance of context for understanding the materials? The challenge for archivists will be finding the right balance between presenting materials in the context we have traditionally thought was critical to an understanding of them and letting the documents stand on their own on the Web.

Archivists have always known that they do not hold the copyright to all materials in their collections. While this was sometimes a thorny issue, it was rarely the responsibility of the archivist to sort it out. If someone wanted to reproduce an image for publication, the archivist would provide the best information available about the copyright status of the item, and the rest was up to the patron. When archives began publishing reproductions themselves—as digital copies on Web sites or by using Web 2.0 tools like Flickr, YouTube, blogs, and podcasts—these issues became the archivist's problem. How comfortable are you publishing something on the Web if you aren't able to contact the copyright holder and get permission? Added to this is the concern many archives have about the illegal copying and distribution of material over which they do hold copyright. Posting digital material on the Web often means that it is available to anyone to copy, as well as to access, and this raises issues for many cultural heritage organizations.

In this climate of uncertainty, many archives with conservative legal counsel and risk-averse management might find themselves unable to digitize and share very much of their collection. While the archival, library, and museum professions are part of a coalition trying to push for legislation that would provide greater freedom to share orphan works, for many in the profession copyright is a large, scary, gray area with no clear answers. Every institution has to find its own comfort level as it weighs the risk of publishing materials on the Web against the benefits of making materials available. There is no "one size fits all" answer or best practice that applies universally. The challenge of using Web 2.0 is finding the appropriate balance between limiting what we make available because of the risk of legal consequences and maximizing the amount of material we share with the public.

Web 2.0 offers a smorgasbord of options for reaching out to new users, but it's important to remember that not everyone has access to the technology necessary to take advantage of Web 2.0 sites. While sharing images, video, and podcasts are wonderful outreach efforts, they will not reach everyone. Part of the challenge facing all cultural heritage organizations as they move more operations online is not to neglect those on the less-fortunate side of the "digital divide."

Some archives also feel that they're on the wrong side of the digital divide themselves. Institutions that lack the resources or the support for new technology projects risk becoming marginalized as their peers, who are more readily able to commit resources to things like Web 2.0, garner all the attention and kudos. In a competition between an archives doing an outstanding job at traditional activities and one producing innovative Web projects, it's possible that the flash of the Web might pull more weight with funders. While it's natural to want to keep pushing forward with our own goals, part of the challenge for us as professionals is to balance our own personal desire to succeed against the need to help our less well-resourced peers.

The commonality in all these challenges is also the last challenge—how to find the right balance? Archives need to find the right balance between meeting user expectations about plentiful Web offers and supporting physical processing, between the conventions of the digital world and traditional archival principles, between concerns about copyright and the desire to make materials available online, and between investing in and recognizing the opportunities of technology while not leaving behind those who cannot afford to keep up. All of these contribute to an overarching need to balance the demands and opportunities that the new digital world presents against the needs and traditions of the physical world.

What makes this challenge so difficult is that no one outside an organization can know what the right answer is. No one unfamiliar with your situation can tell you what your archives or historical society "should" be doing. Not everyone should be doing things with Web 2.0, and certainly no one could ever say that all archives should have a blog or a Twitter account or anything else. Based on what you know about your archives and what you now know about the capabilities and requirements of different Web 2.0 tools, you can judge for yourself what you think your archives should be doing. But your decision will be grounded in an understanding of your organization's mission and strategic goals and based on realistic assessments of your resources. You will figure out where starting something new with Web 2.0 figures into the right balance for your organization.

Having said that no one can tell you what you should be doing, I will say that I hope you *do* find a way to fit Web 2.0 into your balance. Traditionally, archives have been about the "old," but today we have no choice but to be about the "new" as well. If the Web put archives on the same playing field as everyone else, we need to make sure that we get ourselves in the game and don't get stuck on the bench. In the current economic climate, institutions that don't find a way to engage their audiences and stakeholders are going to get passed over for funding, and, with the added challenges brought by the Web, we need that funding more than ever before.

Archives *are* for use, and the way people want to use them is changing every day. The challenge of more people wanting to use our materials is a wonderful one to have, and the opportunities afforded by Web 2.0 technologies are worth exploring as we try to meet these challenges and strike a good balance between the traditional ways we did things and the new ways that we must engage with our audiences.

Additional Resources

In keeping with the intent of this book to serve as a practical resource for busy practitioners on a topic that is changing rapidly, rather than provide a simple list of print and Web resources, I will share my recommendations about what I think are the best ways to learn more about the topics I've covered in the previous chapters.

RESOURCES ON WEB 2.0, SOCIAL MEDIA, THE EVOLUTION OF THE WEB, AND RELATED TOPICS

The books that I would most recommend for learning about Web 2.0 are not guides to any specific tool but ones that discuss the changes in our culture that caused the tools to succeed and the changes that they in turn are supporting. I think in order to understand how your organization can best succeed on the Web, it's helpful to have a broader understanding of the issues that will shape that success. If you have a good understanding of the forces influencing the way the Web is evolving and how that in turn is affecting society, then you will be in a better position to plan how to achieve your long-term goals as software, tools, and policies change over time. These books are aimed at a broad audience of nonspecialists. They are intended to be enjoyable and easy to read, and most of them are.

Two books dating from the relatively early days of Web 2.0 that are still worth reading are *The Cluetrain Manifesto* (Levine et al., 2000) and *Small Pieces Loosely Joined* (Weinberger, 2002). The first was a joint effort by four technology writers (who began collaborating on the original Cluetrain Web site), describing how the environment in which businesses operate had fundamentally changed—hence the subtitle, "The End of Business as Usual." It opens with "95 theses for the people of earth" and in its introduction states that this is unlike other business books because (1) it's not a feel-good book, (2) it's not a how-to book, and (3) it's not boring. These statements are all true. While directed at companies, its lessons are easily translatable to historical organizations, and they still hold true today. The authors have made the entire book available online at www.cluetrain.com/book/index.html. A "Tenth Anniversary Edition" has just been published (2009) with new introductions by the authors and commentary essays. I'm looking forward to reading how they think their work has held up.

Small Pieces Loosely Joined was written by David Weinberger, one of the authors of *The Cluetrain Manifesto*. Its modest subtitle, "A Unified Theory of the Web," belies its purpose—to present a series of short philosophical essays about how the Web is "changing bedrock concepts such as space, time, perfection, social interaction, knowledge, matter, and morality—each a chapter in this book" (Weinberger, 2002: 25). It is filled with personal observations and takes a more abstract approach to the changes the Web is bringing. Not everyone enjoys this kind of writing, and, of the two books, I would recommend *Cluetrain* first. But if you want to see how one influential writer was thinking about the broader implications of the Web in 2002, this is a fairly short and entertaining read.

In 2004, *Wired* editor Chris Anderson introduced his ideas about the applicability of the "long tail" for e-commerce, and he expanded on those ideas in his 2006 book, *The Long Tail*. His argument that "the future of business is selling less of more" has been disputed, but the value of his central theory (built on earlier research studies) is still influential. Although Anderson's book is very much about business and optimizing revenue, I believe (as I said in the Introduction) that the same model applies to archival and historical materials as well. For an overview of the concepts, the *Wired* article is probably all you need, but if you want to dig deeper, I would recommend the book. (Note that Anderson published an updated version in 2008 with a new chapter on marketing. If you want to read the book, try to get this edition rather than the 2006 one.)

If you want to learn about the evolution of the companies behind many of the Web 2.0 tools and the people behind them, Sarah Lacy's (2008) *Once You're Lucky, Twice You're Good* might be an interesting read. It's not a comprehensive overview and the tone is at times rather gossipy, but it will give you a basic overview of how some of the major Web 2.0 companies, like Facebook, got started and grew to be major players in business and on the Web.

One aspect of Web 2.0 and social media that has garnered a great deal of attention in the popular press is the potential the new Web presents for online collaboration and the impact this collaboration will have on society. James Surowiecki's 2004 book *The Wisdom of Crowds* is not specifically about the Web, but his argument is certainly applicable in the Web 2.0 environment. Surowiecki presents a wide variety of evidence that the aggregated decisions of many people produce better results than the opinion of one person. Like many books of this genre, Surowiecki uses examples drawn from many disciplines to make his case; these stories are relevant and he writes well, making the book a pleasure to read. While none of the decision-making stories relates directly to any cultural heritage organization, there are some similarities between the world of scientific collaboration and scholarship in history and related disciplines. As a sidelight, his discussions of group dynamics might also be valuable to managers and others interested in learning how groups work.

Don Tapscott and Anthony Williams' (2008) *Wikinomics* expands on the potential of mass collaboration discussed by Surowiecki (and exemplified by Wikipedia) and places it into a specifically business context. Again, the authors provide many useful stories and examples drawn largely from the corporate world (although they do often reference the open-source development model of the Linux operating system). Their focus on the implications of collaboration on for-profit enterprises may make this a less valuable book for people interested in nonprofit models, but if you work in a large organization you may find its discussions of how to benefit from internal collaboration useful.

Rather than appealing to the market for popular business books, Yochai Benkler (2006), a faculty member at Yale School of Law, delivers complex arguments in *The Wealth of Networks*. This is a dense, scholarly (and rather long) book that is well worth reading but will be much slower going for most people. It may be a cheaper read as well, since Benkler has made the whole book available for free on his Web site: www.benkler.org. This is very much a work of social theory, presenting evidence and arguments about the political and social implications of the "social production" created by the Web's new tools.

In place of (or in addition to, if you prefer) either of those two books on the power of social networking, I recommend Clay Shirky's (2008) *Here Comes Everybody*. I suggest it not only because it's shorter and easy to read but also because Shirky has the ability to communicate complex ideas clearly and concisely. He is skillful at using real-life stories and examples as jumping off points for exploring the larger forces propelling online social networks. For example, he argues:

Every story in this book relies on a successful fusion of a plausible promise, an effective tool, and an acceptable bargain with the users. The promise is the basic "why" for anyone to join or contribute to a group. The tool
helps with the "how"—how will the difficulties of coordination be overcome, or at least held to manageable levels? And the bargain sets the rules
of the road: if you are interested in the promise and adopt the tools, what
can you expect, and what will be expected of you? (Shirky, 2008: 260)

For me, this is the kind of analysis that makes sense instantly and that I can
see supported by my own experiences with social networks—both on and off
the Web. Shirky's discussion of the power of social networks should help you
think about the implications of opening your collections up to "everybody" and
also how you and your organization might want to participate in some of the
larger groups on the Web, such as Wikipedia, Flickr, Facebook, and YouTube.

Not everyone is in favor of the kinds of empowerment Web 2.0 technology
brings. One of the most prominent of the critics is Andrew Keen, whose 2008
book *The Cult of the Amateur* bears the subtitle, "How Blogs, MySpace,
YouTube, and the Rest of Today's User-Generated Media Are Destroying Our
Economy, Our Culture, and Our Values." Keen argues that a society needs cultural gatekeepers to divide worthwhile creative and intellectual products from
the worthless ones. I find his arguments curmudgeonly and elitist, as well as an
attempt to argue for turning back the clock to a Web 1.0 world. I, however, am
biased. If you want to read someone with a different point of view (and a witty,
erudite style), *The Cult of the Amateur* may interest you.

David Weinberger's (2007) latest book, *Everything Is Miscellaneous*,
caused quite a stir in the library community, but I do not recall seeing much discussion of it in the archival world, which is unfortunate. In my opinion,
Weinberger's thesis has just as much—if not greater—relevance for the archival and historical professions than it does for libraries. Weinberger argues that
the ways we impose order on information (as manifested in physical objects
like books, boxes, and catalog cards) are dictated by the limitations of the physical world (for example, that physical objects can only be located in one place
at one time). Many of these systems for imposing order have become so deeply
ingrained that we have forgotten their origins and think of them as being the
only "natural" or logical way to approach the information. In the digital world,
of course, representations of information can "be" at countless places at the
same time, and it is the implications of this "digital disorder" that Weinberger
explores in the book. As in his previous books, Weinberger is skilled at employ

ing examples (including the Dewey decimal system) to illustrate his points, and his style is graceful and witty. I strongly recommend this book, because I think the arguments are supported by the ways we are seeing our users wanting to interact with the information about our collections.

There are three additional topics you might want to explore through additional readings: intellectual property, the characteristics of the so-called digital natives, and the evolution of ideas about privacy. On intellectual property issues, the most respected person writing about the broader implications of the Web is Lawrence Lessig. If you can, I recommend that you read both of Lessig's two most recent books: *Free Culture* (2004) and *Remix* (2008). (Note that all of Lessig's books are available for free download at www.lessig.org/content/books.) In *Free Culture*, Lessig writes:

> . . . an argument for free culture stumbles on a confusion that is hard to avoid, and even harder to understand. A free culture is not a culture without property; it is not a culture in which artists don't get paid. A culture without property, or in which creators can't get paid, is anarchy, not freedom. Anarchy is not what I advance here.
>
> Instead, the free culture that I defined in this book is a balance between anarchy and control. A free culture, like a free market, is filled with property. It is filled with rules of property and contract that get enforced by the state. But just as a free market is perverted if its property becomes too feudal, so too can a free culture be queered by extremism in the property rights that define it. That is what I fear about our culture today. It is against this extremism that this book is written. (Lessig, 2004: xvi)

In *Free Culture*, Lessig lays out the current state of copyright law and describes the attacks he sees being presented to "free culture." In *Remix* he again grounds his arguments about the state of copyright law (and litigation) but focuses on how the current state of intellectual property enforcement is making "criminals" out of a whole generation of our children. He presents a case for a "hybrid economy"—one that is both "RO" ("read only," in which people are restricted from reusing intellectual property) and "RW" ("read/write," in which people are free to reuse others' intellectual property).

In addition to the SAA "Orphan Works: Statement of Best Practices" discussed in Chapter 12, I am also going to recommend a book on copyright that I haven't yet seen but that I know will be valuable to you. Strictly speaking, it doesn't belong in this section because it will probably have little to do with

Web 2.0, but you will probably find it a good practical balance to Lessig's theoretical discussions. Peter Hirtle, the archival profession's leading voice on copyright law, is one of the authors of the forthcoming *Copyright and Cultural Institutions: Guidelines for Digitization for U.S. Libraries, Archives, and Museums*. It will be available as a free download from the Social Sciences Research Network (www.ssrn.com) and "hardcopy" versions will be available through Amazon's CreateSpace subsidiary. I am confident this will serve as a good primer on how current copyright law affects what kinds of materials you might want to digitize and how you might want to share them.

Several books have been written about the culture of people who were "born digital," that is, people who have never experienced life without the World Wide Web. Of these, I think the best are *Born Digital* (Palfrey and Gasser, 2008) and *Grown Up Digital* (Tapscott, 2008). In *Born Digital*, lawyers John Palfrey and Urs Gasser discuss topics such as identity and personal data, privacy, safety, creativity and innovation, copyright, reliability of online information, "information overload," learning, and social activism. In each of these areas, the authors discuss possible opportunities and threats that apply specifically to young people. While the primary audience for this subject matter may be parents and educators, this book offers a useful overview of how digital natives approach a range of issues on the Web. If you are not a digital native, you may find this book helpful for understanding how they expect and want to interact with your institution's resources (as well as a good general overview of this range of issues).

Grown Up Digital is Don Tapscott's follow up to his 1997 book *Growing Up Digital*. In the new book Tapscott outlines how the generation that has "grown up digital" is different from previous generations and explores the implications these differences may have for our society. He postulates eight "generational norms" for digital natives (or the "net generation"), such as "they want *freedom* in everything they do, from freedom of choice to freedom of expression" and "they love to *customize*, personalize" (Tapscott, 2008: 34). In addition to these "norms," he explores possible differences in brain development and cognitive skills in people who've spent their formative years online. He then explores how the net generation is (and will be) different in the areas of education, the workforce, as consumers, and in their family relationships. He closes by discussing the impact the net generation will have in areas like politics and government (citing the Obama campaign's very effective use of social networking) and volunteering and social activism. While Tapscott's sweeping statements about a whole generation are open to debate, it seems clear that there are differences, and this book might help you think about what they are and how you may need to change the way your organization operates to better meet their needs.

An issue that will probably not affect your institution's Web presence, but one that you should be aware of for yourself as well as for the people who visit your site, is online privacy and reputation. I think the single most useful book on this topic is Daniel Solove's (2007) *The Future of Reputation,* which discusses, as the subtitle says, "Gossip, Rumor, and Privacy on the Internet." Like Palfrey and Tapscott, Solove is a lawyer, and this is another well-written book that uses real-world examples to illustrate its complex issues. There are no easy answers, but reading this book will at least make you more aware of how you are managing your own online privacy and reputation.

If you are interested in keeping up with the latest news and thinking on these kinds of Web issues, here are some other recommendations:

- Read *Wired* magazine from time to time—either their Web site (www.wired.com) or the hard copy. (A subscription is not very expensive.)
- Check out Common Craft's "In Plain English" series of short videos that explain Web technologies (and other complicated things) with simple graphics and nontechnical language. They are available at www.commoncraft.com. These are worth knowing about to help you educate others about what you want to do.
- Listen to some TED talks, both old and new, at www.ted.com. "TED" stands for "Technology, Entertainment, Design." This is a very influential conference that is devoted to promoting "Ideas Worth Spreading." I am a big fan of Clay Shirky's talks.
- Follow some technology blogs. Two of the most popular are "ArsTechnica" (http://arstechnica.com) and "Webware" (http://news .cnet.com/webware). I find the *New York Times'* "Bits" column ("Business Innovation Technology Society") very useful as well (http://bits .blogs .nytimes.com).
- Follow some archives and library bloggers who discuss technology. You can find my blog at www.archivesnext.com, and you can see other available archives blogs at www.archivesblogs.com. There are countless librarians who write about technology. Of these, my favorites are Librarian.net (www.librarian.net), "Information Wants to Be Free"

(http://meredith.wolfwater.com/Wordpress), and "Free Range Librarian" (http://freerangelibrarian.com).

- Look for more examples of archives and historical organizations that are implementing Web 2.0 tools. A good source of information is the Archives 2.0 wiki (http://archives2point0.wetpaint.com) that I maintain and keep up to date with the latest examples.
- Sign up for the RSS feed for the Pew Internet & American Life studies to follow the latest research on Internet usage (www.pewinternet.org).
- Most of the authors of the books mentioned in this Appendix have their own blogs you can subscribe to and Web sites where you can learn more.

INFORMATION ON SPECIFIC WEB 2.0 TOOLS

The best place to look for more information on specific Web 2.0 tools is the Web. First, make sure you have read all the information provided on the tool's own site, such as their FAQ or information in their user forums. Some tools, such as Flickr, have their own blogs to provide news, but you should see what others are saying about them. Doing a Google search on the name of the tool or the type of technology will yield the most recent information about it, including posts from technology or business-related blogs and links to Wikipedia articles. Wikipedia articles on topics such as "podcasting" or "micro-blogging" often include a list of the software options that are currently available, including charts of their features.

Web 2.0 tools have active user communities on the Web, and they are really the best sources of information. You can also look for posts on archives, museum, or library-related blogs to find posts about the tool or technology you're considering, and of course you should talk to people at institutions similar to yours who have implemented it. This is an evolving environment, in terms of technology, business models, and policy, and so the best sources of information are the most current. If you need more information on the basics of a tool or technology, you also have many books to choose from. The "For Dummies" and "For Idiots" series of books provide, as promised, easy to understand introductions, but your public library or local bookstore will probably have many other options if you want to supplement the information that's on the Web.

PUBLICATIONS BY LIBRARIANS AND ARCHIVISTS

Hundreds of articles have been published in the scholarly literature of the library community about Web 2.0 adoption and about specific tools. While in some ways these are not applicable to organizations like archives or historical societies, if you are interested in seeing what is available, look for the latest articles in journals like *Library Journal, Reference Librarian, Reference & User Services Quarterly, College & Research Libraries News, Journal of Web Librarianship, Information Technology and Libraries, Library Technology Reports,* and *Library Hi-Tech News.* You might want to start your search by reading Jennifer Boxen's 2008 article in *Reference Librarian,* "Library 2.0: A Review of the Literature." In addition to articles, you may want to read some of the many books published on "Library 2.0." These are among the better ones:

- Phil Bradley. 2007. *How to Use Web 2.0 in Your Library.* London: Facet.
- Meredith Farkas. 2007. *Social Software in Libraries: Building Collaboration, Communication and Community Online.* Medford , NJ: Information Today.
- Ellyssa Kroski. 2008. *Web 2.0 for Librarians and Information Professionals.* New York: Neal-Schuman.

Archival professionals have been significantly less prolific in writing about the impact of Web 2.0 and social media and their adoption. In the *American Archivist*, the journal of the Society of American Archivists, only one article in recent issues has provided any thoughtful reflection on the challenges of the new Web: Max Evans' (2007) "Archives of the People, by the People, for the People." Evans puts forward several ideas for "re-engineered archives," including incorporating scan-on-demand and establishing systems that support and encourage user-supplied metadata. Magia Ghetu Krause and Elizabeth Yakel's (2007) research into improving the design of finding aids and incorporating Web 2.0 tools is described in "Interaction in the Virtual Archives: The Polar Bear Expedition Digital Collections Next Generation Finding Aid." Another interesting article, although rather out of date now, is Michelle Light and Tom Hyry's (2002) "Colophons and Annotations: New Directions for the Finding Aid," which explores ideas about allowing users to add comments or notes to finding aids ("annotations") and providing more information about the archival processing of collections along with descriptive information ("colophons").

The *American Archivist* is one of the places many scholars publish the results of their user studies. To date, many of these studies have centered on assessing topics like the information-seeking behavior of professional historians and the usability of EAD-encoded finding aids. However, two recent articles describe research involving genealogists that I think is more broadly applicable to other kinds of researchers as well. Wendy Duff and Catherine Johnson's (2003) "Where Is the List with All the Names? Information-Seeking Behavior of Genealogists" describes the information-seeking behavior and research process of a small group of genealogists, from which the authors conclude:

> Genealogists represent the majority of users in many archives. And yet, the traditional archival information system does not meet their needs. As previously stated, the content and format of finding aids, whether paper based or Web based, has not changed substantially during the last fifty years even though the archival user population has changed dramatically. (Duff and Johnson, 2003: 94)

In "Genealogists as a 'Community of Records,'" Elizabeth Yakel and Deborah Torres (2007) examine the social network of genealogists. Among their conclusions is the following observation:

> Notable in this community is the lack of participation of archivists and librarians although they are enablers of the community. The interviewees did not place them centrally either in educating genealogists about records and the search process, or in the creation and disposition of family archives. If communities are defined by both participants and nonparticipants, this lack of participation is an important consideration for the archival community. (Yakel and Torres, 2007: 111)

In my opinion issues like these are not unique to our genealogist users. I think many archives and historical societies can begin to address some of these needs with effective use of Web 2.0 tools.

The *Journal of Archival Organization* is an excellent resource for shorter, less densely scholarly articles, including many useful case studies and examples of practicing archivists conducting user studies. Among these are the following:

- Rosalie Lack. 2006. "The Importance of User-Centered Design: Exploring Findings and Methods." *Journal of Archival Organization* 4, no. 1/2: 69–86.
- Cory Nimer and J. Gordon Daines III. 2008. "What Do You Mean It Doesn't Make Sense? Redesigning Finding Aids from the User's Perspective." *Journal of Archival Organization* 6, no.4: 216–232.
- Merrilee Proffitt. 2006. "How and Why of User Studies: RLG's RedLightGreen as a Case Study." *Journal of Archival Organization* 4, no. 1/2: 87–110.

Articles like these can give you ideas about methodologies for your own user studies and often contain a literature review section that can help you if you want to learn about other studies and resources.

Two online publications that often have interesting content are *D-Lib* (www.dlib.org) and *First Monday* (http://firstmonday.org). *D-Lib* focuses on issues related to digital libraries but covers many related areas, including archives. For example, a 2007 article by Lally and Dunford, "Using Wikipedia to Extend Digital Collections," describes the experiences of the University of Washington Libraries as they added relevant links to Wikipedia for items in their digital collections. *First Monday* (named because it comes out on the first Monday of the month), which contains a broad range of articles that relate to the Internet, also features articles on general Web 2.0 issues and occasionally articles about Web 2.0 and archives. In 2007, *First Monday* included "Machines in the Archives: Technology and the Coming Transformation of Archival Reference" by educator Richard Cox and the University of Pittsburgh archives students. This article explores the implications of some common technologies, such as digital cameras and scanners, as well as instant messaging and online chat, on archival practices. One issue (August 2008) was devoted to "WebWise 2.0: The Power of Community: Selected Papers from the Ninth Annual WebWise Conference on Libraries and Museums."

If you are new to the world of Web 2.0 and its tools, catching up on the culture by reading the books and articles I've recommended will help you get up to speed. But to keep up to date on the latest developments and research, you need to find good sources of information, such as blogs and social networks (like Twitter) where both archivists and other users share news. Keeping up with what's new doesn't have to be a full-time job, and I hope that the ideas I've shared in this book will make you want to continue to learn more about how you can use the Web's new tools to connect users to your collections.

REFERENCES

Anderson, Chris. 2004. "The Long Tail." *Wired* 12, no. 10 (October). Available: www.wired.com/wired/archive/12.10/tail.html (accessed July 3, 2009).

Anderson, Chris. 2006. *The Long Tail.* New York: Hyperion.

Benkler, Yocahi. 2006. *The Wealth of Networks.* New Haven, CT: Yale University Press.

Boxen, Jennifer L. 2008. "Library 2.0: A Review of the Literature." *Reference Librarian* 49, no. 1 (August): 21–34.

Cox, Richard, and the University of Pittsburgh archives students. 2007. "Machines in the Archives: Technology and the Coming Transformation of Archival Reference." *First Monday* 12, no. 11 (November 5). Available: http://firstmonday.org/htbin/cgiwrap/bin/ojs/index.php/fm/article/view/2029/1894 (accessed July 5, 2009).

Duff, Wendy M., and Catherine A. Johnson. 2003. "Where Is the List with All the Names? Information-Seeking Behavior of Genealogists." *American Archivist* 66, no. 1 (Spring/Summer): 79–95.

Evans, Max J. 2007. "Archives of the People, by the People, for the People." *American Archivist* 70, no. 2 (Fall/Winter): 387–400.

Hirtle, Peter B., Emily Hudson, and Andrew T. Kenyon. Forthcoming. *Copyright and Cultural Institutions: Guidelines for Digitization for U.S. Libraries, Archives, and Museums.* Ithaca, NY: Cornell University Library Press.

Keen, Andrew. 2008. *The Cult of the Amateur.* New York: Broadway Business.

Krause, Magia Ghetu, and Elizabeth Yakel. 2007. "Interaction in the Virtual Archives: The Polar Bear Expedition Digital Collections Next Generation Finding Aid." *American Archivist* 70, no. 2 (Fall/Winter): 282–314.

Lacy, Sarah. 2008. *Once You're Lucky, Twice You're Good.* New York: Gotham Books.

Lally, Ann M., and Carolyn E. Dunford. 2007. "Using Wikipedia to Extend Digital Collections." *D-Lib* 13, no. 5/6 (May/June). Available: www.dlib.org/dlib/may07/lally/ 05lally.html (accessed July 5, 2009).

Lessig, Lawrence. 2004. *Free Culture.* New York: Penguin Press.

Lessig, Lawrence. 2008. *Remix.* New York: Penguin Press.

Levine, Rick, Christopher Locke, Doc Searls, and David Weinberger. 2000. *The Cluetrain Manifesto.* New York: Perseus.

Light, Michelle, and Tom Hyry. 2002. "Colophons and Annotations: New Directions for the Finding Aid." *American Archivist* 65, no. 2 (Fall/Winter): 216–230.

Palfry, John, and Urs Gasser. 2008. *Born Digital.* New York: Basic Books.

Shirky, Clay. 2008. *Here Comes Everybody.* New York: Penguin Press.

Solove, Daniel J. 2007. *The Future of Reputation.* New Haven, CT: Yale University Press.

Surowiecki, James. 2005. *The Wisdom of Crowds.* New York: Anchor Books.

Tapscott, Don. 1997. *Growing Up Digital.* New York: McGraw-Hill.

Tapscott, Don. 2008. *Grown Up Digital.* New York: McGraw-Hill.

Tapscott, Don, and Anthony D. Williams. 2008. *Wikinomics*. New York: Portfolio.

Weinberger, David. 2002. *Small Pieces Loosely Joined*. New York: Perseus.

Weinberger, David. 2007. *Everything Is Miscellaneous*. New York: Times Books.

Yakel, Elizabeth, and Deborah A. Torres. 2007. "Genealogists as a 'Community of Records.'" *American Archivist* 70, no. 1 (Spring/Summer): 93–113.

Index

Page numbers followed by the letter "f" indicate figures.

About the Author

Kate Theimer is the author of the popular ArchivesNext blog (www
.archivesnext.com), as well as a regular speaker at conferences and workshops
on issues related to the use of Web 2.0 technologies by archives and historical
organizations. In conjunction with her blog, she created and manages the Best
Archives on the Web and the Movers and Shakers in Archives awards, as well
as the Archives 2.0 wiki (http://archives2point0.wetpaint.com). Kate holds a
Master of Information degree with a specialization in archives and records
management from the University of Michigan and a Master of Arts from the
University of Maryland, and she has held positions at the National Archives
and Records Administration, the Smithsonian Institution, and the Historical
Society of Washington, DC. She is also the editor of a forthcoming book from
the Society of American Archivists about the implications of Web 2.0 tools for
the archival profession.